Your Diplomats at Work

For Vance
& Norma
with my compliments.
Frank

MEMOIRS AND OCCASIONAL PAPERS
Association for Diplomatic Studies and Training

In 2003, the Association for Diplomatic Studies and Training (ADST) created the Memoirs and Occasional Papers Series to preserve firsthand accounts and other informed observations on foreign affairs for scholars, journalists, and the general public. Sponsoring publication of the series is one of numerous ways in which ADST, a nonprofit organization founded in 1986, seeks to promote understanding of American diplomacy and those who conduct it. Together with the Foreign Affairs Oral History program and ADST's support for the training of foreign affairs personnel at the State Department's Foreign Service Institute, these efforts constitute the Association's fundamental purposes.

Your Diplomats at Work

A Comedy in Seven Acts

by FRANKLIN E. HUFFMAN

ASSOCIATION FOR DIPLOMATIC STUDIES AND TRAINING
MEMOIRS AND OCCASIONAL PAPERS SERIES

Washington, DC

Library of Congress Control Number: 2011928129
ISBN 978-0-9832451-7-9 paperback (alk. paper)

 An imprint of New Academia Publishing

 New Academia Publishing
PO Box 27420, Washington, DC 20038-7420
info@newacademia.com - www.newacademia.com

"Another damned, thick, square book! Always scribble, scribble, scribble! Eh! Mr. Gibbon?"

> —William Henry, Duke of Gloucester (1743-1805), upon receiving Edward Gibbon's volume II of The Decline and Fall of the Roman Empire

"Diplomats approach every issue with an open mouth."

> —Arthur Goldberg, Ambassador to the United Nations and Associate Justice of the Supreme Court of the United States

"A diplomat is someone who thinks twice before saying nothing."

> —Cited in a talk by Ambassador Charles W. Freeman (March 28, 2008)

Also by Franklin E. Huffman

Monks and Motorcycles: From Laos to London by the
Seat of My Pants, 1956–1958 (2004)

Bibliography and Index of Mainland Southeast Asian Languages
and Linguistics (1986)

English for Speakers of Khmer (1983)

Intermediate Spoken Vietnamese (1980)

English-Khmer Dictionary (1978)

Cambodian Literary Reader and Glossary (1977)

Cambodian-English Glossary (1977)

Intermediate Cambodian Reader (1972)

Modern Spoken Cambodian (1970)

Cambodian System of Writing and Beginning Reader (1970)

Contents

Preface

I resigned as professor of linguistics and Asian studies at Cornell University in 1985 at the age of fifty-one and joined the U.S. Foreign Service. I served tours in London, Burma, Morocco, Paris, Washington, Cambodia, and New Zealand before mandatory retirement at age sixty-five and then accepted post-retirement assignments in Chad and Cambodia.

Your Diplomats at Work is an account of my sometimes comical, sometimes frustrating, but always enlightening adventures as a diplomat in those seven countries. While written in a humorous vein, the book is a critique, not to say exposé, of the stifling bureaucracy and resultant inefficiency of the U.S. Department of State, along with practical recommendations for improvement.

When I was introduced to Ambassador Walter Curley upon arriving to take up my post in the Paris Embassy in 1990, he commented (in jest, I hope): "Huffman, you gave up a full professorship at an Ivy League university to do this? I'm afraid you're not smart enough to serve in my embassy!"

The circuitous route by which I became a diplomat is indeed peculiar and demands some explanation. In the Prologue I have described, perhaps in more detail than is strictly necessary, the peregrinations by which a Virginia farm boy became a professor and diplomat. If you find that saga gratuitous and irrelevant to the topic at hand, I invite you to go directly to Act One: Great Britain—my maiden assignment to the Court of Saint James's.

Much of what follows was adapted shamelessly from the transcript of an interview conducted in 2006 by the Association for Diplomatic Studies and Training (ADST) for their Foreign Affairs Oral History Collection, housed at the Foreign Service Institute in Arlington, Virginia, at Georgetown University in Washington, D.C, and on the Library of Congress Web site as "Frontline Diplomacy." This explains the alternation between a standard written style and the more conversational style of an interview. While such stylistic inconsistency is known to cause heartburn in editors, I have deliberately retained certain conversational segments in the interest of spontaneity.

I must acknowledge my debt to Charles Stuart "Stu" Kennedy, whose expertise as an interviewer (he has interviewed some 1500 U.S. diplomats for the ADST Oral History Project) elicited many of the essential points contained in this book.

Your Diplomats at Work

Prologue

From Farm Boy to Diplomat

I was raised in a farming community with the improbable name of Weyers Cave, in the Shenandoah Valley of Virginia, where hard work and industriousness were considered to be next to godliness, if not a little bit better. My family belonged to the Church of the Brethren, or German Baptists, who, along with the Amish and the Mennonites, had immigrated to the United States in the early eighteenth century as part of the Anabaptist movement. These denominations believed in the "simple life," based on the scripture "Do not love the world or the things in the world" (1 John 2:15). In the church that I attended as a boy, the men wore plain collars, black coats with no lapels, and beards; women wore black bonnets, long dresses, and black stockings. They frowned on such frivolous activities as drinking, smoking, dancing, and card games.

It was regarded as a bit of a concession to let me go to school. I remember that I wanted to go out for baseball like all my buddies but my elders said, "I'm sorry, you don't have time; when school's over you come home and you clean out the chicken house and you pick apples and you help us can peaches" and so on. It was only in my junior year in high school that I persuaded them to let me try out for the baseball team, by which time of course I had not developed much expertise in baseball and made only the second string. Once old enough, I could lead the horses pulling the hay wagon and, later, begin to drive tractors, which were only then becoming common. I looked forward to the time when I could graduate from humiliating domestic chores to working in the fields with the men.

These conservative farmers were, not surprisingly, predominantly Republican. The attitude was, "If he ain't got a job it's his own fault." And, "If you want to work, there's work." A cardinal rule when I was growing up was that you had to have a vegetable garden. Even if you lived in town, you had to have a garden. If a person didn't have a garden, he was considered lazy and not worth much. In the family that lived across the street, the man drove a truck and they didn't have a garden; they had a lot of children, and it was insinuated that they might not even be married. Having a garden was really a litmus test of respectability. We had gardens where we raised so much food that we couldn't eat it all. It was just tradition—that's just what you do—so you canned it to keep it from spoiling and then you gave it away to your neighbors.

One of my jobs as a boy was to go down into the cellar during the winter to clean the sprouts off the potatoes and cull the rotten apples, because there were too many to eat before they spoiled. We had shelves lined with Mason jars of peaches and beans and sausage and corn. My Aunt Mary would go down to the cellar, and when one or two of the jars would have begun to spoil and to spew a little bit, she'd open the questionable ones, scrape away the mold on top to see if it was spoiled throughout. She'd taste it and say, "It's *perfectly* all right!" And if the apples were partly rotten you'd take those up and eat those. As a result you were constantly eating slightly spoiled food; if it wasn't spoiled you left it for later. This is a joke that I share with my brothers to this day—if there is some question as to whether something is spoiled or not, someone says "It's *perfectly* all right," and then we throw it away.

The people in my community were different from the more diverse population in the nearby city of Harrisonburg, the Rockingham County seat. There they had people with foreign-sounding names like McAllister and DeMarco and Gonzales, while our community had typical German names such as Cline, Garber, Huffman, and Miller. And we felt that anybody that was outside our little denomination and our culture, well, they might be nice people but they were outsiders, they were the "other." We had almost no African-Americans. One man in our rural community, Sam Timberlake, went around helping people with threshing and making hay and things like that, and I remember that he was considered "a good worker." He's the only black I ever came in contact with during my childhood. It was very much a European—that is, German—community.

I attended one school, Mount Sidney High School in Augusta County, from the third grade through the third year of high school. Each grade was no bigger than perhaps fifteen or twenty students. The teachers were usually strictly local—they tended to live locally and teach locally. At about that time consolidated schools began to be built, and the authorities would send students from two or three of these small local schools to one centralized high school. What was left behind would typically become an elementary school. So when I finished my junior year I moved to Montevideo High School in Rockingham County, where I took pride in getting myself elected president of the senior class and editor-in-chief of the year-book without having known, or been known by, any of my fellow students. Actually, at that time in Virginia we didn't have twelve grades; we had eleven—seven years of elementary and four years of high school. When my kids laugh at me for not having had a twelfth grade, I tell them it took me only eleven years to learn everything.

My parents divorced when I was six, and my three brothers and I were farmed out to different families, usually families in our church community. Some of us went to relatives, some didn't. I stayed with an uncle and his wife until the age of nine, when I was transferred to a family willing to take a "boy" who would work for his keep. From about the age of nine I felt that I didn't really belong in this family. I had to "earn my salt," which was not a very pleasant feeling for a child.

But the diverse experiences my brothers and I had offer interesting material as to the "nature versus nurture" controversy. My oldest brother Bob went to live with a farm family, where he was expected to work with the poultry operation and with tractors and machinery. He today raises a million chickens a year down in the Shenandoah Valley and has a trucking company with fifty trailer trucks; so you can see how that experience determined what he did. My next older brother, Don, went to live with a blacksmith's family.

He joined the Air Force after World War II and became an airplane mechanic and crew chief on Air Force refueling flights to Morocco. He later became a motorcycle mechanic and today has a successful Harley-Davidson motorcycle dealership in Florida.

I had the good fortune, you might say, to be put with a family who were what could be called the "landed gentry" of the community. They went to college. One of their sons was a professor of religion at Bridgewater College. Another was the general secretary of the National Council of Churches, with offices on Riverside Drive in New York. The patriarch of the family was both a farmer and an itinerant preacher. As I early on showed a certain aptitude for academic pursuits, it was decided that I would be permitted to go to the local college ten miles away, Bridgewater College (provided I could pay for it myself). This led eventually to my becoming an academic and teaching at Yale and Cornell.

My younger brother Bill was quite small when we were split up, and he went from pillar to post, never having a consistent influence of any kind, and he has not followed any particular career. He lives on a mountaintop in West Virginia in a log cabin he built with his own hands (I'm not kidding), raises much of his own food, drives a Porsche, and winters in Florida. Several years ago he invited me to drive down to Costa Rica with him in his pickup truck. In a sense, he is the freest of us all, able to follow his impulses with no constraints.

While all four of us look alike and have similar personalities, our careers were largely determined by the environments in which we grew up. My half-brother Glenn, from my father's second marriage, came along twenty years later, attended college, and had a more normal upbringing, so is thus not part of the paradigm.

Bridgewater College

If I was to attend college, I had to finance it myself, which I did by working ten- to twelve-hour days during the summers for a construction gang and as a "printer's devil" in a print shop in the town of Bridgewater during the school term. I made about $1,000 a summer, which was enough, in those days, to put myself through four years of college and buy my own car. My first year as a graduate student at Cornell cost more than the entire four years at Bridgewater!

The Church of the Brethren is a small denomination, with only several hundred thousand members in the United States. On the other hand they have always been strong advocates of a good education. As a result they founded six colleges, which are rather respectable institutions academically and known for preparing young people for the professions. They're also strong in music, perhaps because of the German tradition of singing. In church the entire congregation would sing in four-part harmony—very different from the Episcopalians or the Catholics, where everybody chants in unison. I remember sitting by my dad, and he would be singing bass. He had never studied music at all but had simply learned that men in church sing bass or tenor—not the melody; that's for the women. So he had learned bass at his father's side, and I learned bass at his, and so on.

Bridgewater College in Virginia, seven miles south of Harrisonburg, is now a fairly big campus with something like 2,000 students, and is well known for its strong premed and teacher training programs. There are two Brethren colleges in Pennsylvania, Elizabethtown and Juniata, one in Ohio called Manchester, one in Kansas called McPherson College, and outside of Los Angeles in California there's one called La Verne. The Church of the Brethren, as its name indicates, has always been interested in the brotherhood of all peoples. In spite of being a fairly fundamentalist sort of denomination, it has always had a very international outlook—all God's children are brothers, we're all "brethren" (and "sistern"?).

Bridgewater College in those days, however, was not strong on international relations. This was the 1950s—the silent generation—and I don't remember a single course on international affairs. We studied world history, American history, English, Shakespeare, math, and biology, but we didn't know much about what was going on in the rest of the world. I'm sure there were some schools in the fifties where you did learn those things; but I was quite ignorant of the world when I graduated in 1955, with a joint major in French and Spanish and minors in English literature and secondary education.

International Voluntary Services

The Korean War had ended when I was in my senior year at Bridge-water (1954–55), but the compulsory draft still required all eighteen-year-old men to serve two years in the military. As the Church of the Brethren, along with the Quakers and Mennonites, is one of the historically pacifist churches, I had registered as a "conscientious objector" to war, but "COs" were required to serve two years in one of a number of programs approved by the Selective Service Board as "alternative service," such as working in hospitals, welfare programs, or relief efforts abroad. International Voluntary Services, Inc., was one of the organizations approved by the U.S. Selective Service for alternative service. IVS was an interdenominational organization that carried out humanitarian and development projects in various countries of Latin America and the Middle East. Its executive director, Dr. John Noffsinger, was on the board that later established the Peace Corps under President Kennedy.

At that time IVS was planning to set up a community development project in Laos, Indochina. Noffsinger had asked the president of Bridgewater College, his close friend, to help recruit "a down-to earth dirt farmer who speaks French" to be assigned to the project as an interpreter. As people with those qualifications were not plentiful in rural Virginia, the president thought of me. When, with some difficulty, I had located Laos on the map and realized that it was about as far away from Weyers Cave as one could get on planet Earth, I jumped at the chance for adventure.

Had we been at war at that time, I am not at all sure I would have registered as a conscientious objector, in spite of my church's position. By the time I graduated from college, I had begun to have some questions about pacifism, as well as about organized religion itself. But the prospect of traveling around the world was infinitely more attractive than two years training at a military base somewhere in the United States

I went to IVS headquarters in Washington to interview for the position. Although my competence in French was more academic than practical, I passed the test and was promised the job, pending finalization of the contract between IVS, the U.S. aid mission in Vientiane, and the Royal Government of Laos.

In the meantime, it was agreed that I would join the Brethren Volunteer Service for work and training at their relief clothing-processing center in New Windsor, Maryland, until my departure for Laos, anticipated for early October. Brethren Volunteer Service was one of the organizations approved by the Selective Service Administration in World War II for alternative service for pacifists. The training school in New Windsor continues to train volunteers for humanitarian and relief work. Many of the volunteers in my unit went to Europe. This was 1955, and Europe was still recovering from World War II, so we sent volunteers abroad who helped with the reconstruction of schools, administration of refugee centers, and various social projects.

At the end of the two-month training period (September–October), when the other members of the training session were leaving for their respective assignments in the United States or Europe, the Laos project had still not been finalized, so my colleague Carl Coppock (an animal husbandry specialist also assigned to the Laos project) and I were assigned as "guinea pigs" (normal control patients) in a cancer research project at the National Institutes of Health in Bethesda, Maryland. Aside from daily injections of radioactive tracer material and frequent blood drawing, this duty was pleasant enough, with plenty of time to read, study, and play ping pong. But Carl and I were impatient to get started on our great adventure, so we proposed to IVS that we be transferred to the Brethren Volunteer Service center in Modesto, California, to work there until our travel orders came through. Having obtained grudging permission for our scheme, Carl and I made arrangements with a car transport company in Chicago to drive a new car to San Francisco in return for gas and a modest stipend paid upon delivery of the car.

My brother Bob agreed to drive me as far west as possible in one day, and I was to hitchhike the rest of the way to Dayton to join up with Carl. On December 9, 1955, we set out in the snow from Harrisonburg, Virginia, in Bob's 1950 Ford convertible across the Allegheny Mountains toward West Virginia. It began snowing heavily, and we had to pile rocks in the trunk to provide enough traction to get up the mountain. At Brandywine, West Virginia, we put chains on the tires and made it as far as Elkins, at which point

Bob decided he had to turn back before the mounting snow made it impossible to get home. I got out beside the road and began hitch-hiking; the temperature was 15 degrees above zero Fahrenheit, and a thick layer of snow had accumulated on my bare head before I got the first ride. After eight successive hitches, I got a two-dollar room in a motel in Athens, Ohio, at midnight. One would think that these circumstances might have been discouraging, but one would have underestimated both my thirst for adventure and my determination to escape from my past.

After delivering the car to its destination in San Francisco, we headed for Modesto, where our work, like that at New Windsor, consisted of receiving and processing relief clothing collected by churches around the country, delivering it to various missions and community organizations in the California area, and shipping it abroad. Finally, after six months of waiting, word came that the IVS contract with the Lao government had been signed, and we left for Laos on February 19, 1956.

In the Land of a Million Elephants

My two years in exotic, landlocked Laos was the beginning of my fascination with foreign languages and cultures. Although I was officially the French interpreter for the International Voluntary Ser-vices community development team, my services as an interpreter were called on only when we were visited by the provincial gov-ernor or other high-level officials who had studied in France. Since the peasant farmers among whom we worked spoke no French, I had to learn some Lao to be at all effective as an interpreter. Other duties included establishing a community library with materials provided by the U.S. Information Service in Vientiane, teaching English, and serving as general assistant for our public health nurse in her childcare clinics in surrounding villages.

In 1956, the prime minister was Prince Souvanna Phouma, a pipe-smoking gentleman for whom I interpreted several times when he came up to visit our project. I admired him enormously, but as a neutralist he was not quite as anticommunist as his U.S. backers would have liked. In 1956 a communist insurgency was taking place in Laos similar to the ongoing war next door in Vietnam. Prince

Souphannavong, half-brother of the prime minister, disillusioned with the failure of the fight for Lao independence from France after World War II, had fled to Hanoi and founded a communist government in exile called the Pathet Lao (literally "Lao State"). With the aid of the Viet Minh, the Pathet Lao had occupied the two northern provinces of Houaphan and Phongsali, which bordered North Vietnam, and were fighting the Royal Lao army. It was in the context of Vietnam and the Cold War that USAID was financing our relatively small-scale IVS project as part of the objective of "winning hearts and minds" and preventing Laos from falling into the hands of the communists. By the end of my tour in 1958 the Pathet Lao and the royal government had come to an agreement that their forces would be integrated, but that agreement fell apart. Then in 1975 the Pathet Lao achieved the communist regime they had been working toward the entire time, and that same regime remains in power today.

The town where we were located, called Phon Savanh (which means "Heavenly Hill"), was a recently founded market village only about fifty miles from the Vietnamese border. The population of the village included not only Lao but also the ubiquitous Chinese shopkeepers, along with Vietnamese refugees who had fled the French-Vietnamese war. Phon Savanh was basically two rows of shop-houses on both sides of a muddy street. The reason we located in Phon Savanh rather than in the provincial capital Xieng Khouang was that they had an airstrip nearby on the Plain of Jars. They had just built a new post office—the PTT (*Poste, Téléphone et Télégraphe*)—which was the most impressive building in town, but since they weren't getting a whole lot of mail, they let us live there. The availability of these quarters was another factor in deciding to stay in Phon Savanh.

Our chief of party, Wendell Ralston, was a retired Iowa farmer who had been quite prominent in Iowa. His wife Frances didn't have an official portfolio other than as a kind of den mother. I was considered the interpreter and education specialist. My friend Carl was the animal husbandry guy from Texas A&M; the idea was that we were going to bring in improved breeds of livestock and poultry to upgrade the local stock. The team was augmented by the arrival six months later of a public health nurse named Martha

Rupel, along with Clyde Searl, an entomologist from the University of Redlands in California. An industrial arts specialist named Wally Brown joined the team about a year after I got there. With six people living in pretty close proximity there were some tensions and personality conflicts, but basically we got on all right, played a lot of canasta on Sunday nights, and had one of the only pianos in the country to indulge our musical interests. And while IVS was interdenominational, it just happened that the team members all belonged to the Church of the Brethren except for Clyde, who was, to put it charitably, nonreligious. So it annoyed him no end when people in the embassy would say, "Oh yeah, you're up there with those missionaries," since, with the rest of us being from the Church of the Brethren they assumed we were some kind of missionary group. That really infuriated him.

I served as interpreter, jeep driver, and general assistant for our public health nurse in her childcare clinics in a dozen surrounding villages. Our patients were typically Hmong women and their babies. While most Hmong men speak also Lao, most of the women speak only Hmong, so I had to learn a certain amount of Hmong medical vocabulary to be effective. Since I would interview the patients about their symptoms and relay this to the nurse, who would then administer the required treatment, the villagers naturally assumed I was the doctor. I remember once we were invited for lunch in the house of the village chief. Now Hmong food is generally pretty good, consisting mainly of fried meat and potatoes, but that day they had discovered a tree of rare yellow jacket larvae, and insisted that we, as the guests of honor, take the first bite of the deep-fried larvae. It wouldn't have been too bad if I had swallowed the thing whole, but I made the mistake of biting it in two, and it oozed a bit.

As the "education specialist," I established a library with materials in six languages: Lao, Thai, Vietnamese, Chinese, French, and English. The U.S. Information Service (USIS) in Vientiane supplied most of these materials. We taught English at night to various ethnic groups. It was clear early on that we had to segregate the English classes, because the Lao were happy-go-lucky and laid back and never did any homework, while the Vietnamese were bright and quick, worked hard, and learned much faster than the Lao. This ties in of course with the whole history of Indochina—the Vietnamese have always had a superiority complex vis-à-vis their Lao and Cambodian neighbors. The Chinese had their own reasons for learning English, mostly commercial. We had some Lao schoolteachers and some local government officials as students, but it didn't work out because the young people would put them to shame, and of course that's a no-no in an Asian society. So the officials gradually fell away and we ended up with classes of Vietnamese, Lao, and Hmong. The Hmong were bright and could learn quite quickly, but they were also illiterate and so had trouble with writing.

Xieng Khouang Province is the primary locus of the Hmong people in Laos. The country at that time had a population of only about two million, a million of whom were ethnic minorities. The Lao themselves typically lived in the plains and small valleys where they could farm wet rice. Government officials and administrators were drawn exclusively from the Lao, so they were the elite of society; but you had the Hmong-Mien, Tibeto-Burman, and Mon-Khmer minorities scattered throughout the country. This was where I first became interested in Southeast Asian languages and linguistics as well as ethno-linguistics—that is, the ethnic groups, the languages they speak, and the affiliations between them.

By and large the ethnic minorities lived separately and did not commingle. For example, the Hmong liked to live at elevations of 4,000 to 5,000 feet in the mountains, where they raised pigs, grew potatoes, and raised opium, the Hmong's major cash crop. USAID was always talking about substituting other crops for the opium, but that didn't work in Laos because no other crop in small amounts brings as high a return as opium. USAID proposed corn, for example, but how could they get the corn to market? There were no roads and no trucks. We had the only truck in the province. So corn was not going to make it as a substitute. A lot of the Hmong themselves were addicts; they took opium as a painkiller and then became addicted. The sale of opium was legal in Xieng Khouang, and sometimes when we were out on the road in the jeep we'd stop and pick up tribes people carrying their opium to market. But they didn't get most of the profit, which went to the middlemen— Chinese merchants—who would buy the opium from the Hmong farmers and then sell it to the French, who would fly it out to Saigon and

Bangkok. Once in awhile they'd get caught, but if they could get just one shipment through they were made for life. There was an inn called *Le Bungalow* in Phon Savanh run by the French. We were supposed to believe that they could operate a twin-engine Beech-craft on the revenue from their inn and restaurant. The problem with that was that there weren't any tourists. Every morning about 5:00 o'clock you would hear their plane take off. We joked about going down there some morning and snapping a flash shot of them loading opium into the nose of the plane, but they would have shot us without hesitation. These were international criminal types— Corsicans, most of them.

A military airstrip right next to us on the Plain of Jars received the wounded troops back from the front. We would see them lying there in the hot sun with just a little bit of canvas as shelter until a military ambulance would come and take them over the thirty kilometers of bumpy road to the provincial hospital in Xieng Khouang. We didn't have much hope for them, because that hospital was an incredibly dirty and ill-equipped place. I really pitied those soldiers. And, like most wars, in the end all of the death and suffering were in vain.

We had very little contact with the U.S. embassy as such. Most of our dealings were with USAID, for whom IVS was officially a subcontractor (as I later learned) and who was thus our parent agency. USAID dwarfed the embassy in size, as was true in many third-world countries at that time. Embassy officers would frequently come up to our project from Vientiane. As we were at an elevation of 3,600 feet and much cooler than Vientiane, officials from USAID and the embassy would seize any occasion to come up, making a pretext of touring our project. The United States was giving Laos about $40 million in aid at that time, and the U.S. mission had approximately 150 American personnel. We were the only six out in the field, so whenever any CODEL (congressional delegation) or any other person who had anything to do with appropriations would come to Laos, they'd shuttle them right up to us, saying "Look what these guys are doing up here—this is a USAID project up here." One such visitor, Senator Allen Ellender of Louisiana, was clearly looking for evidence to use against foreign aid. The word came up from Vientiane that Senator Ellender was on his way and that we should put our best foot forward and show him the wonderful things we were accomplishing. Our little project up there, with a budget of a couple hundred thousand dollars, was a pittance compared to the $40 million in aid to Vientiane. I don't know what Ellender reported about it, but he would have been justified in being fairly critical.

During the 1960s and 1970s, the whole Plain of Jars became an important battleground. Our project was abandoned quite early on, and the city of Xieng Khouang was totally blasted off the map by our bombers during the war in Laos. One event was rather humorous if it hadn't been so sad. We were getting some Brahma bulls from Texas. They had been brought to Texas from India originally and been upgraded and upbred in Texas, whose climate was rather similar to that of Laos. We spent a year building miles and miles of three-strand barbed wire to keep them in. Finally, after almost two years, when our animal husbandry guy was almost due to leave, they arrived. When the boat docked in the Bangkok harbor, these Brahma bulls must have realized they were coming back home to Asia because they jumped off the boat and swam ashore. We had to round them up in the streets of Bangkok. When we finally got them up to the project, it turned out that they could easily leap over our miles and miles of three-strand barbed wire fence. But I'm sure that they made what contribution they could to upgrading the indigenous stock.

From Laos to London by the Seat of My Pants

My friend Wally Brown and I were intrigued by the idea of trying to return to Europe overland by jeep or motorcycle or some other conveyance. Our vacation trip together to Hong Kong, the Philippines, South Vietnam, Cambodia, and Thailand the preceding November had proven that we were compatible, both as friends and as adventurers. But he had arrived a year later than I had and we were thus out of phase. So I tried to get a job somewhere in the U.S. mission in Vientiane for a year so that we could make the trip back together. A lot of IVS alumni went into USAID later on, and there was some interest in hiring me as one of USAID's field service representatives, first in Pakse and then later in Luang Prabang, because Joel Halpern, the field rep in Luang Prabang, had resigned.

But Washington was not too happy about hiring on the ground and said it would take at least six months to get my clearance and so on and so forth. To make a short story long, as my former Cornell colleague John Echols used to say, all attempts to find employment were unsuccessful so I decided to buy a motorcycle and start out on my own.

I didn't know much about the countries I was going to try to go through, but I had a National Geographic map of Asia, which covered such a huge area that Europe was way up in the left-hand corner of the map. From a Lao-French *métis* in Vientiane I bought a BMW motorcycle, single cylinder, 250 cc. It had a shaft drive, which friends told me would be preferable to a chain drive in crossing the deserts of the Middle East. USIS interviewed me before my departure from Vientiane and took pictures of me and my motorcycle against the backdrop of the That Luang, Vientiane's most impressive monument. I headed out for Bangkok, down part of the new U.S.-Thai Friendship Highway that USAID was building in early 1958. When I got to Bangkok and set about the business of getting visas for the countries I planned to go through, the snag was Burma.

The quickest route to Burma was via the Three Pagoda Pass on the Thai-Burma border, but I couldn't get permission from the Burmese to go overland. They suggested that I go down to Victoria Point at the southern tip of Burma and catch a boat up the Tenasserim Coast to Rangoon. I eventually agreed to this plan, but even then it took five or six weeks to get the Burmese visa, because it had to be referred to the Ministry of Foreign Affairs in Rangoon. Finally I got exasperated and pounded some desks. In the Asian context once you do that you've lost already, because it's a positive value in Asia to maintain your composure. Finally, the Burmese consul said to me, "Mr. Huffman, do you have any idea how hard it is to get a visa to your country?" I had never thought about that, because it had never been my problem. Of course he was exactly right.

I finally got the visa and headed down the Thai Peninsula to a little town called Rayong, which is opposite the southernmost point of Burma, called Victoria Point. I went across to Victoria Point and asked about the steamer that was supposed to run once a month from Penang to Calcutta, stopping along the Tenasserim Coast and Rangoon.

They said, "Yes, it come."

"When will it come?" I asked.

"It come tomorrow."

"Oh really? Well, how do we ... Will it stop here?"

"Not stop."

"How can we get it to stop?"

"We go out and stop it."

So, early next morning my motorcycle and I boarded a sampan, went out in the bay, and waved at the 700-ton steamer, which finally came to a halt. I have no idea whether it was going to stop anyhow. When I indicated I wanted to get aboard, the crew put the ship's crane overboard, picked up my motorcycle and me, and lifted us up onboard. We headed up the Tenasserim Coast, stopping off at Mergui and Tavoy and various little ports along the way. Finally, several days later, we made it to Rangoon.

As soon as I started to offload my motorcycle, I ran into problems with Burmese Customs. They said I didn't have a customs document for the vehicle and I couldn't import it unless I had one or unless I paid a bond of 150 percent of the value of the motorcycle. Of course I didn't have that much money to post as bond, so they seized the motorcycle and impounded it. I was stuck in Rangoon and the ship was sailing the next day for Calcutta. I tried to appeal to our embassy in Rangoon for help, and I must say, those were quieter days when Foreign Service officers had more time than they do these days, because the very kind vice consul there actually wrote a letter to Burmese Customs saying, "We know Mr. Franklin E. Huffman and we know that he's traveling across Burma and we assure you he has no intention of selling the motorcycle illegally in Burma."

I thought I was okay, but the Burmese saw through that. They said, "Well, they haven't promised to pay the bond; they haven't made any financial commitment here in this letter whatever."

So I went back to the man and, incredibly, he agreed to write another letter and try to imply financial responsibility without actually saying it. But he said that Customs was perfectly right, and that the embassy was not authorized to make any financial commitment to U.S. citizens. That was my first lesson in just what a U.S. embassy could and could not do for travelers abroad.

The second letter didn't work either. I was staying at the YMCA, in a kind of dormitory situation. I met the British advisor to the YMCA and told him my plight. He said, "Sure, I'll sign a bond for you."

I said, "Why would you do that when my own embassy won't?"

"Well," he said, "I believe your story."

In any case, he signed a bond and that got my motorcycle out of hock. As the steamer had already left for Calcutta, I had no alternative but to try to go overland to India. So I set out up the road to Mandalay. When I arrived in Mandalay two days later, they told me I would have to go in an armed train over to Monywa on the Chindwin River, because some of the ethnic minorities were in revolt in that area and it wasn't safe to go by road. So I put the motorcycle on a train, and when I got over to Monywa I asked, "Where is the road to India?" and they pointed to the Chindwin River.

At this point I began to think, "Hey, there's not much point in having this motorcycle; I've had it on a steamer and I've had it on the train, now I'm going to put it on a riverboat."

Early the next morning I went down to the riverbank and located the large barge-like riverboat where stevedores were loading sacks of rice and jars of fish sauce and various other things onto the boat across a gangplank about two feet wide. Several guys offered to help me put the bike on board, but, wanting to show off my skill as a motorcycle rider, I said, "Okay, stand back, guys, I'm going to ride across the gangplank." It would have worked if the gangplank hadn't sagged way down with the weight of the motorcycle. I stalled going up the plank and fell over into the water along with the motorcycle. This provided a great deal of merriment for everybody. But they all jumped in the water and helped me get the bike back up out of the water and dried off. It started up with apparently no damage done, and this time I agreed to let them walk it onto the boat for me.

We went up that river for about four or five days. I had time to read Tolstoy's *War and Peace* on the way. As this was the dry season, the water was low and the boat kept getting stranded on sandbars; it would take some time to maneuver back and forth and get it off each sandbar. Finally we got up to Kalewa, about eighty kilometers from the Indian border by what was basically an oxcart track. When I reached the Indian border, I crossed over a bridge and was stopped at the Indian customs police. I thought, "Oh boy, we're in for it again!" They showed me into the customs shack in an officious manner and had me sit and make a list of everything I had—articles of clothing, books, money, whatever. There was no place on the form to indicate I had a vehicle, so I didn't mention it. I handed it back to the man and he said, "Okay, veddy good."

Well, I was kind of disappointed, so I said, rather stupidly, "But what about the motorcycle?"

"Oh well, you're not going to sell it, isn't it?" he replied, using the tag question "isn't it?" that typically follows rhetorical questions in Indian English.

"Right," I said, unable to believe my luck. So he set me free, and I proceeded into Imphal, the capital of Manipur State, and made my way day by day across India, sleeping usually in government guesthouses called "dak bungalows." When departing Imphal I wanted to head out toward Assam but was told I'd have to go in an armored convoy because the Naga headhunters take a head once in a while just to keep their hand in.

On that trip through the foothills of the Himalayas I met an Indian businessman who invited me to go along with his family to the Kaziranga Game Preserve, where you can rent elephants to go out and see the wild game. I agreed to go with him, but when we got up there it turned out that the elephants had all been booked for that day. My host insisted that I take his spot on one of the elephants, since I might never get back there again and he could come again from Bombay. I accepted and got on the elephant at 5:00 in the morning. Between 5:00 and 10:00 o'clock we saw some rhinoceros, some wild boar, and other creatures. Though I'm not particularly susceptible to motion sickness, after five hours of swaying back and forth in that howdah, I was green when we alit. I thanked my Indian benefactor, jumped on the motorcycle, raced off, and was sick by the roadside.

When I got to Siliguri, I decided to go up to Darjeeling, which was famous for its tea and where an Australian I had met in Bangkok was teaching at the Mount Hermon Boarding School. So I went up and visited with him, saw the famous Darjeeling tea plantations, and stared at Mt. Everest in the mist. I went back down to Benares (these days spelled Varanasi) on the sacred Ganges River, then on to Agra and the Taj Mahal.

In Agra I was besieged by people who wanted to buy my BMW motorcycle because India at that time was not importing Western motorcycles. As I had had so much trouble with the motorcycle trip, and had taken about two months getting only as far as India, I decided I would sell the motorcycle to two fierce-looking Sikh brothers who offered me roughly what I had paid for it. It turned out later I could have gotten much more than that. But also in India you had a 150 percent import duty, so I told Mr. Harlal Singh, who was buying the motorcycle, "Either you give me the customs duty and I'll pay it, or else you give me an affidavit to the effect that you'll pay it."

He dismissed this with, "Oh, never mind, I have friends in customs, you know."

He never did get the affidavit to me.

In New Delhi I met an Australian graduate student named John Williams, who was traveling to the United States; he had heard about a bus that was supposed to go from Delhi to London for about 500 rupees or U.S. $100, with room and board included. When I saw that 1948 Bedford bus with various parts of frame and bald tires roped on the roof, I should have been suspicious that it wouldn't make it to London, but we couldn't afford to be pessimistic. So, after considerable delay, we set out with a party of about ten Indians and ten Westerners. We had continuous problems with the bus: it constantly broke down, tires blew out, the carburetor gave out, and so on. The Indians on board were worried about getting across the Pakistani border because India and Pakistan, even in 1958, were already at war over Kashmir. Traveling with us was a colorful yogi called the Swamiji Dev Murti, who let steamrollers run over his chest. The Swamiji said he could facilitate things at the border, but he never did help push the bus when it was broken down. We had managed to get over into Pakistan when the radiator sprang a leak. We changed the radiator only to find that the replacement leaked, too, just not as much. At one point there was a mutiny on the bus—the Europeans took over the bus because the Indian owner had spent all our money and was generally incompetent to manage the trip.

Finally when we reached southeastern Iran, my Australian friend and I decided to jump ship and abandoned the bus. We got on some UNESCO trucks that came along and left the bus stranded there in the desert. But later on our UNESCO truck broke down and the bus passed us, and we lost a lot of face. Then the bus got bogged down in the sand and asked the drivers of the two trucks to help push it out. We got them out, but I don't know to this day if that bus ever got out of the Iranian desert.

When we had hitchhiked as far as Kerman, we decided to catch a plane the 600 miles to Tehran. This was the only leg of the trip where we resorted to air travel. On that flight we met the FAO representative in Tehran, a Mr. Philip Thomforde, who invited us to stay with him and his family when we got to Tehran. I asked him if his wife wouldn't be upset by his bringing strangers home unannounced, but he assured us she would not. And she in fact seemed delighted to meet us. "It's a Quaker thing," she explained.

After a couple of days in Tehran, we got on a bus and headed toward Tabriz. That bus broke down, but another bus got us to the railhead of the great Orient Express at Erzurum in eastern Turkey. From Erzurum we took the Great Orient Express to Istanbul, thence across Greece and Yugoslavia to Trieste, Italy, and finally Venice. We had been so cold for so long going through the Himalayas that getting to Venice on a sunny spring morning and having a continental breakfast of croissants and *café au lait* seemed like we were getting back home—it looked like our culture.

I have often thought that it was unfortunate that my first trip around the world was from East to West. Having gone directly to the exotic Orient, on my arrival in Venice I was not as sensitive to the nuances of difference between U.S. and European cultures as I would otherwise have been. John Williams, the Australian I had traveled with from Delhi, was planning to study architecture in the States, and I was fortunate to be traveling with someone who could serve as a guide to the great architecture of Rome and Florence and Paris.

In Paris I said goodbye to John and met up with my brother Bill, who was in the Air Force in northeast France at Chaumont. It was a NATO (North Atlantic Treaty Organization) base, as de Gaulle hadn't yet kicked NATO out of France. When I met Bill, he said,

"Hey, I've got forty days of accumulated leave and a new Simca. Why don't we see a bit of Europe before you go back?"

As I had no specific deadline except finding a teaching job for the fall, I acceded to this marvelous suggestion. Bill rounded up some C-rations and sleeping bags—I didn't question him too closely how he got them—and we set out and traveled around most of western Europe for about a month, going down through France into Spain, across to Italy, up through Austria to Holland. We went to the 1958 World's Fair in Brussels, back down to Paris, and on to Le Mans in southern France for the twenty-four-hour automobile race. Bill was already an enthusiast, but that was my first exposure to sports cars. I was so enamored that I ordered a brand new Triumph TR-3 sports car from a dealer in Paris. Bill lent me the down payment and agreed to take delivery of the car and ship it over from Le Havre to New York at the GI rate. I crossed from Southampton, England, to New York on the last voyage of the liner *Ile-de-France*.

When I got home to Virginia, I needed to find gainful employment to pay for the TR-3, so I walked down the street in my hometown to the local high school and said, "Hi. I'm qualified to teach French, Spanish, and English, and I need a job." The principal said, "Good, we need a social studies teacher; you're hired."

So I spent the next two years, from 1958 to 1960, teaching French, history, geography, and eighth-grade civics in the local high school. To supplement the meager salary, which was $2,800 the first year, I also coached dramatics and drove a school bus, which upped my salary to a generous $4,200.

I think my trip around the world was at least the equivalent of a university degree. Looking back, it's hard to believe I had the temerity to strike out by myself on a motorcycle trip through Asia and the Middle East with only a National Geographic map of Asia as my guide. At age twenty-four we naturally feel invulnerable; by age fifty, we won't even fly to the next city without hotel reservations. Fifty years and two careers later, with the help of a journal that I maintained with German regularity throughout the two years, I published an account of my adventures in a book entitled *Monks and Motorcycles: From Laos to London by the Seat of my Pants, 1956–1958* (available from Amazon.com).

Adventures in Academia

While in Laos, I had the vague feeling that I should go to graduate school, but had no firm idea of what I wanted to study. This lack of commitment to any particular field is suggested by the fact that I applied to Yale and the University of Wisconsin in French literature, to Cornell University in linguistics, to the University of Virginia in history, and to the University of Montana at Bozeman in economics. Wisconsin offered me a fellowship in French for the fall of 1958, but, not fully understanding how graduate school works, I wrote them a letter requesting that the "appointment" be "postponed" until next year, as I had to work another year to pay off the car. They replied, rather stiffly, "If you are still interested next year, Mr. Huffman, you may reapply." I did reapply, and surprisingly, they made the same offer again for the fall of 1959, but again I demurred, feeling I needed to teach another year. By that time, Wisconsin decided I wasn't a serious scholar (not a totally inaccurate assessment) and didn't make the offer a third time.

Fortunately Cornell came through with an offer of a scholarship in linguistics for the fall of 1960. At Cornell I benefited from the National Defense Education Act, passed in the wake of the Soviets' launch of Sputnik I in 1957 and designed to "catch up" with the Russians in science, math, language, and area studies. After my first year at Cornell, I rode the gravy train of NDEA fellowships for three more years of course work (with fellowships for the study of Thai and Burmese). I had decided that my dissertation would be a grammar of the Cambodian language, the only national language of Southeast Asia that had not been described from the standpoint of modern structural linguistics. I obtained a fellowship for six months' study of Cambodian at the London School of Oriental and African Studies (as Cambodian was not at that time taught in any U.S. university), followed by a Fulbright-Hays grant for eighteen months' doctoral research in Thailand and Cambodia. As a result of the availability of NDEA Title VI grants administered by the U.S. Office of Education, language and area studies programs were expanding in the late sixties, so that when I completed my PhD in Southeast Asian linguistics, I received employment offers from Yale, Cornell, American, Washington, and Hawaii universities, not to mention the Ford Foundation and the Foreign Service Institute of the Department of State. I accepted a four-year tenure-track position at Yale as an assistant professor of Southeast Asian languages, with responsibility for supervising Thai and introducing Cambodian for the first time at a U.S. university. As there were no suitable textbooks for Cambodian, I obtained a grant from the U.S. Office of Education, hired a staff, and wrote three textbooks—a beginning spoken text, a beginning reader, and an intermediate reader. When I submitted the first one to Yale University Press, the editor called up my chairman, a good friend of hers, and said, "Who can evaluate his work?"

My chairman is said to have replied, "I don't know, but if he's at Yale, he must be good."

Based on this rather dubious recommendation, Yale published the first of what turned out to be a series of eight books, including an English-Khmer dictionary, which was on the Yale Press best-seller list for twenty-six weeks (it was popular with the 500,000 or so Khmer refugees who came to the United States in the early 1980s). One day my chairman called me in and said, "Three textbooks in three years—that's pretty impressive! But you know, you really ought to get a research grant and publish something a little more substantive if we're going to make a case for promotion." When I left his office I was walking on air, excited by his mention of "promotion." But then I realized, "Wait a minute; he just kicked my butt. What he told me was that if I don't do something more substantive than language textbooks, I have no chance of getting promoted."

Accordingly, I applied to all the usual suspects, such as the Ford Foundation, the National Science Foundation, the Office of Education, among others. I even applied to the Guggenheim Foundation, perhaps the most prestigious of all academic research grants. To my surprise, I was awarded a Guggenheim grant for "Research on Mon-Khmer Languages in Thailand, Laos and Cambodia." They must have reasoned that my rather exotic topic would be a welcome diversion from a heavy menu of grants in nuclear physics, but I also can't discount the influence of the dictum (however unjustified) that "If he's at Yale, he must be good."

While a Guggenheim grant is quite prestigious, for me it represented both a triumph and a failure, since the decision that I would go to Southeast Asia alone while my wife, Marcia Russell, did her doctoral research in Guatemala led to divorce in 1972. My two sons from that marriage both eventually attended Cornell. Russ, the older, did a PhD in neurobiology at the University of North Carolina at Chapel Hill and is now a senior scientist with a major pharmaceutical company. David, the younger, is president and CEO of an Internet company in San Francisco.

Although Yale's Southeast Asia Program folded from lack of funds in the mini-depression of the early seventies, the university took the very generous position that it still owed me salary for a fourth year, since I had obtained my own salary through the Guggenheim grant for the fourth year of my contract. I had no courses to teach, which gave me the time to write my books and to scout about for another position. Fortunately, Cornell took me back as an associate professor of linguistics with responsibility for teaching Cambodian and Vietnamese, as well as a course on linguistic field methods. I was accorded tenure two years later, and promoted to full professor of linguistics and Southeast Asian studies in 1980—exactly twenty years after I had entered Cornell as a beginning graduate student in 1960.

"When you come to a fork in the road, take it!" (Yogi Berra)

In 1985, at the age of fifty-one, after having taught for eighteen years at Yale and Cornell, and having published nine books and some thirty articles on Southeast Asian languages, I decided to resign from Cornell and join the U.S. Foreign Service. Between 1985 and mandatory retirement at age sixty-five in 1999, I was posted to London, Rangoon (Burma), Marrakech (Morocco), Paris, Phnom Penh (Cambodia), and Wellington (New Zealand). In August of 1999 I accepted a one-year post-retirement assignment as public affairs officer in the U.S. embassy in Chad in order to see something of Central Africa, and a second six-month tour as public affairs officer in Cambodia in 2002.

Many people have asked me what motivated me to make such a career change; there are many answers. First, in the early 1980s my students no longer had access to the three countries of Indochina that were my specialty—Cambodia, Laos, and Vietnam—with which we had no diplomatic relations because of their communist governments. So I had very few PhD students to advise.

As a tenured professor, I could have sat there for another twenty years, but one doesn't like to feel like a fifth wheel. I had become increasingly impatient with the ivory-tower quality of my career as well as with the overspecialized nature of my research. I felt a need to prove myself in the "real world" (although my diplomatic colleagues joked that in the Foreign Service I had certainly not tapped into the real world).

I, like many of my colleagues, was disillusioned by the so-called "Chomskyan revolution" that had hijacked the field of linguistics in the sixties. Noam Chomsky influenced a generation of linguists who based their theories almost exclusively on English. They further declared that language was innate and not learned (ignoring the fact that isolated children don't learn to speak), and that no nonnative speaker of a language could provide an accurate analysis of any foreign language. By these criteria, we who had been trained in anthropological linguistics and had specialized in various languages of the world were declared irrelevant. The real revolution in American linguistics, however, had occurred in the early twentieth century, when linguists such as Boaz, Sapir, and Bloomfield, working with the highly complex American Indian languages, advocated the objective analysis of languages in their own terms, rather than in comparison with, or in terms of, traditional European languages. The so-called Chomskyan revolution was in fact a return to the discredited subjective and ethnocentric analyses of the past. Chomskyan linguistics, which is in reality cognitive linguistics, deserves to be studied as one branch of linguistics, but not to the exclusion of other equally important fields of linguistics such as historical, comparative, descriptive, and anthropological linguistics.

Another reason was simple German stubbornness. In Laos I had become interested in the work of the U.S. Information Agency, which, in those days at least, administered American cultural centers and libraries, provided information about the United States, arranged educational exchanges (the Fulbright program), taught English, compiled bilingual dictionaries, and even went about the country with mobile movie-projection equipment. (Lamentably, USIA was abolished in 1999 at the behest of foreign policy watchdog Senator Jesse Helms, of which more later.) Impressed with the enthusiasm and professionalism of the U.S. Information Service personnel as compared to the more reserved State Department officers, I resolved to take the Foreign Service exam, which was the entry exam for both the Department of State and USIA. When I had visited the USIA headquarters in 1959, then located at 1776 Pennsylvania Avenue, they advised me to accept the scholarship offer from Cornell, since someone with an advanced degree in rare languages would be more interesting to them than people with French or Spanish, who were "a dime a dozen."

Based on this advice, I enrolled at Cornell, intending to perhaps take an MA in some exotic languages and then join the Foreign Service. I soon learned that Cornell couldn't be bothered with terminal MAs; as an Ivy League university (even if not in the top ranks of that hallowed company), they were interested primarily in producing PhDs who could be relied on to push back the frontiers of science and bring glory and honor to their alma mater. When I realized that I was expected to go for the PhD, I thought, "Well, if they think I can, maybe I can." At that point the old German work ethic kicked in, and I was constitutionally unable to abandon the project until I had gone from graduate student to full professor. Only when I had succeeded in that endeavor was I free to change careers and join the Foreign Service, which had been my intention twenty-five years earlier. At one time I considered this characteristic a virtue; now I see it more properly as a curse.

Having given all those perfectly logical reasons for leaving academia, the main reason was that my wife, Sanda, made me do it. She had defected from Romania to Paris in 1971, and had come to finish her PhD at Cornell, where I met her and married her in 1974. After her PhD, she was teaching at Cornell when she got an offer from the Foreign Service Institute to be a language-training supervisor in French—and she accepted the offer.

I was horrified; I said, "What do you mean, you're going to FSI? You're the wife of a Cornell professor and I work in Ithaca, New York." I naturally expected that, like any good wife, her career was going to take a backseat to mine, and besides, there was no comparing a beginning job at FSI with a full professorship at Cornell.

"Well," she said, "it's the best thing for my career, so I'd like to give it a try," and she went ahead with it. Part of the explanation was her background in a communist society, where women were "liberated" and expected to follow their own careers. But of course Eastern European women were not really equal with men—they had the right to pursue a career but they also had to do all the cooking and housework. Nevertheless, to facilitate her career we bought a house in Bethesda, and I commuted between Ithaca and Washington for four years so she could follow her career in Washington. I used the situation to justify buying a used Alfa Romeo sports car, and I drove it back and forth between Ithaca and Bethesda every weekend. I could make it in six hours door to door.

I soon got tired of that, and Sanda kept agitating for me to join the Foreign Service. At FSI she was teaching diplomats who were going off to exotic places such as Rome and Singapore and Rio de Janeiro. And so, more to humor her than anything else, I came to the State Department to explore the possibility of some kind of lateral appointment. They said, "Your background is certainly impressive, Professor Huffman, but confidentially you're the wrong color and the wrong sex to come in at midlevel."

I went home and told Sanda, "Ha ha, they're not seriously interested in me. They made the ridiculous suggestion that I should come in through the exam! They did say they were interested in you, though." During the latter years of the Carter administration they had a special emphasis on recruitment of women. My wife was intrigued and interviewed for midlevel entry. She got on the roster, but then Reagan came in and there was a freeze on hiring, so she was never called. But she passed the exam, and made lateral entry, and I couldn't. It hurt.

The Foreign Service Entrance Exam

I swallowed my pride and took the infamous Foreign Service exam. For some reason the Foreign Service has always been perceived (in spite of evidence to the contrary) as a glamorous and desirable career, shown by the fact that every year some 20,000 Americans take the exam for an average intake of 200 officers—an acceptance rate of one percent! (The idealization of the Foreign Service paled considerably during the Bush administration with the pressure to serve in Iraq. At the State Department's Foreign Affairs Day in 2007, Under Secretary for Political Affairs Nicholas Burns denied that FSOs had to be force-assigned to Iraq, bragging that at least a quarter of all FSOs had served in Iraq. I thought that was a sad commentary on our foreign affairs priorities. But I digress.)

I came through the eight-hour written test with flying colors; I made something like ninety, I think, on the first one. But I failed the orals twice. I couldn't seem to get past the in-basket test, I don't quite know why, because as an academic, that was exactly what I was doing in my office every day of the week. When they changed the content of the in-basket test the third time around I finally made it. Not surprisingly, I did best in the cultural cone, but I also did remarkably well in the economics cone on one of my attempts. They changed the exam from time to time and that particular year the economics part was made up of very practical questions about mortgages and bookkeeping and the kinds of things I had done all my life, so I did brilliantly on the economics part. I would not have done as well if they had asked me about theories and curves and things like that.

They tell you that you shouldn't give up your day job just because you passed the Foreign Service exam, since you still have the hurdles of the orals and the background check. I had a Senior Faculty Grant from the Office of Education to go to Thailand for a semester of research. While I was in Bangkok, I learned that I had passed the orals, but they still had to do the background check. In view of my wife's experience in not being hired even though she was on the roster, we had decided to go back to Cornell, and we bought a house in Ithaca in early 1984. Then during the fall term I was invited to join USIA. This caused quite a quandary, as I had begun teaching courses that continued in the spring term, and I didn't feel I could leave in the middle of the year, so I asked USIA to postpone my appointment until the summer of 1985, and they agreed.

It was quite a traumatic decision to give up my position in academia to start over in another career. But my wife said, "You ought to give it a try. If you don't try it, you'll never forgive yourself."

I said, "You mean *you'll* never forgive me!" So I asked the Linguistics Department at Cornell to grant me a one-year leave of absence in order not to burn my bridges, put our house up for rent, and joined USIA in time for the June 1985 training unit.

Indoctrination at USIA

I was a bit sensitive about being, at fifty-one, the oldest member of the class, but they all assured me that it was more and more common for older people to come in. At that time, in 1985, USIA had its own specialized training program. We did some joint things with State's A-100 class, but we had nine weeks of training at USIA. They had an office of training and a director of training, and I thought it extremely well done. We were trained in all of USIA's exchange programs, the Fulbright program, International Visitors, and all those good things; how to be a spokesman for an embassy; and how to be a press attaché. The whole press thing I always found less congenial than the cultural part, but we had to prepare to do both.

When I came in we were told that the press and cultural sides were a marriage made in heaven and that you had to be able to be a good press officer and a good cultural attaché, serve in both jobs, and then work your way up to being the public affairs officer in charge of both sides of the house. I never did quite believe that, and I still don't. An excellent cultural attaché may not have (in fact is not likely to have) the skills necessary to be an excellent press attaché, and vice versa. I always felt that it was an unnatural marriage of convenience. We were vulnerable to attack and division, and in fact many attempts had been made over the years to split up the Agency. USIA was originally established as the official information agency by President Eisenhower in 1953, but it did not include the cultural side until 1978, when State's Bureau of Educational and Cultural Affairs (CU) was moved to USIA. So it was not too surprising to me when we were eventually disbanded through the misguided depredations of Senator Jesse Helms.

During training they put us in front of a camera and had somebody interview us aggressively to see how we would stand up under pressure. We were taught something I've never forgotten and that every politician knows instinctively—decide what points you want to make before the interview and make those points regardless of what the question is. It was an enlightening experience for me. The whole thing had an air of novelty about it, because I'd been in academia for thirty years and this was new. It was also gratifying to expand my horizons a bit. It occurred to me that in academia, you get so specialized that sooner or later you know everything about nothing, while as a diplomat you need to know nothing about everything. I was quite put off when I first began to explore going into the Foreign Service by the fact that they did not seem to value my language and area expertise very much. But I later understood that they're right—they don't want people with an ax to grind or with an inflexible attachment to the countries of a certain area. It was made very clear that you're going to sink or swim as a generalist; if you can't do that, we're not interested in you. And I think that's quite legitimate, although it's useful to have some expertise in the history and culture of a country or an area, especially for cultural attachés. I've always been a bit envious of the expertise that you find in the Goethe Institutes and the British Councils and the Alliance Françaises around the world, where the officers tend to be cultural experts, artists, professors in their own right who stay in a certain country or area for twenty years—there's a great advantage in that, especially on the cultural side.

While training I continued working on a book. There's never a convenient time to switch careers. The book, with the rather pedestrian title *Bibliography and Index of Mainland Southeast Asian Languages and Linguistics,* was to be my *magnum opus* and had been promised to Yale University Press by a certain date in September. So I made a special plea at the end of the training to let me take leave without pay and finish the manuscript before beginning an assignment, and they agreed. I think USIA, being a smaller agency, was always a bit more flexible than State would have been in similar circumstances. So I sat there in our little apartment in Maryland, assiduously typing the final index to the book and managed to get it off to Yale Press by the deadline. Then the pressure was off, and I could turn my attention to the Foreign Service.

There were about twenty-five countries up for bids, some of which would have involved a year or more of language study before going to post. I had tested at the 3/3 level (considered to be "professional competence") or above in three languages—French, Cambodian, and Thai. You were given salary step increments for language competence, ——three steps for a 3/3, two steps for a 2/2, and so on. I tested in Spanish (2/2+) and Burmese (dismal), but I didn't bother to test in Vietnamese because I already had the maximum allowable ten steps that could be brought into the agency.

Thus, unlike many of my colleagues, I needed no language train-ing. (This policy has since been changed, and you receive extra pay for language ability only when assigned to a position requiring that language.)

Deputy Policy Officer for European Affairs

At that time the agency needed an acting deputy policy officer in the Bureau of European Affairs. The agreement was that if I would do a year in the Bureau of European Affairs the *quid pro quo* was a highly desirable follow-on posting in London. They used the argu-ment that this would familiarize me with the workings of the agen-cy and would be a great advantage later in my career. I'm not sure that was right, but I agreed to do it and became the deputy policy officer with responsibility for security and arms control issues in Europe. In 1985 under Reagan and the Cold War, security issues were quite important. We were engaged in a campaign to get our NATO allies to deploy intermediate-range ballistic missiles, which generated a huge controversy in the capitals of Europe.

Not knowing any more about security issues than the average layman, I had to become familiar with the alphabet soup of arms control talks, such as SALT (Strategic Arms Limitation Talks), CSCE (Conference on Security and Cooperation in Europe), and MBFR (Mutual and Balanced Force Reduction) Talks. One of my jobs was to telephone the PAOs (public affairs officers) in European capitals, who were typically rather senior people, and get their views on what was happening and what progress they were making in the promotion of our security objectives in Europe. This information was then fed into our progress reports to the USIA director and the White House. This gave me an acquaintance with many of the im-portant movers and shakers in the agency and I have to admit that I made some contacts that later proved useful.

After serving for about nine months in the European area of-fice, I left for London in July 1986 to spend a year as a JOT (junior officer trainee) at USIS London (the State Department terminology "junior officer" was a bit less demeaning). This was considered the plum assignment among the twenty-five or so posts that were up for bids, and the assignment was perhaps a nod to my academic qualifications and experience. But of course the job did not have any relevance whatever to my background as a Southeast Asian specialist.

USIA personnel had told me, "If you come in through the exam, we can match your salary," an indication of what academic salaries were like in the humanities. I was making about $40,000 at Cornell in those days. They told me, "We can match that under the new Foreign Service Act of 1980 where we can bring you in at the top of a grade four, but with your languages and background, you'll move up fast." And they were right; I made the Senior Foreign Service in eleven years. I will not pretend that I didn't miss the academic life, but I don't regret the decision to leave it, given the opportunity to travel and work in areas of the world other than Southeast Asia, and to have two careers rather than one.

Act One: Great Britain

Living It Up in London

My family and I arrived in London in early July 1986 for my first
overseas assignment. We approached the rather forbidding London
Embassy with some trepidation. The massive building, with the
sculpture of a bald eagle protruding anomalously above the front
entrance, sat in the middle of Grosvenor Square in London's West
End. When I had first visited the Embassy on my way back to the
States from Laos in 1958, I had no idea that twenty-eight years later
I would be assigned there as a diplomat, albeit a low-ranking one.
And even though as an academic I had made five trips around the
world, the phrase "a Virginia farm boy in the Court of St. James's"
kept going through my head, perhaps unconsciously paraphrasing
Mark Twain's *A Connecticut Yankee in King Arthur's Court*.

We were assigned to temporary quarters in an apartment in
the elegant Mayfair section of London, near the Embassy, pending
permanent housing. I remembered having been impressed in 1958
with the opulence of Mayfair and had taken pictures of the Rolls-
Royces, Bentleys, and Jaguars that lined the streets. As I was busy
moving our bags into the third-floor apartment, my ten-year-old
son Christopher, who had been exploring the furnished apartment,
came running down the steps, followed by three-year-old sister
Samantha. He announced breathlessly, "Dad! There's something
wrong with the TV!"

"What do you mean? What's wrong with it?" I asked.

"I can get only three channels," he replied.

The three channels were, of course, the government-supported
BBC1 and BBC2 and ITN, the one independent channel. But we soon

found that the joy of intelligent and commercial-free programming easily compensated for the lack of multiple channels.

In theory, an officer arriving at a first-world post is given a housing allowance based on rank and family size and is responsible for locating his own housing, while at third-world posts, where locating suitable housing is more problematic, all officers are assigned to leased properties in the embassy's "housing pool." In practice, however, every embassy tends to have a number of properties under lease, and the trend seems to be toward accommodating all embassy personnel in embassy-leased properties. We spent the next couple of days looking at various properties. The DPAO (deputy public affairs officer), Jim Hogan, gave us a list of possibilities, among which was an eighteenth-century townhouse in Hampstead, a rather chic and upscale residential area off the spacious Hampstead Heath, just four underground stops from the Embassy. The house was part of a four-story mansion that had been subdivided into four vertical sections, in a street with the quaint name of Windmill Hill. I was not terribly impressed with it, as the kitchen was rather basic and the plumbing was showing its age, but my wife fell in love with it for its quaintness, and the kids liked the hide-and-seek potential of the numerous nooks and crannies resulting from its peculiar architecture. The next day at the Embassy, Hogan asked me how I had liked the Windmill Hill property. "Well, it's certainly an excellent location, but the house is pretty basic. I'd like to look at some other places before making up our minds," I said.

"Oh, really?" he asked with obvious disappointment, "I hoped you'd like it."

It turned out that the embassy had leased the house for another officer who had been sent packing by the ambassador shortly before my arrival, and had already paid the leasing fee for an entire year in advance. It finally dawned on me that what Hogan was trying to say, but was too diplomatic to say outright, was "I hoped you'd like it, because that's where you're going to live." So we moved there and were ultimately delighted with the choice. I later realized what a jewel the property was, both because of its eighteenth-century charm, and because of its proximity to schools for the kids, to Hampstead Heath where they could run and play, and to my office in the Embassy.

One aspect of the Foreign Service about which I have no complaint is the housing—one of the few remaining perks of the Foreign Service. Because of the need to locate embassy personnel reasonably close to their offices, embassy housing tends to be centrally located in areas one could never afford on one's own, especially in European capitals. This was certainly true of our lodgings in Hampstead. Likewise, in Paris, we were assigned to a spacious apartment just five minutes off the Champs-Elysées, and in Wellington, New Zealand, our house and gardens were equally impressive. In the third world, where there is typically no middle ground between slum housing and the upscale houses built specifically for Westerners, the only choice for diplomats is housing of the upscale category. For example, in Burma, our house was a British-built mansion with its own tennis court; in Morocco we had what was essentially a duplex, with a second unit where we could put up visitors; in Cambodia we had a five-bedroom house—one of many built to accommodate the influx of UN personnel during the 1992–93 UN Transitional Authority in Cambodia. The only post where housing was of a dubious standard was Chad, but more about that later.

After moving to the Hampstead house, we explored schools for the kids. We enrolled Christopher in the fifth grade at the admirably equipped American School of London in St. John's Wood, where over the course of the year he joined the Boy Scouts and took up the cello. My wife located a nursery school for four-year-old Samantha in the basement of a venerable old Anglican church nearby, where Samantha, with her incredible ear for languages, was soon saying such things as "Don't be silly, Daddeh" with an impeccable Oxbridge accent.

OK, What Do I Do Now?

Having dealt with housing and schools, I turned my attention to finding out what a fifty-one-year-old JOT (junior officer trainee) was expected to do. A large embassy, such as those in London, Paris, Bangkok, or Manila, typically houses representatives from twenty or so different U.S. government agencies, depending on our interests in a particular country. In addition to the political, economic, consular, and administrative sections of the embassy staffed by State Department Foreign Service officers (FSOs), and the (now former) U.S. Information Service, staffed by USIA FSOs, a large embassy may also house personnel from the U.S. Agency for International Development (which in third-world countries can dwarf the size of the State Department contingent), the defense attaché's office (potentially including officers from the army, navy, and air force, not to mention the Marine Guard Detachment), the Foreign Commercial Service of the Department of Commerce, the Foreign Agricultural Service of the Department of Agriculture, the Department of the Treasury, the Department of Labor, the Drug Enforcement Administration, the Social Security Administration, the Internal Revenue Service, U.S. Customs, the Federal Aviation Administration, the U.S. Park Service, the U.S. Trade Representative, the Library of Congress, the Environmental Protection Agency, the Coast Guard, the Peace Corps, the FBI, and of course, the CIA, which maintains the fiction that it is covert by using various pseudonyms, such as the Political-Military Section, or the Regional Assessment Office.

In a small embassy it is usually an open secret who these people are, but it is a crime to deliberately reveal it to either a colleague or a host country national (as we saw in the "outing" of CIA agent Valerie Plame by an official—or officials—of the Bush administration). Once during our tour in Paris my wife was invited to a coffee klatch for newly arrived spouses (all wives, it must be admitted) of embassy officers. Each woman was asked to identify herself and her embassy officer husband. My wife was working as an assistant in the political section of the embassy and was therefore personally acquainted with all seven political officers in the section. She listened in amazement as some twenty women identified their husbands as "political officers." (Interestingly, USIA never provided cover for CIA personnel, but nobody believed it, especially the Soviets, since KGB agents occasionally called themselves "cultural attachés.").

I was to be based in the U.S. Information Service unit of the embassy, headed by a high-profile public affairs officer named Robert (Bud) Korengold, who had joined USIA after a distinguished career in journalism, including serving as *Newsweek*'s Moscow bureau chief. USIS was divided into a press section, headed by the IO (information officer) and a cultural section, headed by the CAO (cultural affairs officer); at a post like London, these were very senior positions. Under the section heads were a number of AIOs (assistant information officers) and ACAOs (assistant cultural affairs officers). The entire USIS section included some ten American officers and maybe twenty-five locally hired British employees called FSNs (Foreign Service nationals; although they have more recently been baptized LES—locally employed staff—I will continue to use the designation FSN throughout the book).

In principle, a trainee was expected to be rotated through the various sections of the embassy in order to become familiar with the work of each section—the press and cultural sections of USIS and the political, economic, consular, and administrative sections of the embassy. During this rotation, the trainee is typically considered to be "over complement," that is, not encumbering an actual position. However, perhaps because of my ripe old age and academic background, I was continually given rather substantive special assignments, some of which would not have been assigned to an ordinary twenty-something JOT. For example, when Robin Raphel, the Asia watcher in the political section, took unanticipated maternity leave (unanticipated at least from the embassy's standpoint), they needed a temporary replacement, so they said, "Well, you know, there's Huffman down in USIS, he has an Asian background, why not let him replace her?" So rather than looking over the shoulder of the Asia watcher during a stint in the political section, I *was* the Asia watcher, responding to queries and drafting cables in my own right.

This was about the time when the Irangate scandal broke, and Richard Murphy, the assistant secretary of state for the Near East and North Africa, decided to call together eight ambassadors from the Middle East for a damage control confab in the London Embassy. In a normal embassy, the visit of just one ambassador, let alone an assistant secretary of state and eight ambassadors, would demand the attention of the ambassador, or at least the head of the political section. But London was (and is) one of the busiest embassies we have, and high-level visitors were an everyday occurrence. Secretary of State George Shultz was a regular. At the time of Murphy's visit, we had three cabinet secretaries visiting at the same time—Secretary of State Shultz, Attorney General Ed Meese, and a third secretary whose identity I don't recall—

probably Secretary of Defense Caspar Weinberger. Preoccupied with the cabinet-level firemen, the head of the political section, Kim Pendleton, said, "We'll let Huffman handle Murphy's operation." So I went into action, made sure they had appropriate hotel and restaurant reservations, reserved the necessary conference rooms, and set up requested appointments with British officials.

In addition to Assistant Secretary Murphy, the group included U.S. ambassador to Israel Tom Pickering (who was later ambassador to the UN), ambassador to Saudi Arabia Walter Cutler, ambassador to Egypt Frank Wisner, and ambassador to Lebanon John Kelly. One day as I was ensconced in my (Robin Raphel's) office, looking very senior, one of the ambassadors came in and, assuming I was in fact a senior political officer, said apologetically, "I'm very sorry to bother you, but I was wondering if I could use your telephone to make a call back to Washington."

"Oh, sure, go right ahead, Mr. Ambassador; no bother at all," I said expansively, enjoying the moment. I've never been very good at role-playing, but in this instance I couldn't resist playing it to the hilt.

As the press section was two officers short at the time, I was in effect the acting AIO during my rotation there. Duties included arranging press conferences for visiting U.S. officials (such as SecState Shultz, Lt. Gen. James Abrahamson, Strategic Defense Initiative Organization director, and Assistant Secretary for Africa Chester Crocker), and inviting journalists to participate in "WorldNet interactives" (two-way audio, one-way video conferences broadcast from the USIA studios in Washington).

While in the press section, I had the opportunity to lead a group of six British academics on a tour to various NATO (North Atlantic Treaty Organization) facilities around Europe. On this particular tour we visited NATO headquarters and SHAPE (Supreme Headquarters Allied Powers Europe) outside Brussels, both West and East Berlin, and the headquarters of AFCENT (Allied Forces Central Europe) in Brunssum, The Netherlands. These NATO tours were sponsored jointly by NATO and USIA to provide an inside look at NATO for journalists, academics, and officials with a view to enhancing understanding of, and one hoped, sympathy for, the NATO mission. And I must admit that the program appeared to be rather effective in achieving its aims. British academics (like most academics elsewhere) tended to be rather liberal (to avoid the word leftist) and skeptical of all things military, but by the time they finished their ten-day tour of NATO facilities—where they were briefed by high-level military officials of various nationalities, able to ask any question and challenge any position they wished, given an inside look at NATO facilities that effectively "demystified" NATO's activities, and treated to comfortable lodgings and free food at the expense of NATO and the U.S. government—their attitudes and comments had softened, or at least were somewhat less hostile.

"Two Countries Separated by a Common Language"

To further fraternal relations with the British press, we would sometimes have lunch with our counterparts from the print and electronic media for off-the-record discussions of bilateral issues. At one such luncheon we were comparing the broadcasts of the BBC with those of the Voice of America. VOA had the practice, and still does, of carrying editorials at the behest of the State Department, preceded by the statement "The following is an editorial that represents the views of the U.S. government." After reading the editorial, maybe three minutes long, they intone, "The preceding was an editorial which represents the views of the U.S. government." The purpose of these statements is to make a clear distinction between opinion and news reporting in an attempt to reinforce the idea that the VOA is an objective and independent news service—which in fact it is, to a remarkable degree.

The deputy director of the BBC World Service kidded us about these editorials, saying, "You know, you Americans, you're constantly throwing it in the face of your audience that you're putting things on there that represent the views of your government. So people think that you're just a mouthpiece for the government. Now, at the BBC, we editorialize all the time but we just don't admit it. You should quit doing that." And I totally agree; I have always argued that these editorials hurt the credibility of VOA as an objective and autonomous news agency. We have to face the fact that the BBC is more prestigious around the world than VOA. It's considered the last word, the most unbiased, independent voice, and so on, but in fact I found in working with the BBC in various countries that they definitely had a liberal bias, with the freedom to put their own spin on things. I also found that they had more of a tendency to go off half-cocked on stories than the VOA did, sometimes reporting things a bit to the left on which they hadn't done the necessary spadework to verify the stories from various sources and which they sometimes had to retract.

BBC English remains the standard around the world, in spite of major inroads by American English. In fact, there is an absolute mystique that surrounds British English; foreigners frequently say they want to learn "genuine"—meaning British—English. British English is the standard for the American stage, and American corporations like to hire British secretaries to answer the phones for their prestige value. George Bernard Shaw famously said, "England and the United States are two countries separated by a common language." One cultural difference is that the Oxbridge pronunciation is consciously taught and transmitted to the elite of society, thus becoming a mark of sophistication and education. By contrast, Americans see language only as a medium of communication where any accent will do so long as communication takes place. I was once on an academic panel with three Americans and one British member. The three Americans made their presentations first, and when the Brit made his contribution, he sounded so confident and authoritative that the audience assumed he was brilliant, when in fact he was talking nonsense.

The truth, however, is that American English is much more homogeneous than British English. There is less dialectical variation in American English from New York to San Francisco than there is in Great Britain from London to Edinburgh. Thus a greater percentage of Americans than British speak "good" English. But I digress.

Striped-Pants Duty

One of the reciprocal duties of diplomats is to attend the national day receptions of all the other embassies in town. These are pleasant if not terribly useful occasions where you introduce yourself to the host and hostess (usually the ambassador and his wife), make polite conversation with your counterparts and acquaintances from other embassies, and enjoy the usually quite good finger food and wine (except at receptions of Islamic countries, where wine is replaced by fruit juice and other nonalcoholic beverages). Because of the near impossibility of shaking hands with other diplomats while holding a wine glass in one hand and a plate of food in the other, I quickly learned the survival strategy of placing myself within arm's reach of the finger food, holding the wine glass in the left hand and leaving the right hand free to alternately reach for an hors d'oeuvre and shake hands when the occasion demanded. There is a decided pecking order in which the more important the country in question, the higher the rank of the officer(s) assigned to represent the embassy. Surprisingly for a junior officer trainee in an embassy of several hundred American officers, I was tapped to represent the embassy at the Thai, Burmese, and Bahraini national day receptions, perhaps, again, because of credibility conferred by my age and background.

The most enjoyable duty was attending the frequent receptions at Winfield House, the American ambassador's elegant residence in Regents Park and the second largest country estate in London after Buckingham Palace. The neo-Georgian mansion was sold to the U.S. government by Woolworth heiress Barbara Hutton for one dollar and has been the residence of the U.S. ambassador to the Court of St. James's since 1955. Whenever there was a reception at Winfield House, PAO Bud Korengold would insist that all USIS personnel attend the reception in order to deal with any unforeseen problems, make the proper introductions to the ambassador (especially those of our contacts whom he might not know), and in general smooth the wheels of diplomacy. But there was usually such a crowd of guests (typically in the hundreds) that if one steered clear of one's boss, one could schmooze with the frequently interesting guests while enjoying the excellent wine and hors d'oeuvres and the general ambiance of Winfield House.

On one such occasion the cultural section had arranged a concert at the ambassador's residence by the gifted Japanese-American pianist Megume Umene. During the reception that followed, I was congratulating the artist, when former prime minister Sir Edward Heath joined the conversation. Sir Edward was an accomplished musician in his own right and had on occasion been invited to conduct the Royal Philharmonic Orchestra. A USIS photographer snapped a picture at that moment, and I still treasure the photograph of me with Sir Edward.

On another occasion, one of the guests was Ambassador Kingman Brewster, Jr., who had been president of Yale University when I was an assistant professor there (1967–72) during the Vietnam War. Brewster had been U.S. ambassador to Great Britain 1977–81 (Winfield House was thus his former residence) and had later been appointed Master of University College at Oxford. Yale had managed to avoid the worst of the antiwar violence that had taken place on other campuses such as Berkeley, Columbia, and Cornell, where armed protesters actually took over the student union building. I introduced myself as a former member of his faculty and told him I had always admired the way he handled the student protests at that time. Brewster was a towering hulk of a man in failing health, had recently had a stroke, and had difficulty speaking, but in response he simply held up two crossed fingers, implying that he had been lucky. But I don't think it was luck so much as Brewster's skill in defusing the situation. Rather than calling in the gendarmes, he had managed to persuade the students that he was on their side, while at the same time no doubt telling a panicked Board of Trustees, "Just let me handle it, and we'll be all right."

The director of USIA at the time was Charles Z. Wick (formerly Zwick), whose monumental ego and fiery temper were legendary. When Reagan appointed him director in 1981, some of Reagan's staff questioned whether Wick, as a former musician and motion picture financier, had the qualifications to be director of USIA, but as Wick had raised $15 million for Reagan's first presidential campaign, Reagan is quoted as having said, "He can have anything he wants."

Wick had a blacklist of people who were not permitted to serve as U.S. speakers abroad, a list that included Walter Cronkite, Ralph Nader, and Coretta Scott King. He had megalomaniacal ambitions for the overseas television network he set up, called WorldNet, with which he wanted to compete with government-funded operations such as BBC-TV and France-Inter, ignoring the fact that to do so he would have to compete with such U.S. private sector networks as

CNN. PAOs abroad were pressured to inflate the number of viewers being reached by WorldNet in their respective countries so that Wick could brag to the president that his network had an audience of twenty million or so viewers; but what this really meant was that they were the "potential" audience, if they had chosen to tune in. Once while Wick was in London, he was invited to a reception at Winfield House; mistakenly assuming he was the guest of honor, he proceeded to make a rather lengthy speech to the assembled guests. When he finished, a British member of Parliament whispered in my ear, "Who *was* that funny little man?" Little did we know that we would later be nostalgic for the reign of Charles Wick, who expanded the budget and power of USIA enormously through his influence with the White House.

During my year in London, I was given a number of writing assignments, such as preparing a background manual on NATO (useful in leading the NATO tour to Belgium, Germany, and the Netherlands), writing letters for the ambassador's signature, and writing speeches for the ambassador to deliver on various occasions, such as the annual British-American Ball, the dinner for Senator J. William Fulbright and Alistair Cooke, and the opening of the University Forum debates.

The ambassador at that time was the Honorable Charles H. Price II, a wealthy banker and businessman from Kansas City who had been appointed by President Reagan in 1983. (Note: Roughly 30–40 percent of U.S. ambassadors are noncareer, usually political, appointees; the other 60–70 percent are drawn from the ranks of career Foreign Service officers. The most desirable posts typically go to wealthy supporters of the president; some wag actually compiled a list of countries and the cost of buying an ambassadorship in each of them. The prevalence of political appointees as ambassadors causes a lot of heartburn among senior diplomats who have come up through the ranks only to have their elevation to ambassadorships blocked by inexperienced political appointees. While it is true that political ambassadors can be like bulls in the diplomatic china shop, I have served under both good political appointees and bad career ambassadors. Conventional wisdom is that ambassadors to such high-profile posts as London and Paris need to be independently wealthy, since the meager funds provided by the State

Department do not cover the costs of the social obligations at such posts. Raymond Seitz was a notable exception. But I digress.)

Ambassador Price, who later served on the boards of directors for British Airways, the New York Times Company, Texaco, and Sprint, was perfectly capable of writing his own speeches, but when you have 1,000 employees at your beck and call, why bother?

Putting Words in President Reagan's Mouth

One of the most interesting things I did during my entire tour in London was writing a speech for President Reagan. The English-Speaking Union had requested that the embassy send an invitation to President Reagan to come over and address the English-Speaking Union in the famous old Guildhall on the fortieth anniversary of the Marshall Plan. We didn't have much hope that he would accept if it didn't fit his plans or if he didn't already have a European trip planned, but we had to submit the request to the White House anyway. We suggested as an alternative that he might be willing to do a speech on video, which could then be played on a huge screen in the Guildhall. And lo and behold he agreed to do that. Well, who was going to write the speech? So they said, "Let Huffman do it. He's a former professor of linguistics; he ought to be able to write a bang-up speech." So I settled down to doing the research on the background of the Marshall Plan, and I must say I was learning a lot of new stuff. I think it's an advantage when you're learning new material because it's fresh and exciting, whereas if I'd been a specialist in arms control in Europe and the Marshall Plan and so on, I'm not sure I could have brought the same spontaneity to the project. But when I learned that the United States had given over $13 billion, or 6 percent of our national budget, for the reconstruction of Europe after World War II, this impressed me as an event of unprecedented generosity in the history of nations.

An amusing anecdote while I was writing the speech: We had a dinner party one night with some embassy people and some of my contacts in the cultural community in attendance; the phone rang, and my wife said, "Frank, it's for you; it's the White House calling." My guests were highly impressed.

"Oh, thanks. I'll take it downstairs," I said.

It turned out it was some young speechwriter in the bowels of the old Executive Office Building calling me to verify some of my figures and ask where I got them and so on, but of course I didn't point that out to the dinner guests when I came back up. I simply said, "I took care of that. Sorry about the interruption."

They sent us a copy of the video to hand over to the English-Speaking Union, and I must say it was an eerie experience to hear the president speaking my words. At that point I realized why Reagan was considered such a great communicator—he delivered the speech as if he were searching for the right terms and then he would come up, unfailingly, with my words, as if from the depths of his emotion.

The Olney Pancake Race

Great Britain is a treasure trove of forts, castles, cathedrals, abbeys, and historic houses that are a magnet for tourists, especially Americans. Our fascination with castles is easily explainable by the fact that we did not historically have any, except for several imported stone by stone from Europe (although the tracts of ostentatious "McMansions" that dot the countryside of Northern Virginia or Montgomery County rival the castles of Europe in size if not in taste). After exploring the fabled sites of London, such as Westminster Abbey, Parliament, the Tower of London, and St. Paul's Cathedral, we regularly used weekends to visit sites farther afield, such as the castles of Windsor (one of the most impressive castles in the world), Hampton Court, and Dover, the cathedrals of Canterbury, Salisbury and Lincoln, the country homes of Blenheim, Longleat House, and Haddon Hall, and the picturesque towns of Oxford, Cambridge, and Chester. But before we could get out of town, we had to get some wheels. Through a newsletter that listed diplomatic cars for sale, I bought a 1985 BMW 316 from a secretary at the German embassy. (The 316 was the smallest BMW, with a 1.6-liter engine; it was never exported to the States, as it was considered not powerful enough for the U.S. market.)

As she had brought the car from Germany, it had left-hand drive, which I thought might be a problem in England, but in the end I decided it was a definite advantage. Although I had driven on the left in such countries as India, Thailand, and Malaysia, I found that having to focus on staying on the left, passing on the right, and turning right across oncoming traffic, in addition to having the gear shift and turn signal on the wrong side, sometimes caused a sensory overload, leading to such gaffes as turning on the windshield wipers when intending to hit the turn signal. By contrast, having the steering wheel, gearshift, and turn signals where you are accustomed to having them allows you to let your subconscious reflexes do the driving while you focus only on staying on the left side of the road. Besides, I intended to take the car with me to my follow-on assignment in Burma, where they drive on the right. (It is not quite clear why Burma, having been a British colony like India and Malaysia, nevertheless drives on the right—maybe just a finger in the eye of their former colonial masters.)

Because I had developed a bit of a reputation as a speechwriter and speaker, I was from time to time asked to represent the embassy as a speaker at rather low-level events that did not merit the presence of a higher-ranking officer. Some of the venues were the English-Speaking Union in the town of Chester, the Daughters of 1812 in London, the Hemel Hempstead Middle School, and the Junior Officers Association of Lakenheath Air Force Base.

One of the strangest events I attended was the Olney Pancake Race. This race, run every year on Shrove Tuesday in the little town of Olney, reputedly dates back to 1445. It requires young ladies, married or single, dressed in traditional costume, to run a distance of 415 yards carrying a skillet and flipping a pancake. No one knows quite how the race originated, but one story tells of a harassed housewife who, hearing the church bell for the Shriving service, dashes off to the parish church still clutching her frying pan containing a pancake. Following the race, the contestants and townspeople, along with large crowds of tourists, pour into the parish church for the Shriving service, after which the day is given over to celebrations and merriment on the last day before Lent.

The race became an international event in 1950 when the town of Liberal, Kansas, decided to compete with the runners in Olney, and times are compared through a transatlantic telephone call; Olney usually wins. Apparently it was decided that this was an event that could adequately be covered by a junior officer. I note that the

London Embassy Web site features a visit by an embassy officer to the 2006 running of the pancakes.

The Special Relationship

For speaking venues, I had written a speech titled "The Special Relationship: Fact or Fiction?" As can be surmised, it sets up the straw man that maybe the special relationship is in some danger, then in the end puts everyone's mind at ease by claiming, after considerable discussion, that it is still strong and healthy. It is an easy case to make:

- As a former colony of Great Britain, we inherited our language, traditions, legal and educational systems, and philosophy of government from the mother country.
- The U.K. is our strongest ally in the area of security, having sided with the United States in every war since the unfortunate events of 1812.
- Forty percent of the U.S. population traces its ancestry to the British Isles. (According to the 2000 census, while people of German ancestry constitute the largest ethnic group in the U.S., the U.K. wins if you combine the English, Irish, Scots, and Welsh.)
- We share a commitment to democracy, rule of law, human rights and freedoms, free enterprise, free trade, and the dignity of the individual.

The very obviousness of this common heritage can be misleading. There are rather striking differences in our respective value systems. We have some mutually negative stereotypes of each other. Americans generally admire the British as sturdy, self-reliant, stoic, "stiff upper lip," and so on, while at the same time feeling that they are, as a people, cold, reserved, and somewhat arrogant. Conversely, the British generally admire the fact that Americans are open, direct, optimistic, practical, and hard working. At the same time we tend to strike them as loud, uncultured, naïve, aggressive, and materialistic. Though some of these stereotypes are oversimplifications, where there's smoke there's fire.

It was my job to refute such stereotypes, or at least try to explain them, which I did in the following ways: The charge is frequently made, especially by the British, that Americans are a bit naïve in the conduct of world affairs and that, compared to the old countries of Europe, America is too young and inexperienced to bear the burden of being, by default, the world's only superpower. It is usually implicit in this criticism that Britain could really do a better job of it. It's true that Americans tend to believe that every problem has a solution; thus it might be kinder to call them "optimistic" or "positive" rather than "naïve." These characteristics derive, quite naturally, from our colonial experience—the early settlers were faced with a set of entirely new problems that demanded original solutions. They were a self-selected population of "doers" rather than "thinkers." Faced with a hostile environment and the exigencies of survival in a strange land, they had little time for a class of philosophers, scholars, or literati. Daniel Boorstin, former director of the Library of Congress, has even claimed that Americans represent "the triumph of naiveté over learning," and that they succeeded in a whole range of endeavors precisely because they hadn't read the theories of the European philosophers who said it couldn't be done.

It's true that Americans are compulsive problem-solvers. There's a joke that goes as follows: Three men had been condemned to death by guillotine—a Frenchman, a German, and an American. The Frenchman went first, but there was a malfunction and the blade failed to fall; on the principle that it would be inhumane to subject him to such a trauma again, the authorities decided to let him go free; his reaction was a Gallic shrug and the comment, "*C'est la vie.*" Next it was the German's turn; he placed himself on the guillotine with Germanic stoicism, but again the machine failed to function, and the German was released, exclaiming "*Gott sei dank!*" When the American placed himself on the guillotine, he looked up at the blade and said, "I think I see the problem; if I had a screwdriver I could fix that." But Americans' naiveté—or rather their "can-do" attitude—has produced impressive achievements in science, technology, and the arts; to insist that we do it with style and panache is perhaps to apply one society's values to another.

A criticism that I frequently heard in Great Britain was that Americans are "materialistic"—not to say "moneygrubbers"— that we sacrifice quality of life for financial success, and that in the

United States class is based solely on money and wealth. I wouldn't undertake to deny such a charge, but here again there is a historical explanation: the earliest colonists came from the middle ranks of merchants, artisans, and planters. There was no aristocracy—and certainly no royalty—on which class distinctions could be based. On the other hand there was no limit to what one could achieve through initiative, resourcefulness, and hard work, so status was in fact based to a large extent on financial success. This is still true; the "self-made" man or woman is still very much the ideal in twenty-first century America. (Unfortunately, the predominant role of large corporations and lobbyists in influencing political campaigns and legislation has led some pundits to claim that the United States is becoming a "plutocracy" rather than a democracy.)

Some British claim that America is a nation of workaholics—that we are compulsive about work and don't take time to smell the flowers. As the product of a background in which industriousness was next to godliness, if not a bit better, I am the last person to be able to deny this charge. In fact, statistically Americans work more hours per week than any other nationality except the Japanese. American diplomats are known around the world as drudges—when other diplomats are already out on the tennis courts, the Americans are still beavering away at the office. My wife, a European, complains that Americans take a vacation only in order to work more effectively, while Europeans work only to take a longer vacation. It is true that vacations in the United States are typically much shorter than in Europe, where vacations of a month to six weeks are standard. To an American, it seems frivolous and unproductive to take a month's vacation; a European considers it his right.

I frequently heard the charge that Americans are too competitive—that the free enterprise system as exemplified in the United States is a cruel system of cutthroat competition, of the survival of the fittest, and the devil take the hindmost. It's true that Americans believe in harnessing the tremendous power of individual initiative, and understand that the right to succeed entails the right to fail—in other words, the market system cannot work without the failure of the uncompetitive aspects of the economy. There is, admittedly, a delicate balance between that level of social services required to protect the less fortunate of society and that level of government spending that stifles individual initiative. Just where this point on the continuum should be is essentially the crux of the debate between the two major parties in the United States. It also mirrors the debate in Great Britain, where society tends to be even more polarized between the radical right and the "loony left" than in the United States.

In spite of these cultural differences, it is significant that it would take far longer to discuss the similarities between us than the differences—such things as common language and traditions, Anglo-Saxon common law, the dignity of the individual, and a shared philosophy of government. I have never heard it said, but I suppose that the mutuality of political and economic interests between the United States and Great Britain is one of the reasons that we have only one USIS post in Great Britain (London), while in Germany we had, as of 1986, six USIS posts—in Bonn, Berlin, Frankfurt, Hamburg, Leipzig, and Munich (although Bonn and Hamburg have since been dropped). No doubt, Cold War considerations played a role as well. As I write this, the "special relationship" is perhaps at its lowest ebb in recent memory, with a great majority of the British people opposed to the Iraq war and to the British government's support for that war. But there is a historic tendency in American politics for the pendulum of change to swing back in the opposite direction when things have gotten off track, or have swung too far in one direction. I used to tell my audiences, if you don't like current American policies, just wait awhile and they will change. (I fervently hope that this is true. The mandate of the U.S. Information Service was to "tell America's story to the world." It is fortunate that I reached mandatory retirement from the Foreign Service before the election of George W. Bush, as I would have had difficulty defending America's story under that disastrous administration. But I digress again.)

All in all, London was an excellent entrée into the Foreign Service, both because it is a large and comprehensive embassy, and because I was given substantive assignments throughout the year. And London is a fascinating place to live and work. My family and I look back on our London tour with great nostalgia (but I find that the longer a posting retreats into the past, the more nostalgic one tends to feel about it).

Act Two: Burma

Burma in Perspective

I first visited Burma in 1958 when I crossed the country on a motorcycle after spending two years as a volunteer in Laos. At that time Rangoon seemed like a modern city compared with Vientiane, Laos, or even Bangkok, Thailand. It was a bustling, prosperous city with comfortable hotels and numerous good Chinese and Indian restaurants. In spite of my difficulties in getting across Burma (as recounted earlier, my motorcycle had been impounded by Burmese Customs for several weeks before I managed to spring it and continue my journey to India), I had found it a friendly and congenial place. In fact, in those days Western diplomats assigned to Vientiane or Bangkok used to travel to Burma for R and R (rest and recuperation), not only to enjoy its relatively modern amenities, but also to visit the impressive ruins of the tenth-century kingdom of Pagan, which was (and still is) Burma's premiere tourist destination. I was one of the last people to cross Burma by road before General Ne Win took over the government in late 1958 vowing to "restore law and order" (sound familiar?).

Elections allowed by Ne Win in 1960 were won by former Prime Minister U Nu, but Ne Win took over again in 1962, blaming threatened insurgencies by the Communist Party of Burma and several ethnic minority armies. Proclaiming the notorious "Burmese Way to Socialism," Ne Win nationalized all business, turned all commerce over to twenty-three state corporations (leading to a flourishing black market referred to by the people as "Corporation 24"), closed down the media, expelled foreign NGOs (nongovernmental organizations), banned the teaching of English, and instituted the totalitarian military regime that remains in power today. The regime brutally suppressed popular uprisings, typically student-led, in 1962, 1974, 1988, and most recently in 2007. On subsequent trips to Burma on my way to academic research in Southeast Asia in 1965, 1970, and 1979, Rangoon had become a depressing place. Banks, businesses, hotels, restaurants, shops, and transportation had all been nationalized, leading to the departure of Chinese and Indian entrepreneurs who had been the backbone of Rangoon's economy. The infamous "People's Shops" contained cheap merchandise such as toothpaste produced by "The People's Toilet Industry;" hotels and restaurants were dingy and uninviting—a "socialist gray" seemed to have set in.

Burma is the largest country in Southeast Asia, and given its rich natural resources—petroleum, timber, coal, ores, and gems, not to mention opium—it could have become the Japan of Southeast Asia; but as a result of the government's disastrous centralized economy, its people are among the poorest in Southeast Asia.

Arrival in Rangoon

It was thus with mixed feelings that I arrived in Burma to begin a two-year tour as assistant public affairs officer. What would life be like in what was essentially a police state? We were met at the Mingaladon International Airport by Commercial Officer Gary Couey and his wife Mary, who were our "sponsors." Every arriving new officer and his family are assigned an embassy sponsor, whose duties are to meet them at the airport, show them to their assigned housing, stock their refrigerator with some basic groceries, and smooth their introduction to the country. And it is an excellent idea. My family and I had already had considerable experience living and working in third-world countries, but others less traveled than we might be more susceptible to culture shock if they arrived on their own and were confronted by the dilapidated airport, the stifling heat, the cockroaches running around the edges of the floor, and the officiousness of immigration and customs officials on the make for some extracurricular income. Gary and Mary ushered us past crowds of shouting porters and taxi drivers, dressed in the traditional Burmese *longyis* (ankle-length sarongs worn by both men and women) to an embassy van—the ubiquitous Chevy Suburban that is the standard workhorse for embassies around the world, not so much because of its quality as because of the "buy America" regulations under which embassies operate.

When I had first visited Rangoon in 1958, the city was a veritable museum of old American cars kept alive by the resourcefulness of Burmese mechanics; now, thirty years later, the streets were crowded with rickety Japanese Toyotas and Nissans — many of them right-hand-drive as they had been smuggled in from Thailand (Burma, unlike other former British colonies such as India and Malaysia, had converted to driving on the right following independence from Great Britain in 1948). Import duties of at least 100 percent made new cars prohibitively expensive. Taxis and motorcycles competed for the road with ancient buses of World War II vintage, belching black smoke and filled to overflowing with passengers, clusters of whom clung to doorways like bees to a hive. We turned into a narrow lane off University Boulevard and after a few hundred yards, passed through a gate into a compound, where we stopped under the portico of an imposing mansion. "Well, here it is, guys," said Gary, "your home away from home!"

We looked at the house in some dismay. Apparently originally painted a pastel ochre, the peeling paint was streaked with green and black, especially nearer the ground. "Why is it green?" I asked. "That's just mildew," said Gary. "They'll paint it again once the monsoon is over." Burma is so situated that it gets both the southwest monsoon (June–September) and the northeast monsoon (December–April). The result is that by the end of the southwest monsoon, all the buildings in Rangoon begin to take on a greenish black hue from the mildew, giving the impression that everything is in an advanced state of decay. An additional reason that buildings have to be repainted annually is that painting contractors tend to dilute the paint so it goes further and they get more profit.

As we got out of the car, we were met by the household staff, all bowing with palms pressed together in the traditional Burmese greeting. It was apparent that we were to inherit the staff from my predecessor, who no doubt inherited them from his predecessor. They were, in order of seniority, the main cook, the assistant cook, the driver, the gardener, and a guard. Given the state of the economy, the total salary for all five of these people came to less than $60 per month.

Ma Win, the main cook and amah, was a motherly figure who became very dear to my daughter Samantha, somewhat to the chagrin of my wife, who was employed in the embassy. Our driver, Maung Maung Hla, was also a favorite of my daughter. With a B.A. in philosophy, he could find no better-paying job in Burma than that of chauffeur for an American embassy officer. When he was not occupied with driving duties, he would play games with four-year-old Samantha; once I found them making mud pies on the bank of the lake that fronted our yard. Maung Maung Hla was not a particularly good driver and never quite mastered the manual transmission on my BMW 316, which I had shipped out from London. Fortunately repairs were ridiculously cheap, mainly because there were no spare parts, especially for a BMW, so Burmese mechanics would basically manufacture whatever part was needed. At one point the clutch began to give trouble, due no doubt to Maung Maung Hla's mistreatment, so when he delivered me to the office, I told him to take the car and get it repaired at the accustomed garage. When he picked me up that evening at the embassy, I asked him if they had fixed the clutch.

"Yes, Mastuh," he said (he called me "Master," in spite of my objections), "but very dear today."

"How much?" I asked, thinking of what it would cost to repair the clutch of a BMW anywhere else.

"Two dollah," he said, shaking his head sadly.

"*Keisa mashibu* (never mind)," I said.

Maung Maung Hla took great pride in the fact that he was the driver for one of the only two BMWs in Rangoon—the other was an older model 525. My wife had reservations about the safety of Maung Maung Hla's driving, especially with the children, but I didn't have the heart to fire him, both because he was a favorite of my daughter and because he supported a family of five or six. But I must admit that he scared me a bit as well, especially when he would take both hands off the steering wheel and put them together in obeisance every time we passed the magnificent Shwedagon Pagoda on the way to work.

Ma Win, the cook, lived in a smaller house in the corner of the compound with her husband, Ye Myint, a driver for USIS, and their three young children. Ye Myint's English was rather impenetrable and a constant source of amusement for my son Christopher (age eleven) and Samantha (age five). He informed me that my predecessor had fired the former gardener, because he was "bad guy."

I asked why he was a bad guy.

"Because he cut the gee," he replied. "That's why."

It turned out that the former gardener had stolen one of the geese that were kept in the compound to guard against the snakes that were discomfortingly prevalent in Burma, and had presumably cut off the goose's head with his machete. Ye Myint had made the perfectly logical assumption that if you say "two geese," then the singular would be "one gee."

The compound also sported a tennis court—a luxury that I had never enjoyed before and have never enjoyed since. Most American embassy officers lived in rather grandiose mansions that had been built by the British colonials before Burmese independence, and most of them had their own tennis courts. These courts turned out to be a rather important factor in reaching out to members of the Burmese public. It was not wise for Burmese to be seen associating with Westerners, but the Burmese are such sports fanatics that we were able to invite them to tennis matches and organize tennis tournaments between the diplomatic and Burmese communities. My court was made of poured concrete and had a number of rather large cracks and a ragged net, but I worked out a deal, which appeared to be the norm, with a Burmese tennis pro named Maung Maung Lay that he could use the court to give tennis lessons in return for providing tennis instruction to me and my family. He made a living and we got instruction from a pro—in fact he had been the Burmese national champion for eleven years.

All in all, our housing situation was more than adequate. In fact, the generosity of embassy housing in Rangoon led to some complications with State Department bureaucracy. The Bureau of Administration had a set of rules whereby the square footage to which a particular Foreign Service family was entitled depended on the officer's rank, family size, and representational responsibilities, primarily the need to host official receptions and/or dinners. During one of the dreaded inspections of the post by a delegation from the Office of the Inspector General, the inspectors said that embassy housing in Rangoon exceeded the regulations.

For example, someone of my rank and family size was entitled to no more than 2,200–2,500 square feet of living space, while in fact I was living in a mansion with over 3,000 square feet of space and thus was not in compliance with the housing regs. The ambassador pointed out to the inspectors that housing in Rangoon was basically of two kinds—small one-room shacks built of wood or brick on the one hand, and spacious Western-style mansions on the other. Housing of the appropriate intermediate dimensions did not exist in Rangoon, but if the department insisted, they could undertake to build new housing of the appropriate size, which would end up costing two to three times more than leasing existing housing. The inspectors let the matter drop.

The majority of embassy housing was contained in a pleasant, tree-lined housing compound off University Boulevard called Washington Park. The compound had its own tennis courts and playgrounds and fronted on the famous Inya Lake, which was bordered by some of the most elegant housing in Rangoon, including the U.S. ambassador's residence and General Ne Win's residence across the lake. (Word is that the housing compound has been requisitioned as the site for a new U.S. embassy. It can't be denied that a new embassy was in order, as the old one downtown was a rat-trap, but it's not clear how the valuable, and highly satisfactory, housing will be replaced.)

Shrimp in the Bathtub and Other Attractions

Elegant as the housing was, we were not exempt from some of the bizarre incidents that come with living in a third-world country. There was no municipal water supply, so each house had a large metal tank on the roof, which was replenished with water as needed by a water truck maintained for the purpose by the embassy's General Services Office. In principle these tanks were cleaned from time to time, but obviously not often enough—once, to her delight, my daughter found baby shrimp in her bath water. As the tropical sun heated the rooftop tank, all manner of organisms were incubated in the tank. Once we found a frog in the toilet—not clear by what route it had arrived.

Burma is famous for its snakes, with over fifty varieties of poisonous snakes, the most notorious of which is the king cobra. One morning the amah discovered a big black snake in the upstairs of the house. I quickly armed myself with my son's softball bat and located the snake, a black snake about two meters long, in the study. There ensued a tremendous battle, from which I emerged victorious, having smashed the snake's head with the bat. When we took the snake to the embassy health unit, as we were instructed to do, the Burmese technician scolded me for having smashed the snake's head, as they were thus not able to determine whether it was a poisonous variety or not.

In another amusing (?) incident, Mary Couey (one of our sponsors) got into her car and when she started it up, a snake emerged from the engine compartment and climbed up on her windshield. She had the presence of mind to roll up the windows, and sat motionless until someone discovered her trembling in the car and chased the snake away into the bushes. As mentioned before, it was common for housing compounds to keep geese on the property to chase away the snakes. Earl Young, the USAID rep, was so fascinated by snakes that he kept several varieties in cages as pets, including a huge king cobra, and employed his household staff to catch rats and mice to feed them.

The plentiful wildlife in Burma has its upside as well. Burma has an estimated 10,000 elephants, or about one-third of all the elephants in the world. As a result it was an easy matter to hire an elephant to give rides at children's birthday parties. There was even a troupe of dancing elephants that could be hired for national day celebrations. Rangoon had a zoo stocked with a large cross-section of Burma's rich fauna, including elephants, lions, tigers, leopards, bears, crocodiles, snakes, and exotic birds, as well as some non-native animals such as camels and giraffe. But the zoo did not subscribe to the best zoological practices, to put it charitably; the facilities were poorly maintained, the animals scruffy and rather unhealthy-looking, and the common perception in the diplomatic community was that the government did not have enough money to feed the animals properly. In fact, this was one zoo where visitors were encouraged to feed the animals, and some local charities were organized to donate food to the zoo.

A favorite pastime among members of the diplomatic community was scavenging for antiques. Burmese antique dealers had learned that those crazy foreigners would pay as much as 4,000 *kyats* (about $100 at the black market rate of exchange) for old pieces of furniture, carved chests, *kalagas* (colorful brocaded tapestries which had their origin as ornate caparisons for royal coffins), Burmese laquerware, Chinese porcelain, and more. Accordingly almost everything was priced at 4,000 kyats, regardless of its intrinsic value. For example, during our tour we purchased an antique carved Chinese chest, a carved teakwood Burmese chest of recent vintage, a Chinese altar table, a large *kalaga,* an elegant English gramophone cabinet, a Karen bronze drum, a gilded Burmese temple chest, and several beautiful lacquered Burmese manuscripts (containing Buddhist scriptures hand-lettered by monks)—all for 4,000 kyats each. Some of these things might have brought at least $1,000 at Sotheby's, while others, such as the recently carved teakwood chest, would not have qualified as antiques. And the Burmese had become quite skilled at producing "instant antiques," such as the Karen drums that were known from Neolithic times, but which Burmese artisans had learned to counterfeit using steel oil drums. There was an antique dealer named Augustine who was well-known in the diplomatic community because he had an old pickup truck and would appear in front of your house on Saturday and Sunday mornings laden with all manner of enticing antiques, sparing you the bother of scavenging for bargains in dingy, uninviting shops. When we visited Rangoon again in 2004, Augustine had become so prosperous that he no longer had to peddle his goods from house to house; his clients all came to him.

Rangoon's most famous attraction is the fabulous Shwedagon Pagoda, on a hill just north of the main town. The central *stupa* is 326 feet high and plated with over 8,000 gold tiles. The tip of the spire is said to be set with 5,000 diamonds and 2,000 of the rubies and sapphires for which Burma is famous. The base of the monument is surrounded by 100 other smaller *stupas*, shrines, reliquaries, monks' quarters, chapels, bells, and temples on a floor of white marble. The temple is approached by four covered arcades, each several hundred yards long, with elaborately carved wooden eaves painted red and gold, and with tiered roofs snaking up the hill.

One must remove one's shoes and socks at any of the four entrances before beginning the climb up to the temple. Signs at the entrances read "Footwearing Prohibited," reflecting an imperfect control of the language of their former colonial masters. Making our way barefoot up the long approach to the base of the temple, stepping in pigeon droppings and betel spittle all the way, it was obvious that the prohibition of "footwearing" owed more to ritual than to hygiene. Once on top, it is impossible to walk on the marble platform without frying one's feet, especially during the hot season. For this reason, a very welcome hemp runner is provided for pilgrims and tourists to walk on as they circumambulate the monument in their bare feet.

According to the guidebooks, the Shwedagon, at 326 feet, is the tallest Buddhist monument in the world, but apparently the Phra Pathom Chedi in Thailand, at 127 meters, or 412 feet, can more properly claim that distinction. Of the two, the Shwedagon is by far the more colorful and elaborate.

Burma or Myanmar?

Let me address here the confusion surrounding the name of the country. Is it Burma or Myanmar? No Burmese calls his country Myanmar except in a very stilted spelling pronunciation; the usual pronunciation is much closer to "Burma," but with stress on the last syllable. Incidentally, there is no final "r" in Burmese; it is added to Myanmar just to suggest the pronunciation in English. The change of Rangoon to "Yangon," however, is a change in the other direction, from the British pronunciation to its actual Burmese pronunciation. (In defense of "Rangoon," the letter now pronounced "y" was formerly pronounced "r".) So there is no logical or linguistically consistent rationale for the changes; the regime's only interest was change for change's sake. I note with satisfaction that the State Department retains the names Burma and Rangoon, as if to underscore the current regime's illegitimacy.

A note is in order about Burmese names. Burmese typically have a sequence of either two or three given names, but no family names. There seems to be a preference for repeating a given name. My driver was Maung Maung Hla, one of my FSNs was San San Myint, and another was Than Than Nwe. The complication was that the word "Maung" can be either a name or a title for a young man; likewise the word "U" can be either a name or the title of a respected elder, such as "U Nu"; one of my employees was U Taw U. Thus there is the possibility of having someone called "Maung Maung Maung" (Mr. Maung Maung). All very confusing.

The Burmese people, as a result of the British colonial experience, were by and large English speakers, and had one of the highest levels of literacy in all of Asia. But when Ne Win came to power in 1962, he banned the teaching of English as part of his benighted "Burmese Way to Socialism" for about twenty years, so a generation of Burmese in their forties and fifties, some of whom were mid-level officials, did not speak English. The ban was lifted in 1979, reputedly because Ne Win's favorite daughter Sanda failed her English test for admission to a British medical school, and they began teaching English again in the schools. So you could speak English to the old hands and to the young kids, but those in the middle, frequently in very responsible positions, did not know English.

Circumventing the Censors

U.S. embassies around the world tend to be rather impressive affairs, usually located in an elegant or upscale part of town. Thus my first introduction to the U.S. Embassy in Rangoon was a shock. The embassy was located on Merchant Street in downtown Rangoon, off Mahabandoola Square near the ornate Sule Pagoda, which is considered the heart of the city. Although not entirely out of character with the surrounding buildings, it was a grimy, mildew-covered building with what appeared to be barbed-wire barriers and various antennae, aerials, and communications equipment on the roof. Once past the Marine guards at the entrance, the building is a rabbit warren of corridors, passageways, stairs, and offices. The U.S. Information Service, occupying the ground floor of the west wing of the building, had two American officers—the PAO, who at that time was John Fredenburg, and the Assistant PAO, me—and some thirty Burmese FSNs (Foreign Service Nationals). USIS Rangoon had an unusually large complement of FSNs, partly because wages in Burma were so low that it didn't cost much to hire them.

But the main reason we had so many FSNs in Rangoon was our unusually large translation and publishing operation. The role of the USIA, as its name implies, is to provide information to foreign audiences about the United States and its history, culture, society, and policies. To do this, USIA supports a large menu of products and services for use by USIS posts abroad, including educational and cultural exchanges (such as the Fulbright program, the International Visitor program, and performing arts groups), U.S. speakers and experts, seminars on topics of mutual interest, small grants to local NGOs in support of democracy, rule of law, and human rights, translation of U.S. books and articles for publication in the local language, and liaison with the local press. Relations with the press included issuing press releases and arranging press conferences for the ambassador and visiting U.S. officials such as the president, secretary of state, and congressional delegations (codels).

Not all products and services are appropriate for any one country; if programs of one kind are not allowed (or not appropriate) in a particular country, USIS can compensate by expanding programs not specifically forbidden. This was certainly the case in Burma, which imposed severe restrictions on travel and foreign contacts by Burmese citizens. For example, the Fulbright program, which in normal countries sends students, teachers, and researchers from the host country to the United States and from the United States to the host country, was almost nonoperative in Burma. Those few Burmese allowed to travel to the United States were chosen by the regime from those considered sympathetic to the regime and not likely to defect. The U.S. consulate, on the other hand, was forbidden by law to issue exchange visas to applicants who were not likely to return to their home country as required by law. As the vice consul put it, "I can't issue a visa if I think they're going to defect; on the other hand, if they're too dumb to defect when they have the chance, they don't deserve a visa!" During my entire two-year tour in Burma we managed to get approval for only one U.S. speaker, an emeritus professor from Harvard in the field of science education, but students were prohibited from attending the lecture. Only the university staff and preapproved others were allowed to have contact with these dangerous Western ideas.

On the other hand, a number of Fulbright researchers were allowed into the country, so long as they had never written anything critical of the regime and were in nonpolitical fields such as religion, ethnomusicology, or cultural anthropology.

Constrained as we were in the area of educational and cultural exchanges, we were able to ramp up our activities in the area of publications. It was rather risky to be seen going into the American library, but to compensate we put out four different publications. One was a weekly news summary; another was a collection of stories in "special English," provided by scripts from VOA broadcasts. But our flagship publication was a monthly glossy magazine called *Lin Yaung Chi* in Burmese, or *Dawn*. It contained color photos and feature stories drawn from various U.S. publications such as *Time* or *National Geographic* or *Smithsonian*—in other words, Americana in Burmese. *Lin Yaung Chi* was probably the highest-quality periodical published in Burma, and its popularity was attested by the fact that it had a secondary market in bookstalls around the town, even though we distributed it for free. It was rather surprising that the Burmese allowed this publishing enterprise—some 10,000 copies a month—but as long as we didn't overtly criticize the government, we had a rather free hand to put out any information we wanted about the United States. Some articles dealing with democracy, free enterprise, rule of law, human rights, and transparency of the judiciary might have been seen as rather pointed, but we could always claim that we were simply describing the U.S. system, not making recommendations. The only concession we had to make was to cart all of these copies over to the Customs Department and have them stamped, indicating that they had been approved by the Burmese censors. They didn't read them, of course; it was just an exercise we had to go through.

Sports and Music to the Rescue

The areas in which we had the most success were sports and music. The Burmese are great lovers of sports, and in happier times fielded the strongest sports teams in the region, especially in soccer. As noted, tennis tournaments organized by various embassies provided a cover for making contacts with Burmese counterparts. PAO John Fredenburg was a bit of a jock and an avid fan of professional and collegiate basketball and football; during airings of "March Madness" on our satellite TV, he was difficult to find. The proof of John's athleticism was the way he mastered tennis, a game he had not played prior to his tour in Rangoon. I have a pretty good tennis game, if I say so myself, frequently using strategy and guile to defeat younger, stronger, and less devious players. When I first arrived at post, I beat John regularly; as my tour progressed, he got stronger and stronger, and by the end of my tour I was at his mercy. John served as the "Commissioner" of an "International Softball League" that met on the softball field of the American Club; there were two Burmese teams (who usually played barefoot), a British-Australian team, and a Japanese team, in addition to two teams from our embassy. Fierce competition between these teams provided entertainment for surprisingly large numbers of spectators at the American Club on Sunday afternoons.

Ne Win was a great lover of golf and had his military commanders build golf courses all over the country, as a result of which Burma probably has more golf courses per capita than any other third-world country. Arnold Palmer had visited the country in an earlier time, and we brought over golf pro Chris Harney for a three-month tour. Harney held the record for the longest drive in golf and gave demonstrations of his technique at highly popular seminars with Burmese officials. Once he gave a demonstration of his prowess for the embassy staff at the ambassador's residence on Inya Lake. Pointing to a small island about 400 yards away, he said, "O.K., I'll lay one on that little island." Once he drove the ball, we were unable to verify whether the ball hit the island or not, as it was too far away, but at least there was no "plop" into the water anywhere between us and the island. But we discontinued the exercise when we realized that the balls just might reach Ne Win's house on the other side of the lake.

We also brought in a number of performing arts groups that were hugely successful with the Burmese. The bluegrass group the Johnson Mountain Boys was so popular we had to use the national stadium as a venue, and they were feted by the Minister of Youth, Education and Sports. Other groups were hosted solely by USIS, such as the famous jazz group Benny Golson and his All Stars and the U.S. Air Force Band. Some 2,000 people showed up for Golson's concert in the garden of the PAO residence. As we were on the cusp of the rainy season, we built a roof of canvas over the entire seating area in case of rain. After the concert I hosted a reception for the group and local Burmese jazz enthusiasts. My twelve-year-old son Christopher was ecstatic to shake the hand of the great Benny Golson. I play some jazz piano for my own amazement, and the highlight of my evening was to play "Basin Street Blues" accompanied by several of Golson's All Stars and an excellent local Burmese clarinetist who went by the name "Apollo."

An Ethnolinguistic Mosaic

Burma has been plagued by ethnic strife ever since independence from Britain in 1948. It is estimated that Burma has more than sixty ethnic groups and one hundred separate languages (not dialects). Ethnic Burmans (reserving the term Burmese for any citizen of Burma) make up only about 68 percent of the population. At 9 percent, the Shan are the largest minority group; they are related to the Thais with whom they share a border. Next come the Karen along the eastern border, who make up 7 percent of the total population and are thought to be related to the same Tibeto-Burman linguistic family as the Burmans. The Karen claim that although they were the mainstay of the British colonial forces, the British betrayed them when they turned authority over to the Burmans at independence in 1948. The Arakanese along the western border with Bangladesh, also Tibeto-Burman, make up 4 percent of the population. At 2 percent, the Mon in southeastern Burma along the Tenasserim Coast, are the remnants of an Indianized kingdom that predated the coming of the Burmans; they are related to the Khmer of Cambodia in the Mon-Khmer linguistic family. Burmese of Indian descent make up some 2 percent of the population, mainly involved in commerce in the larger cities and towns.

Other smaller ethnic groups (less than 2 percent), mostly in the northern hills, include the Chin, the Kachin, the Pa-O, the Kayah (Karenni), and the Lahu (all Tibeto-Burman); and the Palaung and Wa (Mon-Khmer). Palaung women are noted for the heavy gold rings they wear around their necks; starting in childhood, more and more rings are added until they form a collar ten or twelve inches high, deforming the neck and collar bones, as a result of which they are sometimes called the "Giraffe Women." It is said that if the rings are removed, these women cannot hold up their heads, which simply flop over to one side. A refugee village of Palaung on the Thai side of the border can be visited from Chiangmai. The village supports itself primarily by charging a fee for entering the village and by demanding gratuities from tourists who wish to photograph the women. But some critics consider visiting them not politically correct as it treats the women as freaks and perpetuates a barbaric custom. On the other hand, it is not clear how the village would otherwise support itself without this source of income.

When the British granted independence to Burma, all the ethnic minorities were supposed to come together in a federated "Union of Burma," but it never happened. The central government has been at war with the ethnic armies for decades, as well as with various communist insurgencies and a group of Chinese Kuomintang troops that took refuge in northern Burma when Mao Tse-tung came to power in 1949. These rebel armies and warlords have become pretty powerful over the years, and many were fairly wealthy because they controlled the Golden Triangle, where Burma, Laos, and Thailand come together and where the drug trade has flourished for years. From time to time the Burmese army would go up and burn a bunch of villages, take prisoners, push refugees over the border into Thailand, and make exaggerated claims about the victories of the "People's Army"; but they have never been successful in definitively defeating the multiple insurgencies. Understandably, these tribal groups are intensely loyal to their own tribes and leaders and have no interest in a truce whereby they would come under the heavy-handed control of the Rangoon government.

In the 1990s, the SLORC (State Law and Order Restoration Council) managed to force cease-fire agreements on many of the ethnic groups by promising them limited autonomy and the right to hold on to their weapons. But about a dozen groups, notably the Arakan Liberation Army, the Chin National Front, the Karen National Union, the Lahu Democratic Front, the Shan State Army–South, and the Wa National Organization, continue to hold out, along with the All-Burma Student Democratic Front operating on the Thai-Burma border.

Touring Burma by Road

The contested areas—which is to say the majority of the country—
were off limits to tourists and diplomats. The tourist circuit was
limited to Rangoon, the former royal city of Mandalay in the north,
the ruins of the tenth century city of Pagan, and the mountain city
of Taunggyi in the Shan Hills. But diplomats had to request permission to visit even these sites; in fact, we had to request permission to
travel more than twenty-five kilometers outside of Rangoon.

Once we had permission to travel, however, the trip was richly
rewarding. The ambassador encouraged us to travel to the extent
allowed by the regime, in order to familiarize ourselves with the
host country. Fortunately the PAO also subscribed to this policy
and considered such travel a legitimate expense.

In December 1987, my family and I thus embarked on an orientation trip to Upper Burma, together with the principal of the
International School of Rangoon, his wife, and two children, who
were roughly the same age as our son and daughter. We set off in
the USIS Chevy Suburban with nine people—four children, rang-
ing in age from six to twelve, and five adults, including Ye Myint,
the diminutive USIS driver. I would gladly have driven myself, but
the PAO insisted we take Ye Myint along as driver and interlocutor
with the local inhabitants in case we got into trouble.

We didn't anticipate any danger, as the Burmese are unfailingly
kind and gentle people, but the main challenge of travel by car was
the abominable condition of the roads and bridges. Almost all roads
upcountry were essentially one lane in width—the kind of road for
which we would have a flagman on either end in the States. Thus
you must quickly learn the rules of the road—to get off the road or
stop completely for logging trucks and vehicles larger than yours,
but be fairly ruthless with approaching vehicles of the same size,
oxcarts, motorcycles, bicycles, and pedestrians. Liberal use of the
horn is recommended, not only because it is safer for all concerned
but also because it helps your average speed. Ye Myint was so short
that he could hardly reach the pedals of the big cumbersome van,
but aside from that he drove so slowly and cautiously that I frequently commandeered the wheel in the interest of making better
time. Even so, you could not plan on averaging more than about
twenty-five miles per hour.

Another difficult aspect of travel by road was the uncertain availability of fuel. (The shortage of gasoline in a country that had its own resources of oil and natural gas was testimony to the abysmal inefficiency of the "Burmese Way to Socialism.") As a result we had to carry ninety gallons of gasoline—thirty gallons in the tank and sixty gallons in cans roped to the roof of the van; we were thus a potential traveling bomb. (Due to a leak that we couldn't identify, our food supplies, especially the crackers, tasted of gasoline.)

Whenever the tank got low, we would stop by the side of the road and siphon a new supply into the tank. Ye Myint would insert a hose into one of the cans on the roof and suck on the other end until he got a mouthful of gasoline, and insert the hose immediately into the gas tank before losing the flow. Whenever he was called on to perform this service, I was grateful for the loyal fellow's presence on the trip. We had arranged with the general services office to ship two forty-four-gallon drums of gasoline ahead to the Mandalay guesthouse for the return trip.

We also carried copious food for the trip, as the few Burmese restaurants that existed were of dubious quality and sanitation, especially since the expulsion in the 1960s of Chinese and Indian entrepreneurs, who had operated the best restaurants in the country. (On my first visit to Rangoon in 1958, I recall that tasty food was abundant and cheap in the numerous Indian and Chinese restaurants around the city; but by the time I visited the city again in 1970, after the nationalization of all private enterprise by the regime, it was difficult to get a decent meal in Rangoon outside of private homes.) Ironically, our first experience of a Burmese restaurant was on the evening of our first day in Burma. Our sponsors, the Coueys, had planned to invite us to their home for dinner the first evening, but at the last moment the electricity went off—a frequent occurrence in Rangoon—and for some reason their back-up generator was not working. So they took us to a Burmese restaurant that diplomatic personnel had frequented without adverse consequences. To be brutally honest, Burmese cuisine is not one of the stellar culinary traditions of Southeast Asia. I would rank it somewhere below Thai, Vietnamese, Cambodian, and Malay/Indonesian (in that order of excellence), but above the Philippines, where varied cultural influences seem not to have produced a rich culinary tradition.

One of the more enjoyable Burmese dishes, one that tends to be served on elegant occasions, is *oh noh khao shwe,* a kind of curried soup topped with crispy noodles, coriander, and a slice of lime. One of the more objectionable dishes, from my point of view, is *mohinga,* a soup with a strong fishy taste that is a staple of Burmese breakfasts. With some of my colleagues it was a kind of badge of honor to have *mohinga* for breakfast, but while I love Asian food in general, I need Western things for breakfast, such as bread, butter, jam, and coffee. But I digress.

So whenever we got hungry (which was quite frequent with four kids in the van), we would find some large tree, preferably by a stream but mandatorily with protection from the sun, and have a picnic of bread, ham, corned beef, and other goodies from the small embassy commissary, along with mangoes, papaya, or oranges purchased in local markets along the way. Delicious tropical fruits are one of the delights of Southeast Asia, especially those of Thailand—it is almost worth a trip to Bangkok purely for the mango season. I consider mangoes to be the king of fruits; for my wife it's mangosteens—a fruit whose appearance is stranger than fiction: a thick purple rind, topped by a waxy green caparison, typically containing six sections of delightfully sweet and fragrant white flesh. But again I digress.

At our picnic stops, we would be surrounded by crowds of local villagers, mostly children, who found it highly entertaining to watch a crew of long-nosed Westerners eating those strange foods. Offers to share food with the spectators were usually politely refused, but any discarded containers were eagerly snapped up for their possible use in other applications, or simply for their novelty value.

As we had already visited Pegu, ancient capital of the Mon Kingdom fifty miles north of Rangoon, on a day trip, we headed north through the old Burmese capital of Toungoo and Pyinmana (site of the new administrative capital of Burma declared by the regime in 2006) to overnight at the USAID guesthouse in the town of Yezin. We had reserved the Yezin guesthouse through USAID in the embassy; the rate was 120 Burmese kyat per person ($20 at the official rate of exchange, $3 at the "happy" or black market rate, which everybody used and said they didn't).

The next day we headed for our first primary destination, the mountain town of Taunggyi, capital of the Shan State. The ascent to Kalaw on the edge of the Shan Plateau (called Burma's Switzerland) was spectacular, but the numerous one-lane switchbacks made it slow going.

We spent the night in the Taunggyi Hotel, a dark, cavernous affair in a parklike setting, but as it was in the mountains, temperatures got down to fifty degrees Fahrenheit at night, and they had no heat or even any fires in the huge ornate fireplaces in the restaurant and bar. In the lobby was an office of Tourist Burma, where we purchased tickets for a four-hour tour the next day of nearby Inle Lake, famous for its floating markets and floating gardens, and especially for its leg-rowers—fishermen who row their boats in a standing position, with one leg wrapped around a single oar. A rumor that we would have to supply gas for the boat turned out to be untrue.

The fourth day out we headed for Mandalay, Burma's second largest city and the former royal capital of Burma, where the British in 1886 deposed King Thibaw, the last king of Burma, and paraded him through the streets in a bamboo cage. Some say the Burmese nation has never recovered from this humiliation; little wonder that many Burmese, including the famous General Aung San, welcomed the Japanese during World War II as a way to retaliate against their British masters. The Burmese nationalists were treated so harshly by the Japanese, however, that they eventually changed their minds and switched to the Allied side. But ultimately it was the success of the Japanese in demonstrating the vulnerability of the British in Burma and Malaysia, the French in Indochina, and the Dutch in Indonesia that led to the end of European colonialism in Southeast Asia.

In Mandalay, we had made arrangements to put up at the former U.S. Consulate, an elegant old building that is maintained by the embassy as a guesthouse for embassy personnel, with the proviso that we pay a nominal fee to the household staff to prepare meals and wash the linens. The location of the guesthouse is unbeatable—across the street from the Royal Palace grounds, a huge square surrounded by a moat two kilometers long on each side. The crenellated walls and twelve pagoda-shaped guard towers reflected in the moat, with its colorful water lilies, is a photographer's dream.

Unfortunately, however, the teakwood palace no longer exists, as it was burnt to the ground when British troops shelled it to dislodge the Japanese forces that had made the palace their headquarters during World War II. The "Golden City" is now a Burmese military base, but in recent times the Burmese have built a replica of the palace for the enjoyment of tourists, both foreign and Burmese.

A Mandalay experience not to be missed is a climb up Mandalay Hill, which overlooks the city from the north and appears to be the only significant elevation in the plain on which Mandalay stands. Our driver, Ye Myint, attempted to discourage our plan to climb the hill, no doubt thinking that Westerners, and especially their young children, might not be up to such an arduous climb in the afternoon heat. He did not understand that a hill, especially one with shrines on top and with a view over the city, was an irresistible challenge for a fanatical photographer like me. Huge whitewashed *chinthes*, or mythological lions, guard the entrance to the covered steps leading up to the summit. Taking off our shoes, as demanded once again by the signs reading "Footwearing Prohibited," we started up the stone stairs. Along the way astrologers and souvenir peddlers vied for our attention. Monks and nuns were making pilgrimages to the shrine on top, or returning to their quarters in one of the many temples along the way. Children, dogs, and the occasional monkey scampered about, the children shyly asking for coins to buy cane juice. Two-thirds of the way to the top is a standing Buddha; his outstretched hand is said to be pointing at the site of the Royal Palace—the "Center of the World" for the Burmese kings. After negotiating the 1,729 steps to the top of the 774-foot-high hill, I conceded that Ye Myint had been right to question whether we were up to the challenge; but the stunning view over the entire city of Mandalay was fully worth it.

The next day we made the two and a half hour trip to the town of Maymyo, a hill station built by British colonialists to escape the heat of Mandalay. With its half-timbered mansions and English gardens, one could imagine oneself in the Highlands of Scotland, except for the prevalence of brilliant bougainvillea trellises. Maymyo sports a 432-acre Botanical Garden, an eighteen-hole golf course, and three waterfalls. General Ne Win had a summerhouse here, and there is a large Burmese military presence (something that can be said of almost any city or town in Burma). People who visit Maymyo like to stop at the picturesque Candacraig Hotel, built in 1905 as a resort for the Bombay Burma Trading Company, where you can enjoy a proper British tea by the huge fireplace in the great room. But the most picturesque feature of Maymyo is its horse-drawn carriages, an artifact of the nineteenth century.

On day seven we headed for Pagan via Mount Popa, a volcanic rock that juts precipitously more than 700 meters above the surrounding plain and is topped by an elaborate pagoda. This climb is even more strenuous than Mandalay Hill, but it is richly rewarding. The rock is thought to be the abode of two legendary *nats*, or spirits, that the Burmese people venerate and all Burmese kings consulted. The steep steps to the top are guarded by thousands of monkeys that bar the way unless bribed by handouts of peanuts or other treats; some of them can be rather aggressive, snatching food, hats, or glasses from unsuspecting tourists. But the thing our children enjoyed most about Mt. Popa was the freedom to strike a huge bell with a heavy pole suspended from a rope, the resulting boom reverberating across the plains below.

After descending Mt. Popa on wobbly legs that would be sore for days, we headed for the extraordinary archeological ruins of Pagan, capital of a Burmese dynasty that lasted from the ninth to the thirteenth centuries, and Burma's premier tourist destination. There, spread out on a dry, dusty plain beside the Irrawaddy River are over 2,000 Buddhist temples and *stupas* (some claim 5,000) in various sizes and states of preservation, all that remain from an estimated 13,000 religious structures built between the tenth and thirteenth centuries.

The Thiripyitsaya Hotel in Pagan is perhaps the best hotel in Burma and gives intimations of what tourism could be like in the country. Situated amid the ruins, the reception area and dining room are decorated with traditional lacquer panels, and the rambling bungalows, set in the gardens, are clean and air-conditioned, with occasional hot water. From the hotel one can hire horse-drawn carts that trundle silently from one imposing monument to the next. A favorite experience in Pagan is to climb to the top of the Thatbinnyu Pagoda for a view over the ruins at sunset. In spite of considerable damage to the monuments from a 1975 earthquake,

Pagan is indeed impressive and is considered by some authorities to rival Angkor in Cambodia in importance. Having visited both numerous times, I would say that Angkor wins hands down, in both size and artistic merit. But I admit to bias.

Arriving back in Rangoon on day ten, we felt that our orientation to the country had been a great success, but there was general agreement that we had tried to do too much in too short a time. We had driven a total of about 1,600 miles, or about six days of driving to only four days dedicated solely to sightseeing. Given the condition of the roads, the trip should have been allotted at least two weeks, especially when traveling with four children.

The Massacres of 8/8/88

By far the most traumatic experience of my tour in Burma involved the tragic events of August and September 1988, when massive pro-democracy demonstrations resulted in the massacre of several thousand Burmese citizens at the hands of the brutal military regime. Previous attempts to throw off the shackles of totalitarianism, usually led by students, had taken place in 1962, when Ne Win's police killed several hundred students at the University of Rangoon and dynamited the historic Students' Union Building, and again in 1974, when the regime shot down several hundred students who marched in support of a general strike, arrested thousands, closed down schools and universities, and declared martial law. In 1988, there had been no major uprisings for fourteen years, but astrologers were predicting that dire events would happen on the magical date of 8/8/88—the four eights of August 8, 1988.

Things were coming to a boil. There were widespread reports of students being beaten, raped, and killed in the notorious Insein Prison north of Rangoon. In the ethnic minority areas, rape, beatings, looting, and the burning of villages were commonplace wherever the Burmese army operated. The country's economy was a shambles. In September of 1987, the regime suddenly and without explanation demonetized all twenty-five, thirty-five, and seventy-five kyat notes (whose strange denominations had been established in a previous demonetization), so that people holding cash were wiped out; 80 percent of the money in circulation became worthless. Hundreds of enraged students stormed out of the prestigious Rangoon Institute of Technology, smashed traffic lights, and burned vehicles. The regime's inevitable response was to close schools and universities.

The first major outbreak of demonstrations came in March of 1988, when an incident in a teashop in which a student was killed escalated into a large-scale demonstration on March 18, later known as "Black Friday," in which thousands of students were arrested and scores of students were killed by the hated *lon htein*, or riot police. In June campus demonstrations resumed, and on June 20, thousands of students staged a peaceful protest in Rangoon, joined by some monks, demanding that dismissed students be reinstated and that those responsible for the March killings be punished. Clashes took place in which eighty civilians and some twenty riot police were killed. On June 22, all universities in Rangoon were closed indefinitely, and a 6:00 p.m. to 6:00 a.m. curfew was declared for sixty days. Unrest spread to Pegu, where some seventy were killed. Then on July 23, General Ne Win, who had ruled the country with an iron hand for twenty-six years, suddenly resigned, citing widespread unrest and strife in the country, and proposing a referendum on the rule of the Burmese Socialist Program Party. Some saw this development as a glimmer of hope that democratic change might be on the way, but more pessimistic—and realistic—observers suspected that Ne Win was still in control. That suspicion was borne out when one of Ne Win's henchmen, Sein Lwin, was appointed president and chairman of the BSPP. Sein Lwin was known as "the butcher" for his role in suppressing the uprisings of 1962 and as de facto head of the hated *lon htein*, who had brutally put down the recent demonstrations of March and June.

On August 1, the All-Burma Students' Democratic League called for a nationwide general strike on 8/8/88 to protest the appointment of Sein Lwin. This prompted Sein Lwin on August 3 to declare martial law. My family and I, along with the Air Force attaché and his wife, were scheduled to take a trip up-country to visit Mandalay and Pagan. My son David was visiting from Cornell, and we had reserved an entire train car from Burmese railways, along with a railways chef, which could be done for quite a reasonable price (all right, a ridiculously low price—I think it was on the order of

$50). I don't recall just why we decided to go ahead with it, given the precarious situation at the time, but I recall thinking that the problems were mainly in Rangoon, and it might even be a good idea to get my family out of town for a while. But when we arrived in Pagan we were advised in a phone call from the embassy that antigovernment demonstrations had broken out in twenty-six cities around the country, and that we should make every effort to get back to Rangoon before August 8, as massive demonstrations were predicted. Just as we were preparing to leave the Thiripyitsaya Hotel in Pagan, the situation became even more macabre when our friends received a call to the effect that their only son had been killed in an automobile accident in Denver. I was standing beside the air attaché's wife when her husband took that call; he turned to her and said, "Our son has been killed." I caught her as she fainted and collapsed to the floor.

We left Pagan immediately by car to join up with our train car on the Mandalay to Rangoon line in Meiktila, only to find that the car had been held up in Mandalay. The regularly scheduled train was departing for Rangoon; the stationmaster refused to honor the tickets we had for the special car, so we bought new tickets for the trip to Rangoon, and managed to board the train as it was leaving. The trip to Rangoon seemed to last a lifetime, with my children sitting somberly and silently while the air attaché attempted to comfort his inconsolable wife. I think my twenty-one-year-old son, who had "gone native" on his first visit to a third-world country, matured by about three years during the trip. When our train, barely avoiding tracks that were blown up shortly after we passed, finally reached Rangoon at 8:00 a.m. on 8/8/88, there was an eerie silence in the city, and we were relieved to see the black Chevy Suburban and the faithful Ye Myint waiting for us at the deserted station. Later that day, however, an estimated ten thousand people took to the streets in what was just the beginning of massive demonstrations that were to take place over the next few weeks. Government radio reported thirty-one killed and thirty-seven wounded in "restoring security."

The next day, August 9, the army, acting under martial law, killed between forty and two hundred demonstrators (estimates varied wildly in those days) and arrested fifteen hundred. Estimates of the numbers of demonstrators that day ranged from twenty thousand to a hundred thousand. With Rangoon paralyzed by a general strike, Sein Lwin resigned on August 12 after eighteen days in power. In the following days, pro-democracy demonstrations grew in both numbers and intensity, encouraged by the apparent reluctance of the military to intervene. Lawyers, writers, film actors, musicians, hospital workers, and even policemen joined the demonstrations. Years of pent-up rage, and rumors that military personnel were poisoning the water supply, led to violence in some parts of the city. Some soldiers discovered among the demonstrators were beheaded as spies by enraged civilians. On one occasion, an eighteen-year-old Marine guard from the U.S. embassy was stopped on the way home and forced to take photos of a beheading. U.S. Ambassador Burt Levin ordered embassy officers to stay away from the demonstrators, claiming that U.S. interests in Burma did not justify the death of one American.

Foreign journalists were not being allowed in by the regime; a lone *Time* photographer had made it in earlier but was arrested for photographing demonstrations at the Shwedagon Pagoda. As a result, as the embassy's press attaché, I was being bombarded with calls from journalists representing AP, AFP, Reuters, *Washington Post*, *Daily Telegraph*, BBC, and others from Bangkok, Hong Kong, London, and even Sydney. They would typically ask, "What is your estimate of the number of demonstrators today?" I would look out my window and make a rough estimate of the numbers of demonstrators in Mahabandoola Square in front of the Embassy. On August 23, for example, somewhere between 100,000 and 200,000 demonstrators marched through downtown Rangoon between 8:00 a.m. and 4:00 p.m., ending with speechmaking in front of the U.S. Embassy. Martial law was lifted on August 24, and army troops moved back from their positions in the center of the city. Estimates were that as many as one million people were involved in demonstrations in Rangoon, with similar numbers in the major cities of Mandalay, Taunggyi, and Moulmein.

By August 26, a general strike had crippled Rangoon. Government services broke down completely, and air and rail service halted. To add to the melee, the government inexplicably released 4,800 prisoners from Insein Prison, resulting in widespread looting and violence. As a result of the general anarchy and the uncertainty of continued supplies of fuel, food, and drinking water, the embassy, in consultation with the State Department, decided to evacuate U.S. dependents to Bangkok. Over one hundred U.S. family members, along with dependents from various other embassies, were evacuated by chartered Thai Airways flights on September 9 and 11. As all airport workers were on strike, a Marine guard commandeered an airport tractor to push the flight stairs up to the plane, damaging the plane slightly as a result of his inexperience. This was one of the rare times when a mob in front of the U.S. Embassy was not anti-American; in fact, when the ambassador's car left the Embassy, the crowd would cheer him, chanting "We want democracy!" and "Freedom Now!"

The demonstrators congregated in front of the U.S. Embassy in the hope that it would provide them both publicity and some security. They were mistaken on both counts. On September 18, the military took over the government (overtly), forming the brutal State Law and Order Restoration Council, with the somehow appropriate acronym SLORC. The soldiers, who had been ordered not to fire on the demonstrators in the hope that they would vent their anger harmlessly, were now ordered to shoot to kill, and over the next week killed an estimated two thousand demonstrators in the process of "restoring peace and order." More civilians were killed that day than were killed in Tiananmen Square in Beijing a year later, but the world paid little attention to Burma. Another embassy officer and I filmed the massacres from the roof of the Embassy, and our tapes, smuggled out in the diplomatic pouch, provided the first glimpses in the international media of the situation in Rangoon.

Influenced by the euphoria of the demonstrators during the massive pro-democracy demonstrations, journalists wrote that whatever the future held, Burma "could never go back to the status quo ante."

They were wrong.

In my opinion, two events precipitated the crackdown by the government: a group of demonstrators surprised and disarmed a group of soldiers on top of the bank building adjacent to the Embassy. The soldiers had orders not to shoot and had been drinking, which no doubt facilitated their capture. The demonstrators, enraged by rumors that soldiers had been poisoning the people's water supply, were intent on killing their captives, but cooler heads persuaded the demonstrators to turn them over to their commanders. This humiliation, coupled with the fact that the demonstrators were for the first time marching on the Ministry of Defense, led to the crackdown. The generals no doubt reasoned that if they lost control of the situation, they would lose not only their jobs but their heads as well.

Evacuation from Post

On September 23, the United States cut off all aid to Burma to protest the massacres and ordered all USAID personnel out of Burma. On the same day, I was included among a dozen embassy officers with the unflattering designation "non-essential personnel" who were evacuated to Bangkok. There I worked TDY (temporary duty) in the Bangkok embassy until all American personnel were authorized to return to post on October 24. In retrospect, sending out "non-essentials" after September 18 was closing the barn door after the horses had fled, since once the SLORC had decided to clamp down, the military was firmly in control.

The evacuation itself was quite a bizarre adventure. For the dependents it was a traumatic experience to go off, not knowing when and under what circumstances they would see their spouses again. For the children, on the other hand, it was rather an exciting adventure, tempered only by the fact that they had to leave pets behind. Evacuations from dangerous posts are quite common in the Foreign Service; some families, especially USAID families, have been evacuated as many as three or more times during their careers. The "safe haven" in such situations is supposed to be CONUS (continental United States), but our families wanted to stay in Bangkok in the hope that they would soon be able to return to post, and Ambassador Levin supported their position. But our ambassador in Bangkok, Daniel O'Donohue, did not welcome having a hundred extra personnel using the facilities of his embassy, such as the commissary, the APO (Army Post Office), and the sports club. The principal and teachers of the American School had been evacuated along with the children. At first they were permitted to hold classes

in the American Club on Sathorn Road, but they were eventually
evicted from the club. As most of the families had found lodging in
one apartment building near the U.S. Embassy, they began to have
classes in various apartments.

Things turned nasty when it was rumored that Ambassador
O'Donohue, in his determination to get the Burma evacuees out
of his hair, had reported them to the Thai government for holding "an illegal school" without permission from the Thai Ministry of Education. This was seen as a particularly dastardly deed,
since O'Donohue had previously been ambassador to Rangoon and
should have been more sympathetic to the evacuees' predicament.
The State Department argued that, based on long experience, such
evacuations typically lasted from six months to a year, and in a significant number of cases the dependents never returned to post.

Both the evacuees and Ambassador Levin dug in their heels,
and before the thing could come to a head, the dependents were
authorized to return to post. As it turned out, Levin was right about
the likelihood of returning to post, but he had stood up against the
powers that be, and it essentially ended his diplomatic career. He
won the battle but lost the war. Nevertheless he landed on his feet
as head of the Asia Society in Hong Kong and later as a visiting professor of international affairs at Carleton College. When people go
through a traumatic experience, a kind of bonding takes place, and
our children look back with a certain nostalgia on the time when
they banded together to survive in Bangkok. Because of his support
for his staff, I have never seen an ambassador more popular with
his staff than Burton Levin.

With the staff and dependents back in Rangoon, Ambassador
Levin forbade any contact with the SLORC, commenting that "the
U.S. has so little strategic interest in Burma that we can, for once,
afford the courage of our convictions." However, in this position he
found himself at loggerheads with the Drug Enforcement Administration, which was interested in cooperating with the military regime to interdict the flow of drugs from the Golden Triangle. Levin
actually cashiered one DEA officer who maintained contact with
the SLORC against his orders, but in the end I think the DEA managed to overrule State in Washington. The only USAID officer who
was permitted to stay at post was the AID representative, Col. Earl

Young, a political appointee. As my wife had worked for USAID as a training supervisor, she was the only USAID employee at post other than Young, so when Young was traveling, my wife served as "Acting AID Rep."

USIS was able to continue its publication program, but not much else, for the remainder of my tour there. What was hard to understand was that, after we were forbidden to have contact with the host government, which is what, after all, an embassy is supposed to do, we were just as busy as before. Rangoon was a mid-size embassy, with about sixty American officers. It makes you wonder what we were doing before. It's a rather sad commentary on our efficiency, but I've come to realize that it takes a lot of effort and resources to maintain a diplomatic mission in a foreign country. You can be awfully busy in a mission abroad but a great deal of your work is just self-perpetuation, or bureaucratic wheel spinning.

Nobel Peace Laureate Aung San Suu Kyi

Aung San Suu Kyi, the daughter of Burma's martyred national hero General Aung San, was drafted on August 24 to head a coalition of pro-democracy organizations under the rubric National League for Democracy. Nobody knew much about her, as she had never been politically active. On a visit from Oxford, where her English husband was a professor of Tibetan studies, she was in Burma to see her sick mother. When the demonstrations broke out, she was drafted by the opposition as the daughter of the national hero, General Aung San, who had been instrumental in the struggle for independence from Great Britain and who had been assassinated in 1948. Sanda and I met her once at the airport when she was seeing off her husband and two teenage sons.

Aung San Suu Kyi was more or less forced by the circumstances to accept the mantle of leader of the democratic movement and became increasingly active during the demonstrations, giving speeches to wildly cheering audiences around the city. Although she was put under house arrest in July 1989, her party nevertheless won 82 percent of the parliamentary seats in the elections of 1990, which were never honored by the regime. She won the Nobel Peace Prize in 1991 for her efforts on behalf of democracy. When her husband died in 1999, she was unable to leave Burma to attend his funeral, because she knew the regime would not let her back in, and she felt she had an obligation to accept the role that had fallen on her shoulders. Suu Kyi was recently released from house arrest but is prohibited from political activity. So as I write this, she and the Burmese people are still in jail in their own country.

Before the events of 1988, I used to ask my Burmese friends why they had never revolted against their thuggish government. They would always reply, "As you know, we Burmese are Buddhists, and we don't believe in violence." But I never bought that line, since the Burmese in fact have a pretty bloody history, having been successful in most of their wars against their neighbors and with dynastic changes characterized by the massacre of the families of rival pretenders to the throne. But when they did come out into the streets to demonstrate for democracy in the hundreds of thousands, they were massacred by the thousands.

Apparently the appropriate answer to my question is "They have the guns, and we don't." The truth of this conclusion is borne out by the fact that widespread demonstrations that broke out in September of 2007, led by courageous Buddhist monks, the ruthless regime responded with the same brutality. The sad fact is that in spite of ineffective economic sanctions by concerned countries and unenforceable resolutions by the United Nations, nothing is going to change as long as the regime is willing to shoot down its own people. The recent parliamentary elections are meaningless, as they guarantee a majority for the ruling party. The only realistic prospect for change would be a split in the military, but there is at present no evidence of disunity. One can only hope that a younger generation of military officers will no longer be able to stomach the murder of defenseless monks and students and the world's condemnation.

Act Three: Morocco

Assignment Roulette

One of the most intriguing aspects of the Foreign Service is bidding on one's next assignment. My wife and family also enjoyed the game of imagining in just what country and even on what continent we would next find ourselves. It was always a bit of a letdown when one's destination had been decided and we had to start making plans to go to a specific post. Every Foreign Service officer was expected to bid on at least five posts, ranked in order of preference, of which at least two had to be hardship posts. The purpose of this rule was to ensure that an officer could not serve his or her entire career in cushy posts such as Paris or Rio.

Some officers nevertheless seemed able to circumvent this principle, serving entire careers in Western Europe—the "old boy network" undoubtedly had something to do with this. State Department officers have to bid all at the same time and thus receive their assignments at about the same time. USIA officers, however, could bid at any time throughout the year. Although my assignments to London and Rangoon were fascinating, I did not join the Foreign Service with the intention of capitalizing on my background in Southeast Asia; my purpose was to broaden my horizons and to live and work in areas of the world that I would not have experienced had I stayed at Cornell. Accordingly, during the second year of my tour in Rangoon I began to bid on assignments in Africa and Latin America.

I established a set of criteria by which I evaluated prospective posts. The following three are common among most officers:

1. How desirable is it as a place to live? (This did not necessarily mean how comfortable or how safe, but rather how exciting, adventurous, or exotic in terms of our interests; in short, how does it grab you?)
2. Is the work interesting, challenging, congenial—something that you would be content to do for two or three years?
3. Is the job (and the post) career-enhancing? (Career-enhancing jobs are typically jobs that are high-profile because of ongoing crises or dangerous circumstances, located in countries that are important to U.S. foreign policy interests, or rated at a higher rank than the incumbent's own rank. For example, when my boss and mentor at USIA learned that my follow-on assignment from London would be Rangoon, he said, "Burma, huh? Not too good from a career standpoint. You might get lucky, though; there might be a coup." He was serious! Little did I know how prophetic his comment would be.)

The next two criteria are specific to officers who have accompanying dependents:

4. How good are the schools? Do they have the appropriate level for my children? (This is a make-or-break consideration for families with children. Larger posts typically have American or international schools that run K–12. Smaller posts frequently have only K–8 and inadequate local secondary schools, which rules them out. Other posts may have no American or international schools, and bidders must consider whether the local schools are adequate.)
5. What are the opportunities for spousal employment in the embassy or the local economy? (Some countries have reciprocal agreements whereby a certain number of diplomatic dependents can work; others prohibit it. In such countries the only possibilities are then in the embassy itself; chances for this are much better in larger embassies.)

In addition, I had a sixth unofficial criterion: What are the facilities for tennis?

I had bid on jobs in Maseru (Lesotho) and Mbabane (Swaziland) in Africa, and Lima (Peru) in Latin America. When I heard that Lima qualified for danger pay because of the activities of the Shining Path guerilla movement, I withdrew my bid for the sake of the family. Then I heard that the personnel office was having trouble filling the job of information officer (press attaché) in Kinshasa, Zaire (now called the Democratic Republic of the Congo). At that time, Kinshasa was a more desirable post than it is now, after a series of coups and civil wars. It would have been a two-grade stretch (it was rated two grades above my rank at the time), so careerwise it would have been good. There was plenty of opportunity for spousal employment in the embassy. It was a Francophone post, and I had the required "professional competence" in French, and my wife is a near-native French speaker. It had a reasonably good American school with grades K–12. Thus the job suited me from many points of view, and the director of the Bureau of African Affairs called me from Washington and encouraged me to bid, saying, "I'd like to have you in that job." But Personnel didn't go along with it; they objected that it would be a two-grade stretch and they would like to hold out for an at-grade bidder, even though it was clear they had no other bidders at the time.

Then one morning at 3:00 a.m., I got a call from Personnel (Washington could never seem to figure out what time it was in Rangoon) saying, "How would you like to go to Marrakech?"

I was caught speechless, both because I was half asleep and because Morocco was totally out of my field of experience. But my wife was delighted because it sounded quite romantic and exotic. [And as I look back on all my posts—London, Rangoon, Marrakech, Paris, Phnom Penh, and Wellington—Marrakech stands out as the most exotic (N'Djamena, Chad, is in a class of its own—more later). Now if you ask most people which country they consider the more exotic—Morocco or Burma—they'd certainly say Burma; but for me Morocco, being a Muslim country and in North Africa, was different from the laidback Buddhist cultures I was familiar with in Laos, Thailand, Cambodia, and Burma. I had spent so much time in Asia as an academic that I felt at home there.]

So I agreed, there in bed in Rangoon, to go to Marrakech. The job was to be director of the American Cultural Center in Marrakech. As we had no consulate in Marrakech, I would be the only official

American in the city. (In earlier times we had had consulates in Marrakech, Fez, Tangier, and Casablanca; for various reasons we had closed the consulates in Marrakech, Fez, and Tangier, leaving Casablanca as the only American consulate outside the capital of Rabat.) The position nominally required competence in both French and Arabic, but because the post had been vacant for some time, they dispensed with the requirement that I also have Arabic. In any case, Moroccan Arabic is totally different from the standard Arabic they teach at FSI; as one of my predecessors put it, "Speaking classical Arabic in the *souk* would make you sound like William Shakespeare at K-Mart."

Mysterious Marrakech

After consultations and Middle Eastern area studies in Washington and the required twenty days of home leave between posts, we arrived in Rabat in early August 1989. Rabat has a temperate Mediterranean climate and is not considered a hardship post, as a result of which offices are not air-conditioned, although it gets pretty hot and muggy in the summer months. Marrakech, on the other hand, has a hot dry desert climate that regularly reaches 110 degrees most months of the year. As I was preoccupied with purchasing supplies for Marrakech and loading them into the Peugeot station wagon that we were to drive to Marrakech, I was dressed in a safari jacket. When I went to meet the PAO, John Graves, he observed my attire and remarked, "You know, Huffman, Rabat is not a safari jacket post."

Dress codes tend to differ from post to post, but at most posts, especially in Europe, business suits or at least jacket and tie are *de rigueur*. Only in more remote posts such as those in sub-Saharan Africa or Latin America are the dress codes relaxed. Also, the same terminology can mean radically different things at different posts; for example, in Paris "informal" means jacket and tie, while in other posts it can mean safari suits or open-necked shirts. Likewise, "casual" can mean anything from jacket and stylish shirt—sometimes referred to as "smart casual"—to shorts and tee-shirts. Thus alerted to Graves's attitude, I was always careful to be properly attired whenever he or other embassy officials visited Marrakech. Which was frequently—of which more later.

Graves himself was an enigmatic personality. He had been one of the hostages captured and held in Tehran for 444 days back in 1979. This experience may have unbalanced him somewhat. Having been born a French Canadian, he was an incorrigible Francophile and frequently bragged that he spoke the best French in the U.S. Foreign Service, when in fact he spoke French with a jarring Canadian accent. Although I found the diverse demands of the job in Marrakech challenging enough, he frequently urged me to take various initiatives, both professional and social, that he assured me he would carry out if he were in Marrakech. He loved to say, "Huffman, if you're not having fun, you're not doing it right." He was also rather insufferable about his tennis game, pointing out that he was "classé" (meaning ranked) nationally in Canada. On the one occasion we played at the Royal Racquet Club in Marrakech, he managed to win, but not impressively. (I didn't deliberately let him win, but I had the impression that he would have been pretty upset if he hadn't.)

Whenever you mention Marrakech, people say, "Oh, my favorite city in Morocco!" Well, yes, it is a fascinating place to visit. With its *souk* (market), its desert, its palaces and all the rest, it's very mysterious—where North Africa blends into sub-Saharan Africa. We had a nice house set in a *palmeraie* (a grove of palm trees, but rather pitiful compared to the lush tropical vegetation we were used to in Southeast Asia). In fact, we had two houses. The main house, which sported a colorful tile indoor fountain that occasionally spurted into the living room when the water pressure surged, was attached to an entire second-floor house accessible only by an outdoor staircase. This second house was an ideal place to put houseguests— you had them nearby but not in your hair. It also served as an excellent space to hold the frequent receptions we were called on to give for visiting U.S. officials. Whenever we told local contacts that we lived in the house called Villa Kawtar, a look of slightly embarrassed recognition would cloud their faces, as apparently the house was previously a well-known night club and brothel.

The embassy employed security guards from the international firm Wackenhut, who were posted around the clock at both the American Center and our residence. Since there was not really any serious threat other than possible burglary, our guards didn't have much to do. To amuse themselves they kept various pets, including an Alsatian dog named Luisa and several cats, which they fed in the garage. One of the guards, named Abdulazziz, was a favorite of my children, but there was a rather strained relationship between our dog Teddy and the guards' menagerie in the garage. Teddy was quite a docile pet around humans, but when confronted with other animals his instinct was to "kill it before it kills me." This pugnacious personality was due both to his isolation from other dogs while growing up in a Foreign Service family and to the terrier part of his mixed pedigree. On one occasion there was a litter of kittens in the garage, which, without the benefit of veterinary care or even basic sanitation, had all died off except for one lone and sickly survivor. My daughter, a lover of all animals, had understandably become attached to this lone survivor, which concerned me, as the chances of the kitten's survival were slim. One day, as Teddy was eating from a dish in the garage, the poor kitten wobbled over to his dish to explore its contents. Teddy, with an age-old survival instinct, growled and snapped at the kitten, breaking its neck. There was nothing to do but dispatch the poor thing and bury it in the *palmeraie.* Samantha was away at school, and when she returned home, I lied that the kitten had died and that I had had to bury it, and even took her and showed her where I had buried it, but I never had the courage to tell her the truth, as I was afraid it would forever jaundice her attitude toward the family dog.

Marrakech, as a favorite destination for both tourist and official travel, had about thirty tourist-class hotels and received flights of visitors directly from Paris, Madrid, and other cities in Europe. The most famous hotel is the fabled Mamounia, built to resemble the royal palaces of Morocco. Winston Churchill, in a letter inviting Franklin Roosevelt to come to the Mamounia Hotel following the World War II conference in Casablanca, said, "It is the most beautiful place in the world."

Marrakech is indeed exotic, with its pink palaces, crenellated walls, mysterious *souk,* somnolent camels, and horse-drawn carriages, but the hordes of tourists and the booming hotel industry hardly qualify it as the fabled oasis of many people's dreams. The city's best-known attraction is Place Jemaa el-Fna, a large square at the entrance to the *souk,* where jugglers, snake charmers, acrobats, pickpockets, and social misfits of all kinds blend with and provide nonstop entertainment for backpackers and other tourists.

The *souk* itself is a confusing and slightly ominous warren of corridors and alleyways, where tag teams of guides, peddlers, and pimps vie for your attention, many of them extremely aggressive and overtly threatening, implying that if you don't hire their services, they won't be responsible for what might happen. In fact, it is strongly advised that single women (or anyone else, for that matter) not enter the *souk* without the services of a trusted guide, whose primary responsibility is to ward off other "guides" whose job is to lead you to specific shops in return for kickbacks.

The most prominent landmark of Marrakech is the twelfth-century Koutoubia, the best preserved of three ancient minarets, the other two being the Tour Hassan in Rabat and the Giralda in Seville, Spain. Ironically, non-Muslims are prohibited from entering the Koutoubia or other mosques in Morocco, even though it is known as one of the most liberal of Muslim countries. Apparently this ordinance was instigated by the French colonists and not the Moroccans themselves, but when they gained independence from France in 1956, they left the law on the books. In spite of this restriction, there are plenty of palaces, tombs, madrasas (Koranic schools), and even restaurants where you can see the beautiful and intricate patterns of Muslim architecture and tilework. The annual Folklife Festival, held in the ruins of the Palais el-Badi, is a romantic and ethereal experience that draws spectators from around the world. Perhaps the most spectacular event of the year is the performance called "Fantasia," where troupes of colorfully costumed Berber horsemen dash from one end of the field to another to show off their skills at horsemanship.

Marrakech is about an hour from skiing in the Atlas Mountains to the south and an hour and a half from the beach at Agadir. The change of climate from one to the other is dramatic. The ski resort at Oukaimeden is so cold that the assistant director of the French Cultural Center, the father of one of my daughter's schoolmates, froze to death when he became lost while hiking in the ski area. Conversely, the beach resort at Agadir is a prime destination for tourists from northern Europe. During our tour we made several orientation trips to the desert south, visiting such cities as

Ouarzazate, Taroudant, and Tiznit, each with its crenellated walls surrounding crumbling palaces—all that is left from former desert principalities.

Dar America

Dar America (America House) was located on a palm-lined boulevard in an area of hotels and was quite a pleasant place to work. The staff were excellent; as two of my predecessors had had to curtail their assignments for medical reasons, staff were quite accustomed to running the show on their own. We had a large USIS library with 8,000 members. We had programs, we had speakers, and we showed American films. The clientele for the USIS center were primarily university students and faculty. Marrakech had a major university as well as several lycées. The French, who for historic reasons had a heavy presence in Morocco, had built in Marrakech one of the largest *Alliance Française* installations in all of North Africa. But they charged a membership fee and didn't have as many members as we did—whether because of the fee or a latent antipathy toward their former colonial masters, or both—so we could collaborate effectively with the French. All we had was a small colonial-style house painted pastel pink (as most everything is there), with a library and offices upstairs and a tiny program area; so I would arrange with the French to hold programs in their magnificent auditorium, and they would thus have access to our membership and expose them to the French cultural center.

We were a kind of refuge and rallying point for the Peace Corps volunteers in Marrakech and the surrounding towns and villages. They liked to rendezvous at our library and attend our programs, and we gave them the privilege of checking out books and videos. There was one older couple in the Peace Corps who became our close friends —Bob and Kathy Govier. They lived in a small but charming traditional Moroccan house in the souk. Bob had been a professor of German literature, a music teacher, and a mutual fund administrator, and was teaching American studies at the university. He was one of those multitalented Americans who seemed able to do everything—he even beat me at tennis and bridge. I used him in my U.S. Speakers program. He would give impressive lectures about American literature and American studies in general. I would send him around to our American Cultural Week presentations in outposts in Agadir and other towns in the area. In addition, he was performing a marvelous service to us by directing a chorus made up of Moroccan university students who practiced at Dar America and sang American show tunes. They performed at various venues, such as schools and hotels, as well as at Dar America, and became a virtual arm of our public diplomacy.

Bob later took jobs in the Gaza Strip and Georgetown, Guyana. I lost touch with him for a while until I got a letter from the Peace Corps asking me to write a letter of recommendation for him for a volunteer position in Turkmenistan. Instead of filling out their detailed questionnaire, I told them, "Listen, if you can get Bob Govier, grab him!" To my surprise, I later got a letter from Bob to the effect that he had resigned. He had been required to share a room with a young Turkmen who spoke no English; the room was cold and had a dirt floor that turned muddy when it rained. He told me, "I've lived in some pretty miserable places in my life, but I'm too old for this." Turkmenistan had finally defeated him.

Marrakech was a popular center for conventions and conferences, and I was frequently asked to represent the embassy at conventions on tourism, the environment, or trade relations and things that USIS officers didn't normally get involved in. I occasionally had to provide consular services such as helping tourists report stolen passports to the police, or contacting a son or daughter for a worried parent—usually a backpacker who had been seduced by the mystical charms of Marrakech, not to mention the hashish. Thus I was a kind of "general factotum" for the embassy.

A Proposition in La Palmeraie

Accustomed to the lush tropical vegetation of Southeast Asia, I have a hard time understanding why some people draw inspiration from the sparse and arid vegetation of the desert. On the outskirts of Marrakech is a residential area known as La Palmeraie (it seems that wherever they can coax a pitiful palm tree or two from the sand, they baptize it a *palmeraie*). The palatial pastel-colored villas and azure swimming pools scattered around the dunes are

owned by wealthy expatriates who are mostly retirees or homo-
sexuals (and in some cases both). Various French celebrities of the
fashion world, such as Yves St. Laurent and Pierre Balmain, had
vacation homes there; YSL had endowed a museum in Marrakech
containing pieces from his personal art collection.

One socialite who had a house in La Palmeraie was Frederick
("Fricky") Vreeland, son of the editor of *Vogue* magazine Diana
Vreeland. Vreeland had had a previous career as a CIA agent cum
diplomat and harbored further ambitions in the field of diplomacy. On one occasion he invited Sanda and me to lunch at his villa
to discuss his interest in Burma. He had asked me to recommend
several good books on Burma, confiding, "George wants to send
me as ambassador to Burma." I finally realized that by "George"
he meant President George H. W. Bush. After a lavish luncheon
washed down by excellent wines, Vreeland, apparently impressed
with my knowledge of and experience in Burma, said that if he were
appointed ambassador to Burma, he would like me to be his DCM
(Deputy Chief of Mission). I thanked him for the offer but refrained
from pointing out that it would not be a popular move to elevate me
to the position of DCM in an embassy where I had recently served
as a lowly assistant PAO. But I had no doubt that he could accom-
plish it if he wished, as Fricky was clearly a man who was used to
getting his way — and not a man I would have enjoyed working for.
In any case, I attributed his claim to empty braggadocio. I learned
later that he had indeed been nominated as ambassador to Burma
but was rejected by the generals in Rangoon for having expressed a
fondness for human rights (and perhaps also because of his history
with the CIA). But his influence with "George" was borne out when
he was appointed ambassador to Rabat — a much more important
post than Rangoon.

An interesting facet of the posting to Marrakech was that just
north of the city was a backup landing site for the launching of
space shuttles from Cape Canaveral. So whenever there was a
launch, about fifty NASA people would arrive in town, and in case
of an emergency landing, my office would have become the press
center for the event. That never happened during my tenure there,
but during the Atlantis space shot to Jupiter, the astronaut Dick
Covey came over and we had him to dinner. My son Christopher

was thrilled to meet an actual astronaut and even more pleased when Covey gave him a signed photograph.

Trouble in Paradise

Marrakech should have been an ideal post. One problem, however, was that the king, Hassan II, would spend three to four months a year in his palace in Marrakech (he had sixteen palaces, but was partial to Marrakech). When the king was in residence, Marrakech was essentially the royal capital, and the movers and shakers came to Marrakech. On such occasions I was "our man in Marrakech." Among the visitors I received were former secretary of defense Caspar Weinberger and his party. I helped brief him on Moroccan culture in his luxurious suite in the grand Mamounia Hotel before his visit to the palace. Frequent congressional delegations included Representative Charles Rangel of New York and a party of thirty-seven, whose primary interest in Marrakech was shopping in the souk. I received Senator Daniel Moynihan and his delegation as well, and served as interpreter for Mrs. Moynihan during the delegation's visit to the royal palace.

I also organized a reception for Moynihan and the American ambassador with all the important people of Marrakech. About two hours before the reception, Moynihan's chief of staff, Peter Galbraith (later ambassador to Croatia), called to say that Moynihan was too tired to attend the reception. I was devastated. I pointed out that the most prominent people from Marrakech and the palace had been invited, and it would have serious repercussions for U.S.-Moroccan relations if the senator were not to attend. Finally Senator Moynihan did attend, was quite gracious to the guests (in spite of, or perhaps because of, his well-known love of tippling), and the evening was saved.

A somewhat annoying aspect of my position was that almost every weekend, about 5:00 p.m. on Friday afternoon, I'd wait for it—the call from the ambassador. He would say something like, "Frank, you know, my aunt's in town and we want to come down to Marrakech, and I wonder if you could arrange a tour for us like you arranged when my cousin was over here, and make reservations at that restaurant there in the souk where they have the performance of the belly dancers, and get a guide for us to go into the souk." And he'd say, "Of course I'd like to invite you and your wife to come along." Well, you couldn't use representational funds to accompany the ambassador and his American guests to an expensive restaurant. We went along two or three times and then decided we couldn't afford it any more. So, my job in Marrakech was actually half Foreign Service officer and half tour guide. As one wag put it, in the Foreign Service "there's no job too small." But that is one of the challenges—and appeals—of the Foreign Service: in a single day you might be faced with anything from carrying the ambassador's bags to negotiating the release of hostages.

Curtailment

When we accepted the job in Marrakech, we knew that it would entail putting both of our kids in the French lycée because there was no American school. My francophone European wife was all for this. Our son, Christopher, who was thirteen, had attended the Lycée Rochambeau in Bethesda, Maryland, for kindergarten, but he had been in English-language schools in London and Rangoon. Our daughter, Samantha, who was seven years old, took readily to the French language, since she was at the age at which kids learn second languages with least effort. It was as if she thought, "So that's what you do in school—you talk in this funny language." But Christopher did not adapt at all well to the very prescriptive French system. For example, in math class he might get the correct answer, but if he didn't go through the steps prescribed by the French system, or if he didn't put his name at the right place in the upper right-hand corner of the page, he'd get zero. Furthermore, thirteen is the worst age to take a kid into a new system, and he just couldn't deal with it. He became upset and withdrawn, doing things like breaking out the windows of his room with a baseball bat.

I wrote to Washington and said, "You know, it's not working here." After describing our problems, pointing out that I considered the educational facilities to be inadequate for an officer with children and that there were no employment possibilities for my wife, ending with the rather self-serving statement that "an officer whose family is not content cannot perform his duties effectively,"

I announced that I wanted to curtail after one year in Marrakech. Now curtailment, even when allowed, was not looked on favorably by the powers that be; it causes them problems, rocks the boat, and costs more money in terms of recruitment and transportation of replacements.

The area office (NEA—Near Eastern Affairs) said, "Look, you bid on Marrakech knowing you would have to put your children in the French school, so why are you complaining now?"

I wrote back and said, "Well, you know, I made a mistake. And intelligent people, when they make a mistake, take steps to correct it." In the end they granted the curtailment, grudgingly. I applied for a job in Paris, where my former boss from London, Bud Korengold, was now PAO; he knew me and my work and had said he would welcome me if I ever wanted to work for him again. So, pulling what strings I had, I got the job of director of programs in Paris. The director of NEA, an old Middle Eastern hand, the son of missionaries, and a bit puritanical, was reported to have remarked that it sends the wrong signal when an officer can "shirk his duty" and still get assigned to Paris.

Closing USIS Marrakech

My curtailment was apparently responsible for the decision to close Marrakech as a USIS branch post, or at least for the timing of the closing. In an earlier more affluent period, the State Department had both consulates and USIS posts in Casablanca, Tangiers, Marrakech, and Fez, in addition to the main chancery and consulate in the capital Rabat. State later closed the consulates in Marrakech, Tangier, and Fez, leaving only the Casablanca consulate, but USIS maintained its post in Marrakech. When it was decided that it was more important to have a USIS post in Fez than in Marrakech, the king himself intervened in favor of Marrakech.

When William Rugh, director of NEA, visited Morocco in February 1990, he asked the PAO, John Graves, to make a recommendation as to whether USIS Marrakech should be closed, in light of the agency's budget constraints. Graves, who didn't want to see his domain diminished by the closure of one of his branch posts, instructed me to write a strong justification for keeping the post open to use in his argument to Rugh. I did so, pointing out that Marrakech in effect became the government during the 3-4 months a year when the king was in residence, the importance of the USIS library as a resource for its 8000 members who were mostly university students, and the role of Marrakech as the "gateway to the southern half of the country," facilitating educational and cultural exchanges with the southern cities of Agadir, Safi, and Ouarzazate. At the end of the memo, I played devil's advocate, providing arguments against keeping Marrakech open, just in case the PAO decided on that line of argument. I pointed out that from USIA's point of view, Marrakech was not a fertile place for public diplomacy (as there was not a great deal of local interest in political or security issues), that the USIS library could be seen as simply compensating for the inadequacy of the Moroccan university system, and that the Branch PAO had to spend too much time as a tour guide at the expense of USIA's primary mission. Graves must either have argued the negative, or not have made a convincing case for the positive, because one month before my departure, I was informed that Washington had decided to close USIS Marrakech (again). Rugh used my curtailment as one of his justifications for closing the post, so that my decision to curtail precipitated at least the timing of the closing of USIS Marrakech.

Where Has My Little Dog Gone?

Our dog Teddy played a role in our decision to drive from Marrakech to Paris. Getting him from Rangoon to Marrakech had been a nightmare. I had bought Teddy as a puppy during a trip to Bangkok, and had carried him on my lap on a Burmese Airways flight to Rangoon. When we tried to get him out of Burma, the authorities refused to let him out, on the grounds that he had entered Burma illegally, but the unofficial reason was simple administrative harassment by the military government with whom the embassy was at odds.

The only solution was to leave him with the household staff (who were quite fond of him in any case) and ask my unsuspecting successor, Bob Schmidt, to ship him to us by air once the Burmese had granted permission. Schmidt dutifully arranged to ship Teddy to Bangkok, where the USIS executive officer, Chuck Flanagan, was to put him on a connection to Marrakech via Paris. The problem was that flights from Bangkok to Paris all went to Charles de Gaulle airport, while flights from Paris to Marrakech all originated from Orly airport, so Teddy would have to enter France proper rather than simply go through Transit, and this would require someone to transfer him from one airport to another. Chuck Flanagan, in an act of kindness well beyond the call of duty and for which we will always be grateful, kept Teddy in his own apartment for about two weeks until he located a Philippine Airlines flight that went directly to Orly.

We were notified one night that Teddy was to arrive at the Marrakech airport at midnight, some six weeks after we had left him behind in Rangoon. As the physical exam Morocco required to occur within the prior thirty days had long expired, I took some books along to the airport to soothe any concerns on the part of the customs officer in charge (gifts of booze are not officially accepted in Muslim countries). Teddy, whose normally iron gray fur had not been cut in several months, looked like some kind of woolly ghost. When we let him out of the kennel, he jumped up into my arms in his excitement, nearly knocking me off my feet.

After this harrowing experience in getting our pet back, we decided we would throw the whole family and the dog into my four-year-old BMW and haul them all to Paris. The car had arrived at post even later than the dog, somewhat the worse from its two-year sojourn in Burma. It had flat tires and a dead battery and had to be resuscitated at considerable cost at the local BMW garage.

It was rather an iffy proposition to try to drive such a car 1,500 miles across Morocco, Spain, and France, but I was consoled by the thought that at least we would be driving in the direction of countries that were better equipped to deal with the maintenance of BMWs. In the end, the car performed remarkably well throughout the trip. The dog kept the children entertained, and they in turn kept us informed of their best estimates as to when the dog had to relieve himself, with gratifyingly few cases of inaccuracy. Our route took us via Rabat to the Spanish enclave of Ceuta on the northern tip of Morocco, where we caught the ferry to Tarifa on the Spanish mainland (from which the word "tariff" is derived), visited the imposing rock of Gibraltar (whose British ownership is still disputed by Spain), meandered up the Mediterranean coast to visit with friends in Barcelona, then headed up the center of France via Toulouse, Limoges, and Orléans to Paris.

Act Four: France

Into the City of Light

Paris did not look much like a "City of Light" as we drove into the suburbs on a dark and rainy day, slipping and sliding over the cobblestones as we tried to locate our temporary lodgings in a rather dreary section of the 16th arrondissement. However, after about a month in our temporary digs, the housing perks of the Foreign Service came through again, and we moved into our permanent lodgings in the fashionable 8th arrondissement, just minutes off the Champs-Elysées. The apartment was on the second floor (third floor in American usage) of an elegant old building with an antique cage-type elevator suggestive of the nineteenth century.

Our three-bedroom apartment, with 2,000 square feet of living space in the center of Paris, was what the French referred to as an *appartement de grand standing*. French guests would invariably gasp in astonishment at its size. Included in the package was a guest room across a cobblestone courtyard above a garage that was originally a carriage house. The room had served as sleeping quarters for carriage drivers in earlier times; it was now furnished with a bathroom and a tiny kitchen. When word got around that the Huffmans had a free *pied-à-terre* in the middle of Paris, the room was seldom vacant. We were visited by a steady stream of friends and relatives, some of whom we had not seen in years, if ever. Actually, the setup was ideal—we got to provide our guests with much-appreciated lodgings, visit with them at prearranged times, and not have them constantly underfoot—an arrangement appreciated by both guests and hosts.

Once settled in, we set about getting Christopher enrolled in the excellent American School of Paris, where he was soon happily taking electives in drawing and architecture (he had announced his intention of becoming an architect at the age of seven), and coming home soaked in mud from rugby practice. As for Samantha, we enrolled her in the local elementary school, the Ecole Paul Baudry, where she adapted so easily to the French system that the headmaster did not even realize that she was not French until he met her parents during a PTA meeting. She became so thoroughly integrated as a little French girl that when her friends were having their confirmations at the local Catholic church (St. Philippe du Roule), she assumed that was the thing little girls do at a certain age, so my wife and I decided to let her go ahead and be confirmed with her schoolmates, in spite of the fact that she had been christened in my wife's Eastern Orthodox religion as a baby. What is surprising is that the Catholic priest had no problem with that—proving that he was an enlightened fellow, in my estimation.

As a further advantage, we were located close enough to the Embassy in the Place de la Concorde that I could walk to the office every day, along the elegant Rue du Faubourg St. Honoré with its fashionable designer boutiques, past the French president's residence, the Palais de l'Elysée, and the almost equally sumptuous American ambassador's residence at 41 rue du Faubourg St. Honoré. Walking to work had the great advantage of not having to negotiate the chaos of Paris traffic. I find that charge somewhat exaggerated, however, since driving in Paris is quite doable once you learn the rules. One of the stranger rules is that in a traffic circle you yield to traffic entering the circle, thus negating the purpose of a traffic circle—and this in the land of Cartesian logic! Traffic around the Etoile, or l'Arc de Triomphe, is so chaotic that French law considers any accident to be "no fault."

It cannot be denied that Paris is a beautiful city. Some have complained that Baron Haussmann's wholesale renovation of Paris in the nineteenth century imposed a boring uniformity on the architecture of the city; but this consistency only makes more daring structures, such as the Eiffel Tower and the more recent Beaubourg (Pompidou) Museum, stand out in contrast. Architecture aside, Paris is a pedestrian-friendly city with a uniquely human dimension. It always impressed me that wherever you decide to pop up from the excellent Métro underground system, you unfailingly encounter cafes, restaurants, fruit stands, flower shops, *patisseries*, and boutiques—all the amenities of everyday life. With apologies to Hemingway, it was "a moveable feast."

Our ambassador to Paris at that time was the Honorable Walter Curley. Traditionally, big posts like Paris, London, and Rome are patronage posts usually given to wealthy administration supporters, and Walter Curley was no exception—he was an investment banker who had supported the administration of Bush the First. But he was quite likeable and had an uncanny ability to remember people's names and who they were. He had maybe a thousand employees in the embassy, and when meeting any of them on the steps he'd call them by their first name. With me he'd say, "Good morning, professor, how are you?" He knew my story. He was also quite a joker. When the PAO first introduced me to him, he said, "Huffman, you gave up a job as a full professor at an Ivy League university to do this? I don't think you're smart enough to serve in my embassy." I hope he was joking.

I think he did not have a great deal of access to or impact on the host government. He fulfilled all his duties as ambassador and represented the interests of the United States perfectly well, but he did not have the profile that I think the French would have liked. His successor, Pamela Harriman, by contrast, was extremely well known and had known the major players in French politics socially and called them by their first names. She spoke quite good French and was, I think, a very effective ambassador. She arrived just shortly before I left post.

Telling America's Story

Paris is one of the most coveted assignments in the Foreign Service. This was the big time, and I couldn't help but wonder how I would perform in such a high-profile post. London had been fun, but I had been "over-complement" there, with no specific portfolio. My job in Paris was to be director of programs. USIS Paris was unusual in that it had a tripartite organization. Most USIS posts have a press section headed by an IO (information officer) and a cultural section headed by a CAO (cultural affairs officer), both supervised by the PAO (public affairs officer). In Paris they had press, cultural, and programs sections. As director of programs, I reported directly to the PAO rather than through the CAO or IO.

I was responsible for recruiting U.S. speakers and experts from government, academia, or the private sector as lecturers and participants in conferences and seminars at various French venues, such as the Sorbonne and the Ecole polytechnique, or think tanks such as IFRI (Institut français des relations internationales) and CERI (Centre d'études et de recherches internationales). In this work I was aided by an American APO (assistant program officer), three French FSNs and a secretary. One FSN specialized in political/military affairs, another in economic and trade issues, and the third in American history and culture. These FSNs were highly qualified, had PhDs, and were members of professional societies in their respective fields. They thus enjoyed a certain cachet among their colleagues as gatekeepers of American largesse for the support of conferences and seminars.

Although the demands of the job were challenging, I was perhaps not as intimidated as a younger officer might have been. After all, I had visited Paris numerous times in the course of six trips around the world as an academic, was familiar with the university scene, and had spent some twenty years as a professor at Yale and Cornell. This experience, along with the support of my excellent staff, enabled me to field an impressive total of some fifty speakers and experts a year, drawn primarily from three sources. About a third came from USIA's U.S. Speakers office in Washington, whose job was to recruit speakers in response to requests from posts for specific kinds of speakers (sometimes by name) to meet the public diplomacy challenges of that particular country. These speakers consisted primarily of well-known academics, such as Barry Bosworth from the Brookings Institution, William Chafe of Duke University, and John Lewis Gaddis of Ohio University, as well as various administration officials. Another third came from what we called TOOs, or "target of opportunity speakers." This was a particularly rich source of experts for Paris, where you inevitably have a lot of prominent people passing through town upon whom we would prevail to give one or a couple of talks for the U.S. embassy.

Some of the more prominent speakers we were able to buttonhole in this manner were Librarian of Congress James Billington, Supreme Court Justice Sandra Day O'Connor, and Ambassadors Vernon Walters, Joseph Greenwald, and John Kornblum.

A third source, not quite as prominent as the other two, was expertise in the embassy itself. Whenever I got a request from a university or a think tank for somebody to discuss trade, security, or U.S.-French bilateral issues, I would call up colleagues in the political or economics sections and say, "Look, could you go out on Thursday night and talk to such and such an academic group on such and such a topic?" Those officers who could lecture in French were particularly useful. Several of the embassy officers I programmed later became ambassadors, such as Alexander Vershbow, ambassador to Russia and Korea, and Neils Marquardt, ambassador to Madagascar and Cameroon.

On those occasions when a speaker was not hosted by some French institution outside the embassy, we had the option of programming events in the elegant salons of the Hotel Talleyrand, where the USIS offices were located. This historic building, built in 1767 and named after Charles Maurice de Tallyrand-Périgord, Napoleon's foreign minister, is situated across the Place de la Concorde from the Chancery itself . The building served as the European headquarters of the Marshall Plan following World War II. The Salon de l'Aigle, with its crystal chandeliers and gilded woodwork, was an impressive venue for lectures and programs. The elegance of the setting was undoubtedly a factor in attracting audiences for our programs. That such programs were typically followed by a wine and cheese reception was also not insignificant in attracting an eager audience.

One of the most popular speakers we had was Ambassador Vernon Walters. He was much in demand as a speaker because of his notoriety as General Eisenhower's interpreter and aide-de-camp during World War II, his background as deputy director of the CIA under Nixon, and as U.S. ambassador to the United Nations under Reagan, but especially because of his ability to lecture in French (as well as in half a dozen other languages). I once had an embarrassing contretemps with Ambassador Walters when I was his handler and he was going to be available over several days. He had his own apartment on the Champs-Elysées; he was in Paris often enough to warrant his own *pied-à-terre* there. When he had finished his program at the French Institute of International Relations and the various venues at which he spoke, he was to catch a flight out of town the next day. I sent one of the USIS drivers to pick him up at his apartment and deliver him to Charles de Gaulle airport.

About a half hour later I had a call from General Walters, saying, "Where's that driver?"

I said, "Well, I sent him a half hour ago; I don't know what happened."

"Well you better get somebody here pretty soon or I'm going to miss my plane."

I said, "Yes sir, I'll certainly locate him or if I can't find him I'll send another car."

So I got another car and went up to General Walters's apartment, but the driver had apparently misunderstood exactly where he was supposed to meet the General, and they hadn't gotten together. General Walters was fuming. I managed to get them connected and apologized profusely. As he was getting into the car, the driver decided he would put the window up on the passenger side. But General Walters had his hand on the window, so the window mashed his fingers as it went up.

By that time General Walters, who does not suffer fools gladly, was turning the air blue. "Huffman, who do you work for? I'm going to give him an earful!"

I was devastated, but I learned an important lesson. When I related this fiasco to my colleagues, they said, "Frank, you know, a man like General Walters, you don't send a driver to take him to the airport, you accompany him to the airport." And I realized, "Yes, well, okay, that was a mistake."

It's difficult to assess just how effective all these program were. The French were very polite and civil, they'd have a lively question and answer period, and you'd have an academic discussion—the French love to debate and are masters of rhetoric—but I don't think a lot of our contacts were persuaded against their will. I do think these programs served an important purpose in reassuring certain audiences that we were not totally crazy and in modifying some of the more virulent anti-Americanism that we encountered from time to time. Though a highly desirable post to which everyone wants to go, from the standpoint of my function to "tell America's story to the world," Paris was one of the most difficult of all my assignments in the Foreign Service. The French didn't want to hear America's story; on the contrary, they felt that America could use a *mission civilisatrice* from the French.

The following anecdote is illustrative of the challenge. We had just had a speaker from the U.S. Trade Representative's office talking about the Uruguay round of the GATT (General Agreement on Tariffs and Trade) negotiations and were discussing agricultural supports, still being debated twenty years later. But I overheard my program assistant, the economist, commiserating with one of her French colleagues who had attended the lecture to the effect that the bilateral reduction of tariffs on agricultural trade was not a good thing for France.

I took her aside afterwards and said, "Sylvie, how are we going to be effective if my own staff doesn't support American foreign policy objectives with our French public?" And so we argued and I said, "Look, don't you think that the French would be happy if they could pay less for their groceries at the supermarket?"

She said, "Listen, I've lived in the United States and I've tasted your supermarket tomatoes, and we French don't want any of them."

She had a pretty good point, to be honest. Food plays a far more important role in the daily lives of the French than it does in the United States. You might say we eat to live; they live to eat. But cuisine is an important aspect of French culture, and they would rather pay more for a good tomato than pay less for a tasteless tomato.

Trade issues formed the most contentious area of U.S.-French bilateral relations. Surprisingly, we were pretty much in sync on defense and security issues. Whenever we had specialists in political-military affairs come and talk with the French military think tanks and institutions, the French were in remarkable agreement with our positions. Following the U.S. invasion of Iraq in January 1991, when terrorist incidents increased around the world, the embassy was on high alert and received the full cooperation of the French diplomatic police in protecting the perimeters of the Chancery, the Consulate, and the USIS offices in the Hotel Talleyrand.

After a period of fence-sitting, the French turned out to be pretty hard-nosed on the Gulf War, and the French military wanted to go on to Baghdad at the end. In view of George W's disastrous involvement in Iraq, who knows, maybe they were right. While France had withdrawn its military forces from NATO in 1966, they remained supportive of NATO and were very much interested in interoperability of weapons systems and that sort of thing. (The NATO headquarters in the sixties was in the building now occupied by one of the branches of the University of Paris, University of Paris Nine, also called Dauphine.)

One of the most interesting things I did while in Paris was leading a delegation of French midlevel politicians on a NATO tour of NATO and SHAPE (Supreme Headquarters, Allied Powers Europe) in Brussels, various arms control negotiation groups in Geneva, and a joint NATO military base in Oslo. I had led a similar tour for British academics while posted to London. These tours were cosponsored by USIA and the U.S. Mission to NATO, in the interest of building support for NATO and U.S. defense policies among young politicians, academics, and journalists. In my experience, these tours tended to be fairly effective. Even the French, who are (or at least pretend to be) notoriously jaded and cynical, could not help but be impressed by the joint NATO base in Oslo, for example, where they observed the close cooperation among officers from numerous other European member countries and received detailed briefings by obviously intelligent military strategists.

Cross-Cultural Miscommunication

As director of programs, I occasionally took speaking assignments myself when I felt qualified to deal with the topic. I gave some half dozen lectures in French to such organizations as France-Etats-Unis and the Institut Franco-Américain. Sometimes I represented the embassy at less rarified venues in provincial cities such as Lyon, Toulouse, Nantes, and Rennes. Having been trained as an anthropologist, my topic was usually a fairly humorous comparison of U.S. and French culture and cross-cultural communication, or as is so often the case, miscommunication.

One of my standard talks was entitled *"Qu'est que c'est qu'un*

Américain?: les differences culturelles entre la France et les Etats-Unis." ("What is an American?—Cultural Differences between France and the United States"). I presented these differences in a light-hearted and humorous vein. For example, the French usually describe Americans as open, friendly, and practical and so on, but they also see us as loud, aggressive, and naïve. Conversely, Americans tend to think of the French as artistic, stylish, and sophisticated but at the same time rude, chauvinistic, and cynical. I would point out that there's always some truth to stereotypes. Charles de Gaulle is famously known for having said that the Germans have talent but no genius, while the French, alas, have genius but no talent.

As examples of cultural differences, I would mention that the French shake hands a lot. If a Frenchman meets a friend in the morning, he shakes hands. If he meets him again in the afternoon, he shakes hands again. If he meets him that night, he shakes hands again. In the United States, I said, we don't feel the need to shake hands with each other more than about once a week, usually when we meet somebody once a week at church. Also the French custom of kissing a lady on both cheeks, twice, sometimes three times, sometimes four—four is becoming more and more popular now. I pointed out that most Americans are uncomfortable with that. To me it seems insincere, but if we have a French couple to my home for dinner and he kisses my wife on both cheeks I have to "do as the Romans do," because if I don't he'll think I don't find his wife attractive. These are all trivial differences that don't affect the essential common interests of the two countries.

Another popular topic that generated a great deal of controversy was a comparison of the U.S. and French systems of education. The French system is much more elitist than ours. Entrance to university is much more competitive, as a result of which only about 40 percent of secondary school graduates go on to higher education, as against about 60 percent in the United States. The French like to believe that they have the best schools in the world, but that can be said only of their *"grandes ecoles"* —the Ecole polytechnique, Sciences politiques, Hautes études commerciales, Ecole nationale d'administration, and the like—which are highly competitive and typically attended only by the elite of France. Many of France's top leaders, of whatever political persuasion, boast of being an "X-ENA," which means they are graduates of both the (undergraduate-level) Ecole polytechnique and the (graduate-level) Ecole nationale d'administration. This situation is one of the things that came to a head in the recent ethnic riots in France, where minority and immigrant students were saying that only white French elite can get into these schools and as a result the country is run by a revolving elite at the top regardless of which party is in power.

I used to compare the two systems in my talks on cross-cultural communication. I would explain to audiences that Americans believe that everybody should have access to higher education, but that some educators go too far in claiming that everybody should *have* a higher education. The problem with this is that if everybody gets a higher education, then it is no longer higher. In spite of our problems, foreign students still flock to our universities (or at least did before the Iraq war). We must be doing something right, since 30 percent of all Nobel prizes since the founding of the competition have been awarded to American scholars.

Another contrast between American and French society is the matter of ethnicity. There's something unique about the United States in that we all came originally from somewhere else, and to say you're an American doesn't mean anything ethnically or racially. To give a personal anecdote, when my wife defected from the communist regime in Romania in 1971, she headed straight for Paris, because the Romanians are incorrigible Francophiles—educated people in Romania typically speak French. She got a job at UNESCO, but after six months she realized that she would never be French; she would forever be a Romanian living in France, whereas in the United States she could be an American—she could be one of the thirty million other people in this country who were born abroad. The words "French" or "German" or "English" have clear ethnic connotations whereas "American" does not. I have always thought this one of the most interesting differences between the United States and France, and most other countries, for that matter.

I would typically end my speech with the following homily:

I have spent a lot of time talking about the differences between the French and the Americans, but it is significant that it would take far longer to enumerate the similarities between us. France and the United States are united not only by historic ties, but also by common democratic ideals and goals, enshrined in the French Déclaration des droits de l'homme et du citoyen, and in the UN Universal Declaration of the Rights of Man. Our partnership has not been entirely smooth, but honest differences are inevitable between two countries in which freedom of thought and action are revered with almost religious fervor. The Franco-American relationship is strong and enduring and will not be derailed by anything as trivial as the cross-cultural differences I have been discussing. But I hope that by squarely facing, describing, and explaining the differences between us, I will have made some contribution to mutual understanding and respect.

France and the Iraq Debacle

This line worked all right in the early 1990s. Unfortunately, one could not have been quite so sanguine about the Franco-American relationship following the Bush administration's war of choice in Iraq, when 90 percent of the French people opposed the war. This perceived intransigence of one of our former allies was met by charges that the French were "ungrateful" and "spineless" and by the silliness of referring to French fries as "freedom fries" and refusing to buy French wines. On February 12, 2003, just before the invasion of Iraq, I wrote the following letter to the *Washington Post*:

> As one of the increasing number of patriotic Americans who oppose the war on Iraq, I was disappointed by the *Post*'s recent editorial capitulation to the Bush war steamroller. But your Feb. 11 editorial ("Standing with Saddam") castigating France and Germany for opposing the war is particularly hypocritical. If we wouldn't want our own government to persist in a policy opposed by the majority of our citizens, how can we demand that France and Germany do so? What they are doing is called democracy.

The letter was never published, nor were the others I wrote protesting the stupidity of the war. But I digress.

Oh, what the hell, I may as well show you the others I wrote. They're so good! Since the *Post* didn't deign to publish them, I'll publish them myself. You can decide for yourself whether they should have been published.

On September 14, 2007, I wrote:

Of all the dubious claims that President Bush made during his speech to the nation last night, the most patently false was the following: "The success of a free Iraq is critical to the security of the United States." Quite the contrary, our continued occupation of Iraq creates more terrorists worldwide and ignores the real threats of the resurgence of the Taliban in Afghanistan and of al Qaeda in Pakistan. The tragedy is that all too many Americans will believe the President's claims. After all, he's the President and the Commander-in-Chief; why would he mislead the American people? He misleads the American people in order to prolong the war until he can blame the debacle in Iraq on his successor. But to continue to send our young men and women to be killed and maimed in an unnecessary war to burnish his own legacy is immoral and despicable.

On September 16, 2007, I wrote:

In the article headed "The Disaster of Hasty Withdrawal," Henry Kissinger says, "Vietnam collapsed because of the congressional decision to reduce aid by two-thirds to Vietnam...." Wrong. Vietnam collapsed because the American people will not support indefinitely a costly war against a country that does not pose a clear and present danger to the nation's security. This is the lesson that Henry Kissinger never learned from Vietnam, and that George Bush is learning in Iraq.

Christopher Columbus: Hero or Villain?

As I was in Paris in 1992, the 500th anniversary of Columbus's "discovery" of America, I prepared a speech entitled "Christopher Columbus: Hero or Villain?" There was a heated debate at the time as to whether the anniversary should be celebrated or deplored. The detractors claimed that, far from being a hero, Columbus had ushered in a period of disease, exploitation, slavery, and genocide. They argued that not only did he not "discover America" (the real "discoverers" being the original settlers of the New World who crossed from Asia thousands of years ago, not to mention Leif Eriksson and the Norsemen who landed in "Vinland" in about 1000 A.D.); he didn't even know what he had found and left as his legacy the misnomer "Indians" (thinking he had found the East Indies). And as a final indignity, the land he encountered does not even bear his name; an ill-informed German cartographer had been told that Amerigo Vespucci got there first. (Columbus left his name in numerous other places, such as the District of Columbia; Columbia University; Columbus, Ohio; Columbia, South Carolina; and the country of Colombia.)

The writer Garry Wills wrote in the *New York Review of Books* in 1990, "A funny thing happened on the way to the quincentennial … of America's "discovery"—Columbus got mugged. This time the Indians were waiting for him." But Congress in its wisdom had, in 1984, established the Christopher Columbus Quincentennary Jubilee Commission to coordinate U.S. participation in some 1300 commemorative events around the world, including museum exhibits, parades, symposia, concerts, and movies; and USIA Washington, always the handmaiden of the whims of Congress, had directed all posts to devote programs to the occasion.

So, after pointing out a few positive arguments of the "hero" side of the issue, such as the spirit of exploration and, in the words of Mario Vargas Llosa, the introduction of "the Judeo-Christian traditions, Greece, Rome, the Renaissance, [and]…the notion of individual sovereignty," I had to conclude lamely that if Columbus had perished at sea, the consequences for the Western Hemisphere would not have been much different. The contact would have been made by one of the explorers who succeeded him, such as Vasco da Gama, who actually reached the East Indies, or by Spanish explorers such as Cortez and Pizarro, or by Magellan, whose circumnavigation of the globe thirty years after Columbus was the first to actually confirm that the world was round. But of course this conclusion satisfied the advocates of neither side.

Linguistic Challenges

One evening when invited to give my speech on U.S.-French cultural differences at the office of the mayor of the 16th arrondissement, I was doing fine until my boss, Bud Korengold, walked in shortly after I had begun my presentation.

Now I have a confession to make: I speak more French than I understand. If you ask most people if they speak a foreign language, they will say, "I understand more than I speak." My situation is the reverse. I could give a bang-up speech in excellent French, but I always dreaded the question-and-answer session, as I have difficulty understanding rapid spoken French. The same is true for Cambodian and Thai, which I taught at Cornell. A possible explanation is that I spent so much time drilling students in the production of the language (the most difficult skill for most students) that I neglected comprehension. Another factor is no doubt the onset of hearing loss, which is hereditary in my family.

However that may be, the presence of my boss, whose wife is French and whose spoken French is no better than mine, but who nevertheless has what FSI refers to as "communicative competence" in both speaking and comprehension, increased my dread of the question-and-answer period to follow. Imagine the embarrassment, and possible repercussions for my career, if, after an eloquent presentation, I were unable to understand the questions, and in front of the guy who writes the dreaded OER (officer evaluation report). One strategy I used was to pause after each question as if pondering the wisest response, while asking myself, "What the hell did he say?" Another technique was the well-known strategy of giving long drawn-out answers to cut down on the number of questions that could be asked in the time available. A strategy that we were taught during our training at USIA in how to deal with press interviews was to decide in advance what three points you want to make, and make those points no matter what the question is. In the end, thanks to these strategies, I managed to muddle through with my dignity intact.

The Wrong Interpretation

I once consulted an audiologist, who confirmed that I had incipient hearing loss. He said that experimental evidence showed that people's brains are wired differently, so that some people process auditory signals much more slowly than others. My wife is a prime example of someone whose auditory processing is so efficient that she can do simultaneous interpretation between French, English, and Romanian. Shortly after we were married, I was showing slides of Thailand to her visiting parents, and she kept talking during my presentation.

Somewhat exasperated, I said, "Am I going to talk, or are you?" She said, "I'm interpreting." Properly chastised, I was quite proud to have my own simultaneous interpreter. Over her career she has interpreted for seven heads of state, including U.S. presidents Jimmy Carter and George W. Bush, as well as the presidents of Romania, Moldova, and France.

While we were posted to Paris Sanda received a call from the Quai d'Orsay asking if she would be interested in accompanying President François Mitterrand to Bucharest as an interpreter, on what was to be the first visit of a Western head of state to Romania after the fall of Ceausescu. Sanda asked me whether I thought she should go and without thinking too much about the ramifications, I said, "Sure, why not? It would look good on your résumé."

Once she got there, she had very little to do, as most educated Romanians speak French, and they all wanted to show off their French to the French president. About the only interpretation she had to do was when Madame Danielle Mitterrand visited a Romanian orphanage and asked a little girl what her name was and how old she was. Sanda and I calculated that she had earned something like $1,600 per word on the trip.

But when news of the trip got back to the embassy, all hell broke loose. I was summoned by the regional security officer, who said, "She did *what*? Don't you realize that we can't have the wife of an American officer working for the host government? Think of the security implications!"

But I couldn't really understand their concern; it seemed to me that the French were the ones who should have been worried that their security had been breached by having the wife of an American officer on the inside, but they appeared blithely unconcerned. In fact, it occurred to me that we would do well to imitate the French style of presidential travel: the president and relevant staff just boarded the presidential plane and flew to Romania. What a contrast with travel by the U.S. president, who is routinely accompanied by hundreds of political acolytes and security types and an entire plane devoted solely to the press. When President Clinton attended APEC (Asia-Pacific Economic Cooperation) meetings in Auckland, New Zealand, in 1999, he took over a thousand people with him. With delegations from sixteen countries descending on a city with limited hotel space, the Americans had to lease cruise ships and moor them in the Auckland harbor to house the American delegation and entourage.

Smorgasbord of Tourist Delights

After about a year, the old BMW 316 began to show signs of exhaustion, due in part to the indignities it had suffered in Burma and Morocco. Furthermore, we were planning a vacation trip to Scandinavia, and it was questionable whether the old car would make it. When I learned from colleagues that as a diplomat I had the right to purchase a new automobile duty free, that if you took it back to the States at the end of your tour you paid reduced customs on it as a used car, and that if you picked it up at the factory you could save even more money, I began to consider buying a new BMW. This decision was perhaps influenced by the fact that my American assistant had just bought a new BMW 325i and seemed rather smug about having a more expensive car than his boss. When I asked how he could afford it, he pointed out that his wife made more money in the private sector than he did; it wasn't clear whether he was bragging or complaining. Persuaded by all these perfectly reasonable considerations, I went to the BMW factory in Munich and bought a wine-red 318i—just a small one, in the interest of prudence.

During our first summer we had returned to the States for biennial home leave, for which we were due because we had direct-transferred to Paris from Marrakech. The second summer we decided to take three weeks' annual leave to Norway and Sweden, as they were about the only countries of Western Europe that we had never visited. So we piled the kids into the new car and headed north. We had *moules* in the fabulous Grand Place in Brussels, toured the canals of Amsterdam, drank beer in Tivoli Gardens in Copenhagen, explored the fjords in Norway, and in the beautiful (at least in the summer) city of Stockholm stayed in the lodgings of Foreign Service colleagues David Summers and Bea Camp, who were on home leave. (We exploited their unfailing hospitality on two later occasions, when Bea was consul general in Chiangmai in 2004 and in Shanghai in 2010.)

As the end of our tour in France approached, we realized with remorse that we had not taken advantage of the sights of provincial France itself, other than brief trips to Versailles, Nice, and the Loire Valley. Apparently this is a common syndrome among Foreign Service officers—posted to a country for two or three years, they typically assume that there will be plenty of time for sightseeing, only to leave it until it is too late. Determined to remedy this situation, we began methodically to visit all the regions of France during the last few months of our tour.

France is a veritable smorgasbord of delights. Some of my personal favorites include:

- All the chateaux of France, especially Chambord and Chenonceaux in the Loire Valley.
- Bayeux and the beaches of Normandy, for their historical interest.
- The picturesque cities of Dinan and St. Malo in Brittany.
- The Lascaux caves and the spectacular cliff-top city of Rocamadour in the Dordogne.
- The Papal city of Avignon and the Roman ruins of Arles in Provence.
- The mountainside villages of Eze, La Turbie, and St-Paul-de-Vence, which command incomparable views of Monaco and the Riviera.
- The ski resort of Chamonix and the glaciers of Mont-Blanc in the Alps.

Even when you have seen all the above, you have barely scratched the surface of the attractions of France. And I haven't even mentioned the cuisine.

Curtailment—Again!

The normal tour for a USIS officer in a nonhardship post was four years, but as my wife and I both had elderly parents in poor health and in need of our assistance, after three years I requested curtailment of my tour in Paris and reassignment to Washington in the summer of 1993. I was due for a Washington assignment, as I would have served abroad at four different posts—London, Rangoon, Marrakech, and Paris—for a total of seven years. Although headquarters frowns on curtailments, since it costs more money to move people about more frequently than planned, they granted my request, no doubt because of the ease of finding a replacement for a sought-after post like Paris.

I must admit that some colleagues, when I told them I was curtailing out of the "holy grail" of Paris, looked at me strangely. In fact, I was afraid I might get a "corridor reputation" as a serial curtailer, as I had curtailed out of Marrakech after only one year of a three-year assignment. But the truth is I was interested in serving in as many posts as possible in the limited time I had before mandatory retirement at age sixty-five in 1999. Some officers, perhaps less compulsive than I, like to request an extension when they find a post they like.

When I first joined USIA, my mentor at the agency, Miller Crouch, himself a "wunderkind" who was promoted to the Senior Foreign Service by the age of thirty-eight, advised me, "Huffman, never extend. If you extend, they just forget about you. Move as often as you can, and every time you move, move up."

Another colleague had the theory that three years was the optimum length of a tour. He reasoned, "The first year you're learning the job; the second year you're good at it; by the third year, you're bored with the job and should move on." So we reluctantly gave up the seductions of Paris and our *appartement de grand standing* off the Champs-Elysées and headed back to Washington in the summer of 1993.

Photo Gallery

Huffman family photo from about 1939; Father Rudolph, Mother Stella, children left to right: Donald 7, William 3, Franklin 5, and Robert 9

Frank crowns the Queen of May at Bridgewater College in 1954.

Frank's quartet at New Windsor, MD, 1955; left to right: Tom Schultz, Frank, John Wine, Ed Kindley.

Frank sets out on his journey from Laos to London, 1958.

Frank as a graduate student at Cornell, 1962.

Cousin Kenneth Huffman and Frank with his Triumph TR-3, purchased in Paris in 1958.

With first wife, the former Marcia Russell (married 1962-1971), with son Russell during dissertation research in Bangkok 1965-66

Frank and wife Sanda Iliescu (1974-Present), with son Christopher and daughter Samantha, in Washington, 1985

Christopher on the Alfa Romeo that Frank used to commute between Cornell and Washington, 1982-83

Our lodgings at historic Enfield House on Windmill
Hill, Hampstead, London, 1986-87

With former British Prime
Minister Sir Edward Heath and
pianist Megume Umene after
her concert at Winfield House,
the U.S. Ambassador's residence in Regents Park, London

London PAO Bud Korengold presents a farewell
gift on Frank's departure from post, June 1987.

Our mildewed mansion in Rangoon, Burma, 1987-89

Sanda and Frank with the Minister of Education, Youth and Sports at the American Club in Rangoon

Frank and Sanda with David Shawver, principal of the American School, and wife Amy at Pagan, 1987

Evacuation of embassy officers from Rangoon in the wake of the massacres of demonstrators in September 1988

Huffmans' R and R to China, April 1988

Villa Kawtar, the PAO residence in Marrakech, Morocco, 1989-90

Frank holds a reception for Peace Corps volunteers from southern Morocco; second from left is Bob Govier, Frank's friend, tennis partner and man of many talents.

Christopher and Samantha enjoy the ride during Frank's visit to Agadir, March 1990.

As Director of Programs at USIS Paris 1990-93, Frank and family enjoyed visiting the chateaux of the Loire Valley; pictured here: the impressive Chateau Chambord

A visit to the fortified town of Carcassonne in Languedoc, southern France, 1993

Our house in Phnom Penh, Cambodia, 1995-97

Ambassador Quinn donates USIS books to the National Library

A family visit to Angkor Wat, 1995

Frank presented to King Sihanouk of Cambodia by Ambassador Kenneth Quinn, in the presence of DCM Robert Porter and Cambodian Minister of Foreign Affairs Ing Huot

Frank interviewed as Embassy Spokesman, 1996

The PAO house in New Zealand, across the bay from Wellington

USIA Director Joe Duffy gives Frank his 10-year service pin during a visit to New Zealand

Frank with George Washington University President Stephen Joel Trachtenberg (right) visiting as a U.S. Speaker, and Tim Groser, head of the Americas Division at the Ministry of Foreign Affairs

Dinner in honor of Ambassador Beeman; left to right: Frank; Singapore High Commissioner; Hon. Helen Clark, later Prime Minister; Dame Catherine Tizard, New Zealand's first woman Governor-General; Tom Scott, journalist; Mrs. Gerald Hensley

Huffman family on Milford Sound during annual leave to the South Island, January 1998

Frank's children: Russell, Samantha, Christopher and David, 1999

In N'Djamena, Chad, with Mr. Mahamat Nadjib Amine, Director of Secondary Education, and FSN Magdalene Mbong, 1999

Ambassador Christopher Goldthwait, Les McBride and provincial officials during trip to Mao and Bol provinces, January 2000

Samantha in Waza Game Park, Cameroon, Christmas 1999

Return to Angkor during
second tour in Cambodia,
2002 -- overgrown walls at
Ta Prohm temple

Frank with Director of the
National Museum Khun Samen
(right) and Ouk Lay, Director
for International Cooperation,
Ministry of Cutlure, on the
occasion of the repatriation of
two stolen heads to the National
Museum, April 2002

Celebrating U.S. Independence
Day with (left to right) Minister
of Commerce Cham Prasit,
Deputy Minister of Commerce
Sok Siphanna, and CNN Corre-
spondent Mike Chinoy, 2002

Frank receives a complimentary plaque from the President of the Cambodian Journalists Assocation after a talk on the role of journalism in a free society

Frank with (left to right) Phnom Penh Post publisher Michael Hayes, leading authority on Cambodian history David Chandler, and Asia Foundation Director Jon Summers at a farewell party hosted by DCM Alex Arvizu

Sightseeing in Pagan, Burma, en route back to Washington from Cambodia, August 2002

Frank indulges his life-long interest in sports cars with the purchase of a 1959 Morgan Plus 4 in October 2006

Frank giving a lecture in Phnom Penh after donating his Khmer language library to the Buddhist Institute in December 2004

The family at Thanksgiving 2006; left to right: son Christopher, grandson Max, Christopher's wife Nardia, son Russell, grandson Spencer, son David, mother-in-law Elizabeth Iliescu, daughter Samantha

Frank receives the 2007 Distinguished Alumnus Award from Dr. Philip Stone, President of Bridgewater College, April 2007

Intermission: Washington

Wasting Away in Washington

Immediately upon arrival in Washington, we went on home leave. Foreign Service officers are in theory required to take a minimum of twenty working days home leave after every two years of service abroad. The idea is that to adequately represent the United States abroad you need at least a month to get back in touch with U.S. culture, society, and domestic issues. This requirement, however, is not very popular with FSOs, because in general they have nowhere to live when in the States. If you have a house in Washington or in your hometown, it is likely rented to tenants whom you can't kick out for the short period you will be in the States. Another option is camping with relatives, but this gets old after a while, unless you have enough relatives that you can move from one to another for short periods of time without wearing out your welcome at any one place; but this is a hectic way to live. The only other alternative is to stay in a hotel, but as you are not eligible for per diem during home leave, this gets expensive.

It is not quite clear why FSOs are eligible for free housing when posted abroad but not when posted to Washington. The assumption seems to be that you have a home waiting for you when you come back to the States—but in Washington? This is one reason that Washington is almost universally considered a "hardship post." What some FSOs have been known to do is to check in with headquarters upon arrival, give the address and telephone number of a relative where they will presumably be staying, then take off for Mexico or the Caribbean until time to report back for duty. This provides a nice vacation in a desirable location at well below the cost of a hotel in the States.

Just how we spent our twenty days remains a blur in my memory (I'd have to ask Sanda, whose memory for these things is phenomenal), although I assume we visited various relatives in Virginia and New York before taking temporary lodgings in the rather expensive Georgetown Suites—temporary because when you're posted to Washington you receive a housing allowance of decreasing generosity leading to a final cutoff when it is assumed you have had time to locate permanent housing. (Officers on short-term consultations or training in Washington but posted elsewhere receive full per diem and lodging.)

As a consequence, hotels and short-term apartments in Washington are well aware of what the allowable government rates are and strive to set their rates "within per diem." This is why after about ten days in the luxury of the Georgetown Suites, we moved to more spartan lodgings in an apartment building off Connecticut Avenue, which was more conveniently located for enrolling our son Christopher in the Edmund Burke School on Upton Street and our daughter Samantha in the French International School in Bethesda. Again our dog Teddy managed to impose his demands on our lives. After about a month of trying to accommodate his needs in an apartment, we decided we needed a house with a yard, so two months after our arrival in the States, we bought a house with a fenced yard in the family-friendly Palisades neighborhood of Northwest Washington, just over the hill from the obscenely expensive neighborhood of Spring Valley, where the discovery of buried World War I munitions has apparently not reduced real estate values—one house there is currently on the market for $9.5 million. Our house, today worth about one-tenth of that, still represents an appreciation of almost 200 percent over the purchase price.

I had been appointed policy officer in the Office of Policy and Evaluation of the Bureau of Education and Cultural Affairs at USIA, located at 301 4th Street, S.W., in the shadow of the U.S. Capitol. This was considered to be a "thinking" rather than an "operational" position. Basically the job was to evaluate the effectiveness of various educational and cultural exchange programs and make recommendations for how they could be improved. But in retrospect, it's hard to point to anything I accomplished. A great deal of my time was spent in meetings discussing how to work more efficiently, rather than in working more efficiently. My predecessor in the job explained to me that the great thing about the position was that you could define your own job. Well, if a job needs defining, there is some question whether that job is needed.

Some of the management fads popular at the time were "Total Quality Control," the "team approach," and "flattening the management hierarchy," and each of these approaches required orientation meetings. There were also endless meetings of Task Forces and Working Groups, and in some cases Task Force Working Groups. Mid-Career Training was also popular; I was sent to a "Fundamentals of Management" course at the U.S. Department of Agriculture Graduate School, in the FEMA building just blocks away from USIA. Other training opportunities included indoctrination on "Diversity in the Workplace" and "Writing a Mission Statement" for your office, your bureau, and the agency as a whole. We were also in the throes of Vice President Al Gore's "Reinventing Government" initiative, and we were all encouraged to come up with proposals for improving government performance and eliminating "waste, fraud, and abuse."

Don't Join the Foreign Service to See the World

One issue that I felt (and still feel) strongly about was the inefficient and wasteful nature of Foreign Service travel regulations. I had already lived, worked, or traveled in some sixty countries as an academic. But after joining the Foreign Service, my flexibility and freedom to travel was drastically reduced by federal regulations. A Foreign Service officer cannot spend three days in a city en route if the contract fare calls for only a six-hour stopover. If you are posted to the Far East, you must go and come via the Pacific because it is something like 100 miles shorter. Furthermore, there was at that time no American carrier between Bangkok and Bombay; if you didn't agree to return via the Pacific, you became liable for the cost of the entire leg between Bangkok, Jakarta, or whatever, and the nearest city served by an American carrier. Under these regulations, you certainly shouldn't join the Foreign Service to see the world!

So I wrote a memo to the USIA's Reinventing Government Task Force, criticizing such ridiculous regulations as submitting detailed travel vouchers for travel, lodging, meals, and incidental expenses; the Fly America Act, which requires that federal employees travel on U.S. carriers; and the mandatory use of contract fares that have been negotiated by the government with specific airlines for specific city pairs (many of which are higher than can be obtained on the open market). The Fly America Act makes no sense, since all airlines now have code-sharing agreements with other airlines, and in any case the revenue from the use of American carriers by government personnel is negligible, given the size and scope of airline operations. I recommended that the U.S. government adopt the practice of countries such as France and Great Britain and simply give the traveler an allowance based on the cost of economy travel between points A and B, and let him decide how to get there. One day I ran into Rob Nevitt, the USIA representative on Vice President Gore's Reinventing Government team and asked him about the fate of my proposal. He told me that I was not the only one who had suggested scrapping the Fly America Act, but that it would not happen because the power of the airline lobbyists would prevent the passage of sensible legislation. *Plus ça change...*

The Waiver Review Board

One of the more interesting things I did in Washington was to serve on the Waiver Review Board for the J Visa Program administered by the E Bureau (Educational and Cultural Exchange) of USIA. J visas are issued to foreigners who come to this country on official government exchange programs, such as the Fulbright program, the International Visitor program, and various other short-term training programs. One of the requirements of the J visa is that recipients return to their own country for at least two years following their training or study in the United States. The rationale for this rule is that the purpose in bringing them over here for training is to have them go back and help their own countries, but many of these people have a tremendous desire to stay put once they get here. Holders of the J visa can petition to have the two-year return-to-country rule waived on several grounds, such as the threat of political persecution or danger if they were to return to their country, or the fact that they could contribute to the needs of the U.S. government in some capacity that could not be filled by a U.S. citizen.

Another basis for a waiver of the return-to-country rule was a letter from the visitor's home country stating that they had no objection to the visitor's continued stay in the United States. It was rumored that foreign embassies in Washington produced considerable revenue selling "No Objection" letters to their citizens who wished to avoid the return-to-country rule, and we consequently considered such letters the weakest basis for a waiver.

We were directed to be extremely tough in applying the rules. Some of the subjects had managed to remain in the United States for twenty years. Although they might have a family and children here, sometimes we had to apply the law and send them back, because, after all, they had not observed the requirements or the intent of the visa.

The President's Traveling Circus

When President Clinton visited Normandy and Paris in June 1994 to commemorate the fiftieth anniversary of the World War II invasion of Normandy, I made the mistake of volunteering to go to Paris to assist with the visit. Bad decision. I had already participated in three presidential visits and found them the most unpleasant experience in the Foreign Service. Jaunts by the secretary of state were bad enough, but presidential visits are the worst. They consume the efforts and personnel of the entire embassy for weeks preceding the visit. Temporary duty officers are brought in from other posts to swell the ranks. Pre-advance teams come out from the White House Travel Office as soon as there is a possibility that such a trip will be put on the president's schedule. Then when the visit is confirmed, an advance team comes out, the ambassador and all the personnel of the embassy snap to attention, and sit through interminable meetings where every possible step of the visit is discussed, along with all possible permutations. Embassy personnel and their White House counterparts go out and make "site visits" to all the places that the presidential party is likely to visit, then come back and make detailed drawings and blueprints of each site. And frequently the president, unaware of the minutely calibrated schedule his minions have prepared, changes his mind on the spur of the moment, and goes off-schedule. In fact, the least onerous presidential visits are those where the White House adds a certain country to the itinerary at the last minute, thus depriving the advance teams of the time to work their mischief.

The worst aspect of such trips is the arrogance and self-importance of the advance teams. Usually quite young, and heady with the power conferred on them by being from the White House, they treat all embassy personnel, from the ambassador on down, as their personal staff. They run roughshod over matters of protocol, ignore diplomatic sensitivities, and refuse to go through proper channels when dealing with high officials of the host country.

In spite of all these reservations, I volunteered to go, perhaps out of the mistaken belief that at least I would enjoy Paris. The agency agreed to send me because of my French and my familiarity with the post. I was assigned as the USIS site officer, along with embassy and White House counterparts, to both Orly airport (for the arrival of the press plane and departure of the presidential party) and to the Palais de l'Elysée (for the visit of the presidential party to dine with President Mitterrand).

A serious contretemps with Orly airport security developed during the arrival of the press plane. Two young White House advance travel officers, both aged 24–25, ordered the buses to drive right out on the tarmac to meet the journalists, against the instructions of airport security and the advice of the embassy FSN who had been our embassy liaison with Orly for twenty-five years. The White House cowboys ordered the cavalcade of nine fifty-passenger buses full of tired and irate journalists to leave the airport through the secure area simply because it was shorter than leaving by the public exit. Shortly thereafter an airport police car screeched to a halt in front of my lead vehicle, and the chief of airport security pointed out to us that we were on French soil and were in violation of airport security.

They were accompanied by the embassy's liaison, José, who was enraged by the actions of the White House guys. I said, "José, what are you doing?"

He replied, "I'll be damned if I'm going to let those two young imbeciles wreck twenty-five years of good relations with Orly security!"

Although I admired his courage, I said, "José, you can't win this one!"

"I don't give a damn," he shouted, and retreated behind the police lines.

Through diplomacy and artful translation of the obscenities shouted by the White House security officers, I managed to mollify the French and get an official escort out of the secure area of the airport.

The enraged White House officers said to me, "What's that guy's name? We're going to have his head!" And they had the power to get a long and faithful embassy employee fired. I later heard that our ambassador, Pamela Harriman, who had some clout of her own, had intervened to save his job.

During a meeting with French officials at the presidential palace, the advance team members, rather than negotiating with their hosts, were instructing them on how the visit should proceed. Two of the three advance team members, who had obviously struck up a liaison during the trip, were actually smooching with each other, ignoring the proceedings. It was as if they were 800-pound gorillas in a colony of ants. On the day of the visit to the palace, I received a radio call from the PAO, Bud Korengold, to the effect that Mark Gearan, chief of White House communications, was on his way to the Elysée Palace to join the president's party and, as he had no credentials, the White House site officer should get him through palace security. When I tried to relay this message to my White House counterpart, he was on his radio and imperiously waved me away.

As he continued to make calls on his radio, I approached him again, and said, "I think you really need to hear this."

"Shut up!" he yelled at me, stamping his foot petulantly. At that point I wanted to say, "You little shrimp, I'll kick your butt all the way to the Seine!" But of course I had to swallow my pride. Later, when he had been chewed out by Gearan, he had the gall to criticize me for not giving him the message. I simply grinned at him.

During an earlier site visit to Orly to rehearse the departure of the presidential party, one of the White House advance team spied a man with a camera and asked me who he was. I was told he was the official Orly photographer.

"Get him out of here," he ordered. I explained to the Orly official that the White House had requested (as I put it) that we not have any photographers in the press box of the *Salon d'honneur.*

The White House guys then insisted that I negotiate with the airport official to have the moving press risers that would follow the president along the red carpet to the plane go along the right, rather than the left side of the carpet. I don't recall just what the rationale was, if there was one.

With barely concealed fury, the Orly official pointed out that the risers would be backwards if the sides were reversed. He asked me to point out to the White House team that Orly had been receiving international visitors for years and didn't need any advice on how to do it. When the White House guys, ignoring my translation of that remark, continued to make demands of the official, he suddenly became very agreeable, smiling pleasantly, and in response to each new demand, said, *"Bon, pas de problème. Comme vous voulez."*

I thought, "Wait a minute; there's something wrong here." I was proved right when, on the actual day of the departure, French officials proceeded to do as they had always done, ignoring all the instructions that had been given to them during the site visit. The official we had dealt with was not even on the scene.

White House security came to me and asked, "What the hell's going on?"

I shrugged. "That's the French!"

In addition to my personal experiences, there were stories that the DCM, Avis Bohlen, had been shouted at by one of the WH advance team; that Madame Chirac, wife of then-mayor, later president, Jacques Chirac, had been insulted; and that Ambassador Harriman was "upset" by the behavior of the White House crew. Mary Gawronski, CAO and embassy control officer for First Lady Hillary Clinton, commented to me that the whole thing had been a "nightmare." At the end, we congratulated ourselves that, from a media point of view, the visit was a success. Although it was certainly the most unpleasant presidential visit that I had participated in, the behavior I have described is unfortunately not atypical.

Bailing Out of Washington

In general, I found working in Washington rather unfulfilling, not to say boring. I didn't resign from Cornell to work behind a desk in Washington. So after only about six months in the job I began to bid on other assignments. (I should mention that my wife's father had passed away in the meantime, so that was no longer a pressing issue.) One way of getting out of an undesirable job was to bid on "immediates," positions that were vacant because the incumbent had resigned or had been shipped out for medical reasons, or because the position had been vacant for a long time or was difficult to fill, or both. When the job of PAO in Cambodia came open, I thought, "Ah ha, here's my ticket out of Washington!"

When I joined the Foreign Service, I did not intend really to try to maintain any expertise in Southeast Asia; in fact, I wanted to live and work in parts of the world other than Southeast Asia. But I saw this as an opportune moment to trade on my background in Cambodia, which had been my academic specialty.

In the end I served only eighteen months in Washington, so you could claim that I had curtailed out of a job for the third time (after Marrakech and Paris). The normal pattern was six to eight years in the field followed by two or three years in a Washington assignment, but there were many deviations from this rule of thumb. I had met officers who bragged that they had been in the field for fifteen years and managed to avoid a Washington assignment for that long. State and USIA had different cultures in this respect. In State, at least for the most ambitious, the theory was that you had to be in Washington, near the center of power, to advance your career, usually by attaching yourself as a "special assistant" to a high-ranking mentor. In USIA, by contrast, you earned your spurs — and burnished your corridor reputation — by proving your skills in the field, especially in difficult posts.

My appointment as PAO-designate to Phnom Penh was confirmed in March 1994, but as I was not due at post until January 2005, I began to undertake activities that would better prepare me for the job, somewhat to the neglect of my duties as policy officer, which were in any case rather vague. I had visited Cambodia as a tourist in 1957 and had periods of research in the country in 1965 and 1971, so I was familiar with the country; but I had never yet been a full-fledged PAO for any country, so I enrolled in the PAO training course. (My jobs had been junior officer trainee in London, assistant PAO in Rangoon, Branch PAO in Marrakech, and director of programs—basically a CAO—in Paris.) I had lunch with Bob Porter, deputy chief of mission in Phnom Penh and in town for consultations, who gave me some tips on the politics of the embassy in Phnom Penh. (Every embassy has its own internal dynamics, driven by the personalities of the ambassador and his subordinates. It is particularly important for a PAO to know whether the ambassador wants him to be the spokesman for the embassy, insulating the ambassador from the press, or whether he likes to talk to the press himself.)

When visiting Cambodian foreign minister Prince Sirivudh and Cambodian ambassador to the UN Prince Sisowath were hosted by Deputy Assistant Secretary for East Asia and the Pacific Peter Tomsen at a luncheon on the eighth floor of the State Department, I was introduced as the PAO-designate and gave a presentation on the kinds of educational and cultural exchanges that USIS could provide to Cambodia. At the same meeting, they signed agreements on sending Peace Corps volunteers to Cambodia (an agreement that for security reasons was not implemented until some ten years later) and on restoring the former Cambodian Embassy on 16th Street NW (abandoned when the Khmer Rouge took over Cambodia in 1975) to the Cambodian government.

I also took advantage of the two-week Southeast Asian area studies course at the Foreign Service Institute. Although most of this was well-traveled ground for me (I had already spent some eight years in Laos, Thailand, Cambodia, and Burma), the area studies courses at FSI are in general excellent introductions to an area, with speakers and experts from both government and academia. I had taken the course on the Middle East and North Africa before going to Morocco and found it highly informative and useful. And while I had taught the Cambodian language at Yale and Cornell for eighteen years, I had not used it for almost ten years, so I persuaded the training division to allow me to enroll for a six-week "refresher course" in order to brush up on the specialized vocabulary of diplomacy. During the course, rather than being "taught" by the Cambodian staff, I used them as resources, or informants, for the kinds of information I thought I needed to know.

Throughout all these career moves, my wife Sanda was admirably patient and adaptable, cheerfully subordinating her career to the exigencies of the Foreign Service and finding interesting employment at each post (although I used to point out that it was her interest in the Foreign Service that had led to my resigning from Cornell and joining the Foreign Service in the first place). In Burma she was hired by USAID as their director of training; in Paris she worked in the political section of the embassy, and in Cambodia she was the director of a Georgetown University training project funded by USAID. As she had worked as a linguist at the Foreign Service Institute from 1979 until we left for London in 1985, the Institute immediately offered her a job as a French language textbook consultant when we returned to Washington from Paris in 1993. Now, just eighteen months later, we were moving again—this time back to the exotic Orient!

Act Five: Cambodia

Please Don't Throw Me into the Briar Patch

Cambodia has played an inordinately large role in my life. I visited Cambodia for the first time in 1957 while taking a vacation from my job as a French interpreter in Laos with International Voluntary Services. My friend Wally Brown and I stopped by Angkor en route from Saigon to Bangkok, more or less as an afterthought and on the advice of colleagues in the embassy in Vientiane who had said, "You absolutely *must* see Angkor Wat." Although duly impressed with the awesome ruins, I had no inkling at that time that I would ever visit it again, let alone that I would eventually write my dissertation on Cambodian grammar, teach the Cambodian language at Yale and Cornell, and serve two tours as public affairs officer in the U.S. embassy in Phnom Penh.

Chance played a role even in the choice of Cambodian for my dissertation. I had planned to write on some aspect of the Lao language, which had been my first Southeast Asian language, but my thesis advisor felt (erroneously) that Lao was not sufficiently different from Thai to justify a dissertation. He insisted that if you were going to get a PhD in general linguistics you needed to write a dissertation that described all levels of a language, from the phonetics through the phonology and grammar to the syntax. It turned out that the only major national language of Southeast Asia that had not yet been described from a modern structural linguistic point of view was Cambodian.

When he suggested I do Cambodian, I said, "You know, there is a grammar of Cambodian done by a Frenchman, Henri Maspero, called *Grammaire de la langue khmère.*"

He said scornfully, "That's not a grammar of Cambodian, that's a description of how Cambodian differs from French." (In this he was correct.)

So I decided to do my dissertation on the Cambodian language, not only because it is a fascinating language in its own right, but also because Cambodian is the major modern representative of what was probably the earliest linguistic stock in Southeast Asia, the Mon-Khmer or Austro-Asiatic language family, comprising some 150 languages spoken by minority groups across an area that extends from India to Vietnam (Vietnamese itself is now thought to belong to this family).

As Cambodian was not at that time taught at any U.S. university, I obtained a grant to study Cambodian for six months at the London School of Oriental and African Studies, to be followed by eighteen months' research in Cambodia (1965–66). However, as Sihanouk had been at odds with the United States since 1963, the Cambodian government would not grant me a research visa; as a result I had to do my research with Khmer speakers based in Bangkok, and to content myself with short trips into Cambodia on two-week tourist visas, during which visits I was constantly shadowed by Sihanouk's security police.

In 1970–71, after three years at Yale, I obtained a Guggenheim Fellowship to study Mon-Khmer languages in Thailand, Laos, and Cambodia. Unlike my previous research in Cambodia in 1965–66, this time I was able to travel freely to Phnom Penh under the U.S.-friendly (and U.S.-supported) Lon Nol government. But the Khmer Rouge campaign of terror in the provinces made it unsafe to travel outside of Phnom Penh. My solution was to work with speakers of various minority languages who had fled their villages for the safety of refugee camps on the outskirts of the city. Their misfortune was thus my good fortune. Toward the end of my research period, however, even Phnom Penh was a safety hazard.

In January 1971, I stopped in Phnom Penh on my way back from the 28th International Conference of Orientalists in Canberra, Australia, to pick up the galley proofs of the Cambodian text for one of my books. On the evening that I planned to fly back to Bangkok, Bill Stubbs, a friend in USIS Phnom Penh, invited me to dinner at his home. They had an excellent cook, and I decided to postpone my flight to Bangkok until the next day. That night the Khmer Rouge blew up the airport at Pochentong, as well as the South Vietnamese ambassador's residence near the Stubbs's dinner party. As a result I had an enforced stay of another ten days until the damaged airport could be restored to limited service.

Thus while I had made numerous trips to Cambodia and had focused on research on the Cambodian language and culture for some thirty years, I had never actually spent an extended period of time in Cambodia. My two-year assignment to Cambodia would be my longest uninterrupted stay in the country of my specialization.

The Five-Minute History of Cambodia (OK, Ten)

Cambodia is unfortunately best known to most Americans through the movie *The Killing Fields*, which portrayed the brutal Khmer Rouge regime of 1975–1978 under which an estimated 1.5 to 2 million Khmers lost their lives through starvation, forced labor, and execution. But the country has a long and illustrious history that is worth recounting.

Cambodia is the modern descendent of Funan, the earliest Indianized kingdom in Southeast Asia (first to sixth centuries A.D.), of Chenla (sixth to ninth centuries), and of the great Khmer Empire (ninth to fifteenth centuries), whose power at its height included present-day Cambodia, southern Vietnam, southern Laos, and eastern Thailand. The Khmer Empire, sometimes called "the Rome of Southeast Asia," left behind the monumental complex of temples at Angkor, one of the most impressive archeological ruins in the world, as well as hundreds of other stone temple ruins across Cambodia, Thailand and Laos. Angkor Wat itself—the main temple at Angkor—is the largest religious monument in the world. I've visited the pyramids in Egypt, Machu Picchu in Peru, Borobudur in Indonesia, and Pagan in Burma, and in my opinion none of them compares with Angkor in either scope or artistic quality.

There are many competing theories about who built Angkor and what caused the decline and disappearance of that civilization. Uneducated Khmer peasants attribute the monuments to a race of giants, but since many of the inscriptions at Angkor, and at many other sites around Southeast Asia, are in Khmer (the others being in Sanskrit, the literary language borrowed from India), it is safe to conclude that the temples were built by the Khmer. Khmer, incidentally, is the ethnic term that Cambodians use to refer to themselves and to their language, while Cambodia (Anglicized from "Kampuchea") is the formal name of the country, so the two are basically interchangeable.

What caused the decline of the Khmer Empire? One theory is that there was a prolonged drought that destroyed the intricate system of irrigation that supported the empire. Another is that Jayavarman VII, the last great builder king, who built the walled city of Angkor Thom and many other temples throughout the empire, exhausted the treasury with his building campaign. A third theory is that, when Mahayana Buddhism was replaced by the more ascetic Theravada sect of Buddhism, the new religion did not support the cult of the *devaraja,* or god-king, which required great temples. While all of the above may have played a role, the immediate cause of the fall of Angkor was that the Thais invaded and destroyed Angkor in the fifteenth century. When the Thais had moved south from China in the eighth to twelfth centuries, they came into contact with an established Khmer civilization, and they borrowed heavily from Khmer religious, cultural, linguistic, and literary sources. As the Thai capital at Ayutthaya grew in power and influence, the Thais turned on their former teachers.

After the fall of Angkor to the Thais in around 1440 (the exact date is debated), the Khmers moved their capital south to Lovek; but in 1594 the Thais again invaded and sacked Lovek and burned all its archives. The Khmers again moved their capital southward, this time to Phnom Penh, at the confluence of the Mekong and Bassac rivers, where it remains today. During the seventeenth and eighteenth centuries the territory of the Khmer empire was eroded from the east, as the Vietnamese encroached into what is now southern Vietnam, and from the west, as the Thais helped themselves to the western Cambodian provinces of Battambang and Siem Reap, which included the ancient monuments at Angkor. Although these two provinces were restored to Cambodia in 1907 under pressure from the French, there is a large-scale model of Angkor Wat in the Royal Temple compound in Bangkok.

I once asked a Thai guide for an explanation, and he said, "Well, you see, Angkor used to belong to Thailand."

I thought, "No, you got it backwards; Thailand used to belong to Angkor," but I did not say it, as he would have thought I was crazy.

In 1863 the French established a protectorate over Cambodia and incorporated the country, along with Vietnam and Laos, into French Indochina. The French rode roughshod over traditional Khmer culture in the process of imposing their *mission civilisatrice* on the country. At the same time, French epigraphers and archeologists did important research in deciphering ancient Khmer inscriptions and restoring the crumbling monuments at Angkor.

After imposing their will on several hereditary monarchs, the French in 1941 installed Prince Sihanouk as a malleable playboy. But Sihanouk turned out to be a stubborn fellow who wrested Cambodian self-rule from the French in 1953, even before the Geneva Conference in 1954. This won him the title of "Father of Cambodian Independence," and he commonly referred to himself as "Royal Father" and the hapless Cambodian people as "my children." A master of the common language—not to say a demagogue—Sihanouk adopted the habit of other dictators in delivering four-hour speeches around the country. In fact, during my dissertation research in 1965–66 I recorded Sihanouk's speeches to use as texts for grammatical analysis of the Khmer language; one of his frequent lines, delivered in his high screechy voice, was "*Amerik cia satrow tii-muey reboh loke!*" ("America is the number one enemy of the world!").

Threatened on his eastern border by the increasing influence of the Vietnamese, who were supporting the Khmer Rouge rebels in the north, Sihanouk in 1963 suspended the U.S. military aid program that had supported his own forces. He proclaimed neutrality in the Vietnam conflict but secretly signed documents allowing Vietnamese bases inside the country. Members of his government and the military began plotting against him, and when he left the country for Paris in early 1970, the National Assembly voted 86-3 to oust him in favor of then-Prime Minister General Lon Nol. Rumors that the CIA was involved in the coup have never been proven, but the United States certainly didn't oppose it, as they had become increasingly frustrated with the vacillations of Sihanouk's policy. Shortly before the coup he had actually tried to reestablish ties with the U.S. military. While most of the urban elite and the military supported the coup, Sihanouk remained popular among the rural people, and his ouster no doubt led to the increased success of the Khmer Rouge in the countryside. Nixon's secret invasion of Cambodia in 1970 and the subsequent bombing of the Ho Chi Minh trail along the Cambodia-Vietnam border also contributed to the success of the Khmer Rouge insurgency.

From 1975 to 1978, the Khmer Rouge led one of the most radical agrarian revolutions in history. They emptied the cities, destroyed money, and murdered all those people who were educated, or who were in any way associated with the elite of society. Just how many people lost their lives under the Khmer Rouge continues to be debated, but estimates range between 1.5 million and two million, which would have been roughly 30 percent of the population of the country at that time

The intensity of the violence differed from one part of the country to another, depending to a certain extent on who was in charge. A lot of getting even took place, with the poor people rising up and saying look, it's really okay to kill these wealthy people and these white shirts and these urbanites who have always oppressed us. Some experts on the situation feel that it was not so much that Pol Pot personally ordered all of the executions, but that things got out of control. Ironically, Pol Pot, Ieng Sary, and Khieu Samphan and all of the leaders of that revolution had acquired their revolutionary ideals studying in Paris, but they took it to a much greater extreme than even the Maoist agrarian revolution in China.

After the Khmer Rouge had been in power for almost four years, the Vietnamese invaded Cambodia in late 1978 and basically pushed the Khmer Rouge westward toward Thailand; many of them escaped over the border into Thailand. The Vietnamese installed a puppet government, made up of people who had been in exile in Hanoi. The U.S. government supported the three Cambodian opposition groups along the Thai border—basically the royalists, the democrats, and the Khmer Rouge. In one of the darker periods of U.S. policy, for political reasons we supported the Khmer Rouge for the Cambodian seat at the United Nations rather than that of the Vietnamese puppet government installed in Phnom Penh, because we were still piqued about Vietnam. The rationale was that Vietnam had invaded a sovereign country and their puppet government should not be recognized. But some contrarian historians, such as Michael Vickery, think that the Vietnamese should have been thanked for what they did. In the end the Vietnamese were not able to expel the Khmer Rouge completely. It became such an economic and military burden to run the country that they withdrew a decade later, in 1989, leaving in power the people they had installed. A major reason for their withdrawal was the collapse in the mid to late eighties of monetary support from the Soviet bloc. Thus weakened, the government of Cambodia agreed to a peace conference of all parties held in Paris in 1991.

In accordance with the Paris Agreements, the UN Transitional Authority in Cambodia, usually referred to as UNTAC, from 1992 to 1993 mounted one of the largest UN operations in history, with 20,000 personnel and an estimated cost of $2 billion. In the election they succeeded in administering in May 1993, there were three major parties. The Cambodian People's Party (CPP) was represented by Hun Sen, head of the former communist regime installed by the Vietnamese; the FUNCINPEC (royalist) party was headed by Rannariddh, son of Prince Sihanouk; and the BLDP (Buddhist Liberal Democratic Party), headed by Son Sann, was perhaps the party favored by the United States. In the elections, the Royalists won and the CPP, Hun Sen's party, came in second. But the CPP refused to accept the result, and six eastern provinces threatened to secede from the country. Finally, with the help of the king they compromised, with the king saying, "Look, we'll have two prime ministers and you can share power; let's just overlook the fact that the Royalists won; you boys be good now and Rannariddh will be the first prime minister and Hun Sen will be the second prime minister." They also had two ministers of defense and two ministers of the interior. After at one point declaring his intention of becoming prime minister himself, Sihanouk was made king as a symbol of the unity of the country, but he was pretty much a figurehead.

The history of the mercurial Norodom Sihanouk has shown him to be both an opportunist and a survivor—first a thorn in the side of the French, he then suppressed democratic movements inside the country, broke off diplomatic relations with the United States in 1965, and proclaimed his neutrality in the Vietnam war while cultivating relations with Hanoi, Peking, and Pyongyang. Deposed by the republican regime of Lon Nol in 1970, he sided with the Khmer Rouge, who used him to gain power, then put him under house arrest and killed seventeen members of his family. Seen as a useful symbol of unity by the Paris Peace Conference of 1991, he was reinstated as king of a coalition government in Phnom Penh, where he was a powerless figurehead under the control of the dictator Hun Sen until he stepped down in 2004 in favor of his son Sihamuni. Quite a career! But I digress.

In the Wake of the Khmer Rouge

When I arrived in Phnom Penh in January 1995, the two main parties—the former communists and the royalists—were competing for power and not much was getting done in terms of the efficient running of the country. Things were pretty tense, given that the struggle against the Khmer Rouge was still going on. They were still holding out in the mountains of the north and west, and the Royal Government troops were unable to definitively wipe them out. From time to time they would kidnap some Westerners; in one notorious case they kidnapped three backpackers—a Frenchman, a Brit, and an Australian—off of a train heading down to Sihanoukville and eventually murdered them. It was a pretty dangerous time, with 200–300 people a month getting their legs blown off by landmines left behind from the various wars. It was estimated that there were roughly ten million landmines in a country of only nine million people, creating some 30,000 amputees in Cambodia.

The United States had reestablished diplomatic relations with Cambodia following the Paris Peace Conference in 1991, setting up offices in the cavernous Cambodiana Hotel, built during the communist period in the style of a humongous Buddhist temple. Our first chief of mission was Charles Twining, whom I had met when he spent a year as a special student from the State Department in the Southeast Asia Program at Cornell. (One consequence of joining the Foreign Service after a career as an academic was that I was frequently older than my bosses.) He and the members of his staff lived and worked in the hotel. Twining was a charming and congenial man, with a justifiable reputation as a workaholic. The story from contemporaries of the time was that Twining, without his family at post to occupy his time, would spend his evenings writing instructions to his staff and slipping them under the doors of their hotel rooms in the wee hours of the morning.

By the time I arrived on the scene, Ambassador Twining had set up the embassy in a collection of ramshackle houses that had been converted to offices. The State Department's Foreign Building Operations (later the OBO – Overseas Buildings Operations) and Diplomatic Security were horrified that the compound did not even have a wall, let alone the 100-foot setback from the street required by department regulations. A terrorist could easily have lobbed a grenade from the street into any of the various buildings. Furthermore, Twining rejected the stationing of a Marine Guard Detachment in the embassy, as he felt it sent the wrong message to the local people. I rather agreed with him on this point, as there was little danger of terrorist activity toward the U.S. Embassy in Phnom Penh. The only possible danger might come from the Khmer Rouge, but they had been essentially confined to the provinces.

However, one did have to be careful in traveling outside Phnom Penh not to wander off the road for fear of stepping on a land mine. USAID was rebuilding the highway from Phnom Penh down to the port at Sihanoukville, but you were encouraged to drive only in the daytime and not get off the road because of the danger of landmines. Siem Reap was considered fairly safe, but driving there was not recommended, as there was a danger of being killed or kidnapped by the Khmer Rouge who operated in the mountain areas along the route. The monuments themselves had theoretically been de-mined to facilitate tourism, but it was not recommended that you go wandering off the path into the woods. The exquisite sandstone temple of Banteay Srey, some thirty kilometers north of Angkor, was considered off limits, since a tourist—a professor of anthropology from Texas—and her driver had been ambushed and killed on the road there shortly before my arrival. My predecessor as PAO—David Miller—had just gone up to Siem Reap for his first (and last) visit to Angkor, when he was tasked with accompanying the woman's seriously injured husband by helicopter back to Phnom Penh, whence he was medevaced to Singapore. David told me that the old gentleman, obviously in shock and not aware that his wife had been killed, kept apologizing to David for ruining his weekend.

Trial by Fire

I overlapped with Miller for just one week, but he and the entire embassy were preoccupied with the upcoming visit of Deputy Secretary of State Strobe Talbott four days later, so I had no briefing whatsoever from my predecessor and had to reconstruct the status of ongoing projects and programs from the haphazard stacks of papers on his desk and scattered around the office. On the second evening after I arrived, Ambassador Twining held a "hail and farewell" reception at his residence to mark Miller's departure and my arrival. A group of several hundred guests from the embassy's official, diplomatic, academic, cultural, and press contacts had been invited. The ambassador introduced me, and I couldn't believe my ears, in my jet-lagged fog, when he announced that, as a well-known scholar of the Khmer language, I would make my remarks in Khmer. Not sure if there were members of royalty whose presence would require highly specialized honorifics, I adopted a neutral level of vocabulary and somehow muddled through this baptism of fire; if I made egregious mistakes I'm sure the Americans didn't know it, and the Cambodians were too polite to mention it.

The startup from scratch of an embassy and a USIS post where they had not existed for almost twenty years is extremely challenging and time-consuming, but it was hard for me to believe that my predecessor had not found time in two years to visit Angkor, the premier tourist attraction in the country. However, my own experience in continuing the job where he left off soon lent credibility to his claim. USIS occupied one of the houses in the compound, and David and his staff of five had their offices on the ground floor, while David actually lived on the upper floor.

After spending our first week in the Cambodiana Hotel, my family and I also moved into the upper floor of the USIS building and lived there for six weeks until we could move into the house that was being renovated as the PAO residence. This arrangement might be good for efficiency, but it is certainly not to be recommended for one's mental health, for it is impossible to distance oneself from the demands of the job. As we were twelve hours ahead of Washington, headquarters tended to telephone at about nine or ten o'clock in the evening in Cambodia, when they were just getting to work in Washington. The PAO house, which we moved into after our sojourns at the Cambodiana and above the office, had five bedrooms, each with its own bath. The explanation for such luxury was that the house was one of many that had been built three or four years earlier to take advantage of the need for housing some of the 20,000 or so UNTAC personnel, and was designed to be rented room by room. Chinese entrepreneurs had made a great deal of money in rents and caused a ruinous inflation of housing prices, although prices had fallen somewhat since the departure of UNTAC. Every house leased by the embassy had to have a standby generator for the frequent power failures, and my house had a huge generator—40 KW, I think—in what was supposed to be the garage. Since there was no city power in my street, and the electric company was demanding an extortionate price for supplying a line to the house, GSO decided that they would simply power my house by running the generator full time. As a result, there was a constant roar from the monstrous machine, which was a serious challenge to conversation during representational events at the PAO house.

My wife, a woman of many skills, was promptly hired as an English trainer for a business law project run by the University of San Francisco and funded by USAID. Shortly thereafter she was hired as the training supervisor for a Georgetown University project at the School of Business, also funded by USAID. When the director of the program was fired for general incompetence, she became director of the entire project. Our daughter Samantha, who had been in French schools since the age of three and was consequently fluent in French, enrolled in the Petit Lycée Descartes, where she was in a class of fourteen students from twelve different Francophone countries. She found the diverse backgrounds of her classmates fascinating, and the undercurrent of danger in the city added to her sense of adventure. Our son Christopher, in his first year of architecture studies at Pratt Institute in New York, also found his family's posting to Cambodia advantageous. During his summer visits he managed to obtain an internship with the World Monuments Fund, which was involved in the restoration of the Preah Khan, one of the major temples at Angkor. He felt that such an exotic internship would look very good on his résumé and would be an experience that none of his colleagues at Pratt could duplicate.

Methodical Madness

Traffic in Phnom Penh is chaotic, as there appear to be no traffic rules, and everybody just heads to his destination without regard to any inconvenient constraints. There were at the time only two traffic lights in this city of one million inhabitants, and those were seldom working. The result was that you had to play chicken at each intersection. The most disconcerting thing is that people don't stop at intersections; they barrel right out from cross-streets, and just adapt to whatever oncoming traffic they meet. They do have their own mutual understandings; otherwise there would be more traffic deaths than there are. The problem is that foreigners simply don't understand the rules.

One of the most important things in arriving in a foreign country is to learn the traffic conventions — the unwritten rules of the road. I learned this lesson early on while living in Thailand in 1965–66. Driving from Bangkok down to the beach at Pattaya one fine day in my tiny Fiat 500 on a narrow two-lane road, a bus bore down on me from behind and began blaring his horn at me. I was driving at 80 kph (50 mph), which was about the top speed for the little Fiat, and being an American, I naively believed that I had just as much right to the road as the next guy. Wrong! The bus simply pulled alongside me in the other lane and moved over, forcing me into the ditch.

I quickly learned the vehicular pecking order, just as valid in Cambodia as in Thailand: large trucks take precedence over buses, followed by large cars (SUVs, Mercedes, and the like), followed by small cars, then motorcycles, and finally bicycles. Once in Phnom Penh as I was making a left turn, I stopped and waited for a rapidly approaching motorcycle, which would in our system have the right of way over a vehicle turning left. The motorcyclist, however, seeing a BMW about to make a left turn, stopped and waited for me in accordance with the pecking order. We both sat there waiting for each other like Alphonse and Gaston, until I realized my mistake and proceeded to turn left in front of him.

For some reason Phnom Penh had no taxis (I assume it was because no entrepreneur had yet been able to come up with a suitable bribe to get the concession), so the standard method of getting around if you didn't have a private car was to jump on the back of a motorcycle — called "moto-dup" for "riding double"; most rides were a dollar. This mode of transportation was discouraged by the embassy as being unsafe, especially since women passengers were particularly vulnerable to having their purses snatched by ride-by motorcycle bandits. But what choice did a visiting tourist or businessperson have? My own children cheerfully broke the rules and found moto-dup quite satisfactory, not to say exciting.

Phnom Penh for the Tourist

Aside from power outages, chaotic traffic rules, the lack of modern health care, the danger of banditry, and the mental anguish of seeing so many land-mine amputees begging in the streets, Phnom Penh was a fairly interesting place to live. The conversion from a socialist to a capitalist economy following the UNTAC-administered elections generated an abundance of ethnic restaurants—French, Thai, Chinese, Mexican, Korean, Australian, even Russian—and night spots, much appreciated by our teenage children and their friends. Phnom Penh has become a major destination for back-packers, who flock to the restaurants along the riverfront, especially those serving "happy pizza"—pizza laced with marijuana. Major attractions include Wat Phnom, a tall stupa on top of a hill in the middle of a broad traffic circle. On the façade of a bank in front of the temple was a working clock with numbers composed of flowers. In the park surrounding the temple, astrologers had laid out their paraphernalia, ready to tell fortunes or prescribe auspicious dates for weddings or trips, based on one's horoscope.

According to local legend, the stupa of Wat Phnom contains a relic of the Buddha discovered floating in some driftwood in the Mekong River by an old lady named Penh. She had an artificial mountain built (as the land was completely flat) and erected a stupa on top to house the relic. This is the origin of the name Phnom Penh—"Penh's Mountain." Phnom Penh is situated at the confluence of two rivers, forming what is called cattomuk, or "the four faces." The rivers involved are the Mekong, which rises in the Tibetan plateau and runs for 2,700 miles through China, Burma, Thailand, Laos, Cambodia, and Vietnam; and the Bassac, which flows to the South China Sea to the west of the Mekong; its northern extension is the Tonle Sap, which flows into a huge lake in the middle of the country. (An interesting geographical fact is that the Tonle Sap river, which flows southward during the dry season, actually reverses course in the rainy season and flows northward into the Tonle Sap lake, which expands to seven times its normal area, providing an important source of fish and irrigation for the country.) A wide esplanade runs along the riverbank, creating an appealing promenade where families stroll in the evening, buying balloons and snacks from food stalls that line the quay. This treatment of the riverbank no doubt reflects French attention to town planning, unlike Bangkok, where, as the result of helter-skelter development, ugly warehouses and commercial piers block views of the river.

Farther down the river is the elaborate Royal Palace compound, dominated by a beautiful and graceful throne hall, surmounted by a spire crowned by the four faces of the Hindu god Brahma. One theory among many is that the four faces represent the god-king and symbolize his authority over the four cardinal directions of the kingdom. In an adjoining compound is the ornate Vihear Preah Keo, also called the Silver Pagoda for the five thousand tiles, each made from two pounds of silver, that cover the floor of the pagoda. You leave your shoes and cameras at the door and enter the coolness of the dark interior. The most valuable treasure in the temple is a life-size Buddha image made of solid gold, and inlaid with 9,584 precious stones. The central altar contains a replica of the emerald Buddha in Wat Prakeo in Bangkok. (It is ironic that Cambodia should have copied one of its images from Bangkok, since the Thais originally copied almost every aspect of their Buddhist culture from the Khmer empire.)

One of the most interesting outings is to stroll through the New Market (commonly, but incorrectly, called the Central Market). Under a vast concrete canopy, an infinite variety of merchandise is for sale—tooled silver, jewelry, watches, antiques, fruits and vegetables, fish of all kinds, canned goods, clothing, and small appliances. Outside the covered part of the market, soup stalls, benches, and tables are set up for evening diners. Shortly after our arrival we stopped at one of the cleaner-looking stalls and pointed to some noodles. After a few minutes the bowls of soup arrived, along with small side dishes containing condiments—bean sprouts, lime slices, fried garlic, and sliced chili peppers. We looked dubiously at some of the ingredients of the soup, which included various parts of the pig not normally eaten in the Shenandoah Valley, such as intestines, internal organs, and congealed blood. But when we had added the condiments and cautiously tasted the concoction, we had to admit that it was delicious. (Differing versions of this *kuai tiaw*, or "soupe chinoise," are found everywhere throughout Southeast Asia and can be consumed for breakfast, lunch, dinner, or supper—the functional equivalent of the hamburger in the United States.)

Tourists interested in the darker aspects of Cambodian history can visit the infamous Tuol Sleng prison, whose walls are plastered with the photos of some 17,000 prisoners tortured and executed there during the Khmer Rouge regime. Those interested in even more shocking sights head for Choeng Ek outside of town, site of one of the "killing fields" referred to in the movie of the same name, where one can visit the burial grounds of executed prisoners and where a glass-enclosed tower is filled with thousands of skulls of Khmer Rouge victims.

How I Saved the Khmer Language

I was surprised to find that I was a bit of a celebrity in Phnom Penh because of my books on the Cambodian language, most of which had been pirated and were for sale in the New Market, with colorful covers in pink, mauve, or chartreuse. And while one of my duties as PAO was to support the idea of intellectual property rights, the pirates obviously didn't understand such a vague concept, since the pirated versions contained even the Yale Press copyright page of the originals. My dictionary in particular provided me unique entrée, since every government official had it on his desk. When I was introduced to the minister of culture, he actually genuflected before me and said, "So you're the Professor Huffman! You've saved our language."

That was a bit of an exaggeration, but it is true that my dictionary had provided an authority, right or wrong, for the translation of myriad English documents concerning democracy and human rights into Khmer during the UNTAC period. As a result of this notoriety, I was in some demand as a speaker (in Khmer) at such venues as the Buddhist Institute; but my duties as PAO limited the time available for participation in various events having to do with Cambodian culture. I was like a kid in a candy store with no money. I was accustomed to teaching Americans about Cambodia, while my duty as a PAO was to tell Cambodians about America.

Challenges of the Job

In spite of my background in Khmer studies, the job of PAO Phnom Penh was the most difficult of my foreign assignments so far. There were several reasons for this.

First of all, since the post had opened up only two years before, my staff was not as experienced as you would find at a typical post, where American officers come and go, while local staff carry on and do the work and usually know more about the work and the country than do their American bosses. Thus I was constantly forced to choose between training staff to do a job and doing it myself in order to meet looming deadlines. The best thing my predecessor did was to hire three FSNs who became some of the most valuable and capable FSNs in the embassy: Mr. Chau Sa as cultural assistant, Mrs. Nhim Pheakdey as admin assistant, and Mr. Chrea Vanrith as information assistant. They were indispensable to me during both my tours in Phnom Penh and to my successor PAOs. (I paid tribute to them in a talk I gave in 2010 on U.S.-Cambodian educational and cultural relations, and the audience in the Chattomuk Conference Hall broke out in spontaneous applause in recognition of the contributions they had made to public diplomacy over two decades.)

Second, Ambassador Twining was both a workaholic and a popular envoy. He attended five or six ceremonies, lunches, and dinners a day, and liked to have press coverage of whatever he did. He also insisted on my putting out frequent press releases to the local and international print and broadcast media to publicize U.S. development efforts and the ways in which some $40 million in annual U.S. aid to the country was being spent, a great deal of it channeled through several hundred NGOs funded by USAID. In addition, the DAO (defense attaché's office) was involved in military training and mine awareness programs and assisting with the de-mining of some of the approximately ten million mines still buried in the countryside.

Furthermore, as Ambassador Twining had been in country for four years—longer than most of the embassy staff—he knew more about the current situation than anyone else, which contributed to his tendency to micromanage every dollar spent in whatever agency. He liked to personally approve every one of the some twenty-five educational and cultural exchange visitors that USIS was sending to the States each year.

Third, because of the large UNTAC operation and the international involvement in the country at that time, there was a lot of interest in Cambodia on the part of the international press. I had frequent requests for interviews with the ambassador from prominent journalists, such as Ron Moreau of *Newsweek*, Keith Richburg of the *Washington Post*, Peter Arnett of CNN, and Seth Mydans of the *New York Times*. All of the major news services—AP, Reuters, AFP (Agence France-Presse), and the BBC—had bureaus in Phnom Penh and tended to be rather antagonistic toward the policies of the U.S. government. I never understood quite why that was the case, but I think it was mainly because they knew the kind of corruption that was going on, and the attitude of the press is frequently highly moral; they have the luxury of saying to us that we should not have dealings with these people at all, though we're there precisely to have dealings with them and if possible to influence them in the right direction.

Another factor that complicated my life in Cambodia was the computer. I am a person of normal intelligence, but not a computer whiz, as was my predecessor. He had placed all his contacts and their phone numbers in the computer; if you wanted to call someone urgently, you had to fire up the computer (which was not a speedy operation in Phnom Penh), locate the program for listing contacts, and scroll through the list until you found (or not) the person you were looking for. The first thing I did on a trip to Bangkok was to buy a good old-fashioned Rolodex for my office—a much more efficient way of finding a phone number.

Computers are marvelous for certain tasks, such as word processing, manipulating data, and searching texts, but it never occurs to computer enthusiasts that some tasks are inappropriate for computer applications. Case in point: every year the PAO has to come up with a country plan listing the leading public diplomacy objectives for the year and what USIA programs and products he intends to use to achieve those objectives. This used to be a matter of some three or four pages of running narrative, which could then be faxed or cabled to Washington. But the computer nerds at headquarters decided that they should develop specific software that would guide the PAO through the process of submitting the country plan—and, as is typical of bureaucracies, use of the software was obligatory, not optional, in the interest of keeping up with the brave new world. I embarked on the project one night and immediately hit a snag—you had to fill in the name of the post, chosen from a pull-down menu, in a specific slot. The problem was that Phnom Penh was not on the list, and you couldn't proceed until the slot was filled, so I put in Abidjan, which was the first post on the list, and proceeded down the prescribed path.

Since every bit and bite of information had to be compartmentalized into a honeycomb of specific slots, it took me at least a week of torturous work, accompanied by unprintable comments, to complete the monstrosity, which in the end was full of mistakes wrought by the defective software. I found that when printed out, the computer-friendly, "paper saving" country plan came to seventy-five pages rather than the three or four narrative pages of the previous system. At this point, I redid the country plan by the traditional method and cabled it to Washington, with some blistering comments such as, "If someone in Washington wishes to convert this report into the new format, be my guest, but I don't have time to play this kind of electronic crossword puzzle here at post. Whenever it takes longer to do something by computer than it would to do it with a number two pencil, you need to reconsider your approach." Instead of getting me fired for insubordination, it turned out that my cable struck a resonant chord with many of my colleagues, and I was amused to find a copy of my cable tacked to the bulletin board when I returned to Washington between posts.

Obstacles to Development

Our objectives in Cambodia were basically to support the transition to democracy, an independent judiciary, transparency in government, and respect for human rights. We had a speaker who said that there's an inverse relationship between foreign direct investment and the amount of corruption in a country, and that if all the fundamentals were in place, foreign direct investment would dwarf any aid that USAID was giving the country. But if the fundamentals were not right then any aid that USAID might give was money down a rat hole. This did not make the USAID people too happy because the speaker worked for one of their grantees. But this was the kind of thing that the Cambodians needed to hear, because corruption was rampant, judges were for sale, and democracy existed in name only.

Much of our work in supporting freedom of the press and journalistic ethics focused on the local press, but there weren't really any genuinely independent local media. There were usually thirty to forty local newspapers—some would start up and others would close—but every one was the mouthpiece of a particular political party or interest. There wasn't anything like an independent newspaper that presented the unbiased news. Two local English-language newspapers were relatively independent. One, the biweekly *Phnom Penh Post*, was started as a commercial venture by an American named Michael Hayes, and it was quite a good newspaper, But Hayes had to struggle to make ends meet, as he had to have it printed in Bangkok and there were not enough English-speaking buyers to make it profitable. And then there was *The Cambodia Daily*, which had been started by an NGO supported by the Japanese. Michael Hayes used to complain, "They don't have to make a profit, they're supported by an NGO, and here I am trying to run a newspaper and make enough money to stay in business."

These two English-language papers provided excellent training for young journalists, both Cambodian and American. They enjoyed a modicum of freedom of the press if one didn't go too far—I think the Cambodian press was freer in those days than it had ever been in the past. But they didn't understand that freedom of the press entailed the responsibility to print only the truth, to check your sources, and not engage in libel. In an authoritarian country, you can't get away with calling the dictator's wife "a pig." There were incidents of editors having grenades thrown into their offices or shot by "unknown" assailants if they got too outspoken.

One of the most serious obstacles to the country's development was the lack of expertise. There were no doctors, there were no teachers, there were no technicians—they had all either been killed or exiled. And curiously, as we've seen in several countries, when expatriates have come back to try to help develop their country, it doesn't work. The attitude is, "We stayed here and suffered under the Khmer Rouge and the Vietnamese regime; we didn't run away, and now it's our turn. You ran away and had a better life; now don't come back and tell us what to do and how to run the country."

One such organization was called CANDO, a clever acronym that stood for the Cambodian American National Development Organization. They brought over young Cambodian-Americans who had degrees in health and education and various useful fields. They were coming back to their country to be a Cambodian Peace Corps. Well, they weren't accepted. These young people weren't making much—maybe $700 a month—but it was about twenty times what a government minister was making (officially, at least). Furthermore, in Asian culture you can't have young people coming in and telling the elders what to do. After about two years they gave up and the organization was disbanded. This was the case with many expatriates who came back and tried to help; they were just not accepted. There was one who had been a minister in the Lon Nol regime and had come back, trying desperately to find a niche where he could be useful, and the poor guy had been pushed from this job to that and basically humiliated; he used to come to my office and complain, but what could I do? It was unfortunate, because the country desperately needed the expertise of such expatriates.

Given the coalition government and the competition between Hun Sen's CPP and Prince Rannariddh's FUNCINPEC, everything was politicized. If the ambassador attended a FUNCINPEC function, it was seen as supporting the royalists. If he had a meeting with a CPP minister, he was in collusion with the CPP. When Sanda and I were invited to lunch at the home of Prince Norodom Sirivudh, the king's half-brother, we were torn between compromising the embassy's neutrality by accepting or insulting the prince by refusing. We eventually went and had a delightful time; they served a delicious French meal, and the prince and I took turns playing jazz on his baby grand. Six weeks later Sirivudh was placed under house arrest for an alleged plot to assassinate Hun Sen. (I doubt that our visit with the prince had anything to do with it.) Diplomatic guests leaving the prince's house were stopped. After the Philippine ambassador was ordered out of his car and searched, he announced the cancellation of a Philippine state visit to Cambodia. We had to try to strike a balance between the parties in the people we selected for Fulbright scholarships and international visitor slots, although since many of the royalists had lived and traveled abroad if not to the United States, we did tend to favor the CPP as more in need of foreign exposure.

As press attaché, my duties included organizing press conferences for visiting U.S. officials, such as Under Secretary of State Strobe Talbot or Assistant Secretary for East Asian and Pacific Affairs Winston Lord. Lord, who had not yet been appointed ambassador to China, asked me to participate in a "murder board" for his press conference, and I said here's what they're going to ask: "Why are we dealing with this thug government, who have subverted the elections?" "Why are we granting visas to officials known to be corrupt?" As it turned out, he was asked exactly the questions I had anticipated.

So it was a rather tough job from the standpoint of press relations. The pressure of press work during office hours was so great that I had to work evenings and weekends on trying to establish a U.S. Information Service, American studies center and library, recruiting Fulbright students, and trying to get some educational and cultural exchanges going. It was impossible to meet all these competing demands for my time, and I soon found myself working 12–14 hours a day seven days a week to keep my head above water. Some duties were more pleasant, however, such as taking Senator and Mrs. John McCain to dinner one night when the ambassador (Kenneth Quinn, who had succeeded Charles Twining) had a conflict, and lunching with Sam Waterston of *Law and Order* fame, who was visiting Cambodia with a delegation looking into charitable ventures.

What Do You Do for Fun?

As at all my preceding posts, I used tennis as a welcome antidote to the pressures of the job. Sanda and I purchased a membership at the Cambodiana Hotel, where my family could swim in the pool overlooking the Bassac River. The hotel had two imitation-clay courts (sand over a rubberized base), and I organized tennis matches with embassy colleagues, Cambodian contacts, and anybody I could cajole into playing. My favorite time to play tennis has always been about 6:00 p.m., when I could take out my office frustrations on the ball; I always played my best at that time. This contravened the perfectly reasonable custom in tropical countries of playing either in the early morning or, if lighted courts were available, late in the evening. But the lights at the Cambodiana were so weak and unpredictable that night play was a dubious venture. And I have never been a morning person—as was clearly illustrated during a period of residence in Bangkok in 1976 when I played a Japanese friend who preferred early morning; we were so close in ability that he invariably won in the morning and I always won in the evening.

Unlike my predecessor, I took my family to Angkor early in my tour and took advantage of every opportunity to accompany official and unofficial visitors to Angkor. We also made several trips to neighboring Vietnam during our tour in Cambodia. Vietnam is an ideal place to visit—it is safe, it is cheap, it has an interesting history and culture, and the food is good. What else do you need in a tourist destination?

In November 1995, I took my wife and daughter on their first trip to Laos. Vientiane hadn't changed much since I visited Laos during my research trip in 1970; at that time it had already changed from a sleepy little town where buffalo carts trundled slowly along the Mekong under the palm trees to a city marked by socialist architecture of dubious quality. But Luang Prabang, the ancient royal capital, seemed frozen in time. With its dozens of carved wooden temples and processions of saffron-robed monks taking alms from the villagers in the calm of the morning, it appeared not to have changed since my first visit there forty years earlier in 1956. But now that the entire town has been declared a UNESCO World Heritage Site, the influx of tourists threatens to undermine the UNESCO objective of preserving its beauty and tranquility.

However, Phon Savanh, where I had spent two years of my life as a volunteer in 1956–1958, had changed so much that I couldn't even identify the house we had lived in. A noisy Russian-built helicopter operated by Air Lao flew us from Vientiane to Phon Savanh. U.S. bombs had wiped out the former provincial seat of Xieng Khouang during the Vietnam War, and Phon Savanh had become the provincial capital. It had acquired a paved main street, multistory buildings, and an airstrip free of the water buffalo that had plagued attempts to land in the 1950s.

At this point I hit a string of bad luck. While staying at a hilltop inn run by a Frenchman, someone lifted $1,000 from my briefcase (cleverly leaving the remaining $1,300 in bills so the loss would not be conspicuous). When we got back to Vientiane, I received a call from the DCM reporting that my USIS van—a very popular Mitsubishi Pajero—had been stolen from the embassy compound. Since trouble comes in threes, I was almost relieved when the motor of my BMW blew up after our return to Phnom Penh. So things were back to normal.

The Prodigal Pajero

There was an interesting—if rather comical—follow-up to the theft of my USIS vehicle. As it had disappeared through two locked gates, it obviously had to have been an inside job. Car theft was rampant in Cambodia, especially during the UNTAC era when the influx of expensive Toyota Land Cruisers posed an irresistible temptation to luxury-starved bandits. Although we reported the theft to the police, we had no reasonable expectation of ever getting it back; in fact it was highly likely that the police had been complicit in its disappearance. I replaced it with a new Jeep Cherokee built in China and purchased from a local dealer. I had to justify this noncompliance with the "Buy American" rule by pointing out that a U.S.-built Cherokee would cost twice as much and take six months for delivery. We had no problems with the Chinese-built one.

To our great surprise, about a year later, we were notified by the Interior Ministry that they had recovered our stolen Pajero, along with some vehicles stolen from other diplomatic missions, and would like to turn the vehicles over to their rightful owners at a ceremony at the Interior Ministry. Accompanied by the embassy's RSO (regional security officer), I went over to the Interior Ministry, where we were conducted to a room filled with TV cameras and presided over by the deputy minister of the interior. As the deputy minister handed over the keys under the glare of the cameras, a representative from the embassy of Singapore, whose stolen vehicle had also been recovered, expressed his gratitude by trying to hand over a $2,000 "reward" to the ministry; the deputy minister desperately shooed him off, whispering, "Not now!" The next day, government-run papers praised the Singaporean embassy for their monetary expression of gratitude and criticized the American embassy for not being similarly forthcoming. When interviewed about this lack of gratitude on the part of the Americans, I told the press that we were indeed grateful for the recovery of our property, but pointed out that the U.S. embassy had contributed sizable amounts to police training, that in America we considered it the duty of the police to recover stolen property, and that it should not be necessary to reward them for doing their duty.

We managed quite a bit of travel during our two years in Cambodia. In addition to trips within the country to Angkor, Sihanoukville, and several other provinces and an annual leave trip to Laos, we went to Australia for R&R, visiting Sydney, Melbourne, Canberra, and the Great Barrier Reef; to the island of Koh Samui in Thailand; and to Sri Lanka, one of the few Asian countries we had not visited, and especially interesting to me as the historic source of the Theravada Buddhism of Cambodia, Thailand, Laos and Burma. In addition, I made official trips to Bangkok (once to assist with a visit by President Clinton), to Vietnam (with USAID Director Joe Goodwin to look at USIS-USAID collaboration in their Fulbright Center), and to Honolulu for a PAO conference.

Letters from Phnom Penh

One of the best ways to describe what was "normal" in Phnom Penh is to quote the Christmas letter that I wrote to my family back home in December 1995:

> Things have been pretty hot here lately, with the Second Prime Minister Hun Sen going a bit crazy, encouraging villagers to come into town and sack the offices of an opposition newspaper, and arresting the younger brother of

the king on trumped-up charges of plotting to assassinate him. All this resulted in a spate of articles in the Western press—the *New York Times*, *TIME*, the *Far Eastern Economic Review*, the *Wall Street Journal*, the *Economist*, the *Washington Post*, etc.—criticizing the deteriorating human rights situation here. This criticism caused Hun Sen, already a bit paranoid, to go ballistic: he gave a speech in which he claimed that the 1970 American invasion and bombing had killed 800,000 Cambodians and had brought on the brutal Khmer Rouge regime of 1975–78; he claimed furthermore that the U.S. should pay at least $20 billion in reparations, and called on his listeners to organize violent demonstrations against the American and French embassies for "interfering in Cambodia's internal affairs." The embassy has been on high alert ever since, discussing contingency plans, and reminding the Ministry of Foreign Affairs of their obligation under the Vienna Convention of 1961 to protect the inviolability of diplomatic missions. But when an action is ordered by the Prime Minister, there's not much point in going to his underlings for protection. Hun Sen now says that the newspapers misquoted his speech, that we will be given a week's notice of any demonstrations, and that they will be peaceful; but if any violence should occur, it would be the responsibility of the newspapers that printed "false" news. Nobody can figure out if Hun Sen is really loopy or whether it is a deliberate decision to abandon any pretence of democracy in Cambodia and establish a dictatorship—he has already managed to embarrass the king and emasculate the coalition royalist party. He doesn't seem to realize that his actions will no doubt produce the very thing he is upset about—human rights conditions on U.S. aid and on the bill granting Most Favored Nation trading status to Cambodia, now under consideration by the Senate.

The following paragraph from that same letter describing a royal ceremony illustrates some of the more colorful aspects of serving in Cambodia:

Life here can be quite picturesque; recently I had a chance to represent the embassy at the inauguration of a new dam in southern Cambodia by the king and queen. Cambodian ceremonies are good theater and include a wide range of events. A cheerleader led the crowd of several thousand villagers in cheers for members of the royal family as the king and queen descended from the helicopter and advanced toward the red-carpeted pavilion of honor, shielded from the sun by royal umbrellas held by attendants in traditional palace costume. Next followed chanted blessings by the assembled monks while the king and queen and government officials knelt before them. The next event was a presentation of classical Khmer dance by the royal ballet company, imported for the occasion. Speeches were then made by the governor of the province, the minister of agriculture, the representative of the Asian Development Bank (which was footing the bill for the whole thing), and finally by the king himself. Speeches made in the presence of the king require such elaborate language that they take a long time; the governor had been speaking for about five minutes when the British ambassador leaned over to me and asked, "What's he saying?"

I replied, "He has just finished 'Ladies and Gentlemen.'"

Then came the presentation by the queen of gifts of clothing material to approximately 500 disabled persons, widows and orphans. Finally, a military band played martial music while the king and queen, high officials, and the diplomatic corps proceeded to the dam site. The king and queen gave out souvenir publications from the 1960s Sihanouk era, while the two prime ministers clasped the outstretched hands of the villagers lining the route. At the dam site, the king cut the red ribbon, and the queen released four white doves from a cage as a merit-making gesture; they flew off among the thousands of balloons that had been released when the king cut the ribbon. Too bad I couldn't have filmed the whole thing, but that would have been a bit too touristy for the official representative of the U.S. embassy.

A Tale of Two Ambassadors

In Cambodia I served under two very different ambassadors for roughly equal periods of time. Charles Twining, who was our first ambassador to Cambodia following the UNTAC elections, was a modest, unassuming man who insisted we call him "Charlie" rather than the customary "Mr. Ambassador." He was content to house the U.S. embassy in a ragtag collection of buildings with very little security, not even Marine guards. He explained that we were there to help the Cambodians, not to make ostentatious displays of wealth and power; he poked fun at the French, who had renovated their impressive prewar embassy compound at great expense. He conscientiously attended a constant series of diplomatic, official, and social events, where his use of a serviceable level of the Cambodian language was much appreciated. But after four years of hard work, he had understandably become emotionally involved in the futile struggle to midwife some kind of nascent democracy in a country that was not ready for it. He had developed the well-known disease of "clientitis" to which long-term ambassadors are prone. Once, when I remarked in a country team meeting that my informants estimated that at least 80 percent of Cambodians thought Hun Sen was a Vietnamese stooge, he retorted that my sources were suspect and my methodology unscientific; but you didn't have to use scientific methods to verify the Cambodian people's widespread hatred for, and fear of, Hun Sen and his thuggish party.

By contrast, Ambassador Kenneth Quinn, who arrived early in my second year in Phnom Penh, was a burly Irishman who had the proverbial "silver tongue" of the Irish. I have always considered verbal and written expression my forte, but Quinn easily put me in the shade. When he first arrived, he disarmed everybody by inviting us all to a brainstorming breakfast at the residence to brief him on the situation in the country and to give him advice as to how he should proceed. It was particularly refreshing after Twining's "democracy is working" stance to be asked whether a policy of "constructive engagement" or "principled confrontation" with the Cambodian government would be more successful in fostering democracy, transparency, and respect for human rights. Having seen the futility of trying to negotiate with Hun Sen, the consensus of the embassy staff favored confrontation.

Unlike his predecessor, Quinn immediately set about agitating for a Marine Guard Detachment to provide security. Arguing that it was a scandal that the U.S. Embassy in any country should present such a humble appearance, he invited the Overseas Building Operations to send a delegation to explore locations for a future new embassy; in the meantime, he asked for OBO approval to build a nine-foot wall around the embassy compound.

A major disadvantage for Quinn was that he had a Vietnamese wife. This was anathema to the Cambodians, who saw a Vietnamese behind every bush. Historically there has been a great deal of enmity between the Cambodians and the Vietnamese, and the Cambodians tend to ascribe all kinds of skullduggery to the Vietnamese. That Hun Sen himself had gone into exile in Vietnam compounded Cambodians' suspicions. He was a former Khmer Rouge who in the early days defected to Hanoi and became part of the regime the Vietnamese installed.

Cambodians strongly suspect that the Vietnamese are pulling the strings in the government and that a lot of government officials are really Vietnamese who have taken Cambodian names. Conspiracy theories are rampant. The joke is that whenever you have two Cambodians you'll have three political parties. During the UNTAC period there were stories of Vietnamese bodies floating down the Mekong River—Vietnamese who had been killed in local conflicts or by the Khmer Rouge. A senior FSN told me that he had incontrovertible evidence that the second in command of the Ministry of Defense was an undercover Vietnamese; when I asked him the man's Vietnamese name, he couldn't say.

During Twining's tour, the embassy had been invited to prepare an insert in the *Phnom Penh Post* in commemoration of our national day of July Fourth. Twining had pooh-poohed the idea, saying that was the kind of self-promotion that smaller countries might engage in and that the United States did not have to advertise itself. But when the issue came up during Quinn's administration, he mentioned that it sounded like a good idea to prepare such an insert to publicize what the United States was doing for Cambodia. I was overwhelmed with other duties, as usual, and when Quinn left for one of his frequent trips back to Washington at the end of April, I was hoping he would forget about it. Imagine my

dismay when, upon returning from Washington in the middle of
May, he asked me how the insert was coming along! I had to drop
everything and concentrate on writing the columns and choosing
photos for an eight-page insert in the *Phnom Penh Post* before July
1. I solicited photos and captions from every section of the embassy
and featured a "Message from the Ambassador," U.S. assistance to
road-building, USAID support for some seventy NGOs, humanitarian military assistance by the defense attaché's office, the search
for POW/MIAs, and finally, the activities of the U.S. Information
Service. The ambassador and his family were featured in six of the
photos.

There is a unit at the State Department called the "Art in Embassies Program," which provides artwork by U.S. artists to ambassadors' residences upon request. Ambassador Quinn decided to
request an exhibit of pictures from the loess hills of his home state
of Iowa; this particular kind of windblown soil deposits are found
in only three places in the world—the Rhine River in Europe, the
Yellow River in China, and the Missouri River in Iowa—but rarity
doesn't necessarily guarantee aesthetic interest.

Quinn decided to take advantage of the visit of the director of
the Art in Embassies Program to hold an open house at the residence to showcase multiple paintings of barren Iowa landscape.
He showed me a glossy catalog from an Art in Embassies exhibition held in Manila, where he had been DCM before coming to
Phnom Penh (and where they had about ten American USIS officers
to produce such niceties), and suggested that I should produce a
similar catalog. I was flabbergasted, both because I was extremely
busy with real work and because I didn't feel that the ambassador's
exhibition of Iowa dirt justified such a glorified presentation. But
again I did the necessary. On the appointed evening we had invited
the entire official, academic, and cultural community to the reception. I watched with mixed amusement and embarrassment as the
bewildered Cambodian guests wandered from room to room and
stared at multiple versions of sand dunes in brown and grey, probably saying to themselves, "This must be the kind of stuff that turns
Americans on."

Ambassador Quinn had served as a rural development officer
near the Cambodian border during the Vietnam War, had written

a doctoral dissertation on the origins of the Pol Pot regime, and was apparently fascinated with military history. In May 1975, in the last action of the Vietnam War, the Khmer Rouge captured the U.S. container ship SS Mayagüez off the Cambodian coast; unaware that the crew of the ship had already been released, the U.S. military launched a rescue operation on the island of Koh Tang in which eighteen Marines were killed. Quinn decided to organize a ceremony to coincide with Veterans Day on November 11, 1996, to commemorate the loss of these eighteen Marines during the Mayagüez incident. He invited Senator John McCain to visit Phnom Penh and give the keynote address. The ceremony was held in the front yard of the Residence at 3:00 p.m.—the hottest time of the day. A large audience of invited Cambodian officials, dressed in their formal black suits and ties, sweated through long-winded speeches by Quinn, Senator McCain, and the FUNCINPEC (royalist party) co-minister of defense, after which a plaque honoring the dead Marines was unveiled. I couldn't help but be embarrassed by the irony of requiring a captive audience of Cambodians, who had lost an estimated 1.7 million of their compatriots to the Khmer Rouge, to sit through this tribute to eighteen U.S. Marines who had died more than twenty-one years ago.

In the end Ambassador Quinn reportedly became as much of an accommodationist to the status quo as his predecessor. Neither Twining nor Quinn, both good and capable men, was able to advance the cause of democracy and human rights in Cambodia very much. But this illustrates the classic conundrum of diplomacy: which works better —"constructive engagement" or "hard-nosed confrontation"? The answer depends on the specific situation, but in the case of Cambodia, neither could succeed. Constructive engagement is ineffective in the face of Hun Sen's determination to retain power, and confrontation, such as the threat to withhold aid, is futile when—as shown recently—Hun Sen can turn to China to more than compensate for any aid withheld, with no human rights strings attached.

Art and Politics

Even art and culture were not immune to this deadly competition.

Early in my tour the National Gallery in Washington began negotiating with the Cambodian Ministry of Culture to mount an exhibit
of Khmer sculpture to be shown in Paris, Washington, and Tokyo.
Helen Jessup, who was representing the National Gallery in Washington, solicited my help as cultural attaché to facilitate the project,
and meetings with my counterparts at the French embassy began
early in 1996. The CPP early on saw the publicity value and commercial advantage to Cambodia of having its rich Angkorean trea-
sures exhibited in the leading museums of the Western world. But
Nouth Narang, minister of culture from the FUNCINPEC party,
opposed the project, primarily because it was favored by his rival,
Vann Molyvann, Cambodia's most illustrious architect and head
of APSARA (French acronym for Authority for the Protection and
Management of the Historic Site of Angkor; this acronym is particularly felicitous because it is the Sanskrit term for the ubiquitous
celestial dancers represented in the *bas reliefs* at Angkor.)

Nouth Narang managed to enlist the support of King Sihanouk against the project. The king issued an edict to the effect that
it would bring bad luck for Cambodia if its national icons were to
be alienated from the country. Rumors were even spread that the
French intended to hijack the art objects and sell them to the highest
bidder, when in fact the French were not only training the staff of
the National Museum on preservation techniques but had agreed
to perform vital repairs to some of the neglected art objects, using
advanced techniques not available in Cambodia.

On May 30 we were informed by Vann Molyvann that First
Prime Minister Rannariddh had ruled that "in conformity with the
concerns of the King," the priceless statues of Jayavarman VII and
Siva's mount, the bull Nandin, would not be permitted to leave the
country, but that the exhibit could go ahead without these two objects. On July 18, Minister of Culture Nouth Narang suddenly ordered the packing for the exhibition to be halted, pending approval
from both prime ministers. As transport planes were already on the
way to Phnom Penh to pick up the art objects, this announcement
precipitated panic, especially by the French ambassador, whose
country was to receive the exhibition first. He summoned Ambassador Quinn and me, along with our Japanese counterparts, to an
emergency meeting at his residence, declared that the delay was

unacceptable, and obtained the agreement of Ambassador Quinn to help put pressure on Hun Sen—the only person who really mattered in Cambodia. Quinn duly called Hun Sen, explained that to back out of an international agreement at this late date would bring discredit to the Cambodian government, and Hun Sen gave his go-ahead for the packing. Later that day, back at my office, I received a call from Prince Rannariddh's chief of staff, saying that Rannariddh was considering our request that the packing continue and would deliver his decision later.

I told him, "Thanks very much, but Samdech Hun Sen has already given his approval." The fellow said the equivalent of "The devil you say!" and slammed down the phone.

In the end, the Khmer art exhibit (officially titled "Sculpture of Angkor and Ancient Cambodia: Millennium of Glory") was eventually mounted and was a great success in Paris, Washington, and Tokyo.

I met King Sihanouk several times—once when I accompanied Ambassador Quinn to the palace to present his credentials to the king, and again when Quinn and I went to the palace to turn over two small stolen Khmer sculptures that had been recovered by U.S. Customs officials in San Francisco. The king gave me a copy of his most recent movie, *An Ambition Reduced to Ashes*. Making movies was one of Sihanouk's passions, and he liked to both produce them and star in them himself. Before he was overthrown in 1970, he held annual film festivals where the winning film was invariably— surprise!—one of Sihanouk's own films.

My most amusing visit to the palace was during an audience with the king by visiting Secretary of State Warren Christopher. I was in charge of the press corps that accompanied SecState visits. The press area, along a side aisle of the throne hall, had been roped off, and I had been warned by my palace contact that under no circumstances would the press be allowed to cross the ropes and approach the throne. But Western journalists are notoriously aggressive, not to mention dismissive of the rules of a third-world country, so when the king appeared, they crossed the barrier into the center of the throne hall to get closer pictures. Palace officials immediately informed me that if they didn't retreat to the press area they would be removed by the king's hefty North Korean guards.

I communicated this to the journalists, who either ignored me or only sluggishly obeyed. At that point, the North Korean guards picked up the offending journalists and gently but bodily removed them from the center of the throne hall.

This infuriated some of the journalists, who abandoned the enterprise and returned to their hotel in a huff. Those who remained, however, were rewarded by the rare spectacle of a full moon illuminating the glistening curved roofs and spires of the fairyland world of the palace.

Reconstituting the BMW

I ruined two BMWs through the rigors of the Foreign Service. The first one, a 316 purchased in London in 1986, lasted through postings to Burma, Morocco, and the first year of Paris. The second—a BMW 318i purchased in Munich while posted to Paris—had traveled back to the States and had now been shipped to Cambodia. It suffered from the effects of dry season dust and monsoon mud. During the rainy season the street in front of my house, like most streets that crossed the main thoroughfares, became a sea of mud. On several occasions my wife, who was the primary driver of the car, stranded it in the middle of deep puddles and had to be pushed out by gangs of laughing children happy for the diversion of playing in the mud to help a foreigner. The car gradually lost most of its appurtenances to vandalism—first the side mirrors, then the moldings, and even the turn signal lamps. One day when my wife left her office in the compound of the School of Business, she noticed that one of the parking lamps was missing. She alerted some of her students, who searched a suspicious-looking amputee and found the missing lamp concealed in his empty pant-leg. We were advised to report the incident to the police station, and while we were there a disgruntled husband threw a grenade into the police station in an unsuccessful attempt to kill his unfaithful wife, so we decided to abandon the case. Someone told me that the stolen parts had no doubt been taken to a certain car parts market near the School of Business; I went there and paid $80 for two side mirrors for a 1992 BMW. Since I had the only 1992 BMW in the city, I was undoubtedly buying back my own mirrors.

When they were promptly stolen again, I decided to give it up, and bought two dime-store compact mirrors and glued them to the electronically controlled adjustment mechanism. We drove the car in its denuded state until the end of my tour, when the dean of the Business School expressed an interest in buying it. I went down to the car parts market and bought back all the missing parts and reinstalled them, and then negotiated a price of $13,000 with the dean. He came to the house with the money in $100 bills in a paper bag, asking only that I give him a bogus receipt for a lesser amount for tax purposes. I had him sign a receipt showing the correct price just to protect myself.

Democracy in Retreat

The political atmosphere in Cambodia was one of constant tension between the government and the opposition, with the government using every trick in the book against the opposition, including false charges, intimidation, and violence. Opposition journalists were intimidated or arrested, and offending publications were shut down under the cynical charge of *lèse majesté* if they insulted the king (a handy pretext that the government could use to suppress the opposition), and in some cases a grenade was thrown into editorial offices by "unknown assailants." In one instance a bomb exploded during one party's political rally and some eighteen people were killed.

During my two years there Hun Sen, the former communist and the one who had refused to accede to the royalist victory in the 1993 elections, gradually consolidated his power until finally, in 1997, he engineered a coup against the royalist co–prime minister Rannariddh and sent him into exile. In the next election, in 1998, five years after the UNTAC election, the CCP won again, basically by intimidation, and the royalist party, which had won the first election, was now in a subservient position to the CCP. And that's basically the situation today. Hun Sen continues to consolidate his power, and what used to be referred to as one of the UN's few success stories—establishing a democracy in Cambodia—has turned out to be less than successful .

I was sent back to Cambodia on TDY from New Zealand to cover the 1998 national elections five years after the UNTAC elections. Scores of international observers came in. They watched the voting in the various districts and provinces and decided, "Well, you know, it seemed like it was basically a free and fair election."

What they didn't understand was that the fix was already in before they got there. Dictators become very proficient in learning the jargon they have to use to satisfy the international community and get the donors to give them money—the buzz words are "progress toward democracy," "respect for human rights," "development of civil society," "transparency in government," "an independent judiciary," etc. etc. Meanwhile, under the table, they've got the fix in already, and they do whatever is necessary to perpetuate their power. It is easy to follow the reasoning of such dictators: "I already have power. Why should I subject it to an election? I didn't achieve my present position by being stupid!"

The State Department has never officially given much credence to the excuse of "Asian values" by dictators such as former President Lee Kuan Yew in Singapore to justify authoritarian rule; but authoritarianism and patronage are seen as the proper way to run a government, not only in Cambodia but also in Asia in general. The problem for U.S. diplomacy in touting Western-style democracy is that in Asia, harmony between the peasants and the power elite (who are thought to be powerful because of their *karma*, or good deeds in past lives) is more important than the right of individuals to challenge the power structure; in fact to do so is considered somewhat improper in most Asian cultures. (This impression seems to be contradicted by the current pro-democracy uprisings in the Middle East, but these countries are not, strictly speaking, "Asian" countries.)

Act Six: New Zealand

Out of the Frying Pan

I was extremely fortunate to be posted to Wellington, New Zealand, for my last two years of eligibility for the Foreign Service. I was sixty-three, and had only two years before I would have to quit. You have to resign from the Foreign Service at the end of the month in which you turn sixty-five; there are no exceptions. From the point of view of economics they should not send a guy to a four-year post who has to quit in two years. But Frank Scotton, director of the Bureau of East Asian Affairs, was being pressured by budget cuts to close a certain number of posts, and he felt that to have someone in New Zealand who had to leave at the end of two years might provide him the rationale for closing the post rather than sending a new officer there. So I was fortunate that they were willing to send me to New Zealand for two years, because I didn't want to serve out my last two years in Washington.

While in Cambodia I had been promoted to the Senior Foreign Service with the rank of counselor, so in Wellington my title was Counselor for Public Affairs. (That's "counselor," not "consular." It's disgraceful that even some diplomats don't understand the difference; they say "consular" when they mean "counselor" and vice versa; that works until you have to say "Counselor for Consular Affairs." But I digress.)

I had an excellent staff in Wellington. My Kiwi cultural assistant was the equivalent of an American CAO. We had a library that was state-of-the-art and an administrative assistant who was so good that the agency in Washington kept sending him to other posts around the world to train other Foreign Service Nationals.

I had worked twelve hours a day, seven days a week in Phnom Penh and was determined to avoid that in New Zealand. Happily, my staff told me that if I was in the office after 5:00 o'clock, it was my own fault, as they were perfectly capable of running the program, and had done so in the gap before my arrival.

I was pretty stressed at the time about my wife and daughter, who had remained in Phnom Penh for an additional six months so my daughter could finish the school year at the Petit Lycée Descartes and my wife could finish her contract as director of the Georgetown University training project. They were still there when heavy fighting broke out in July 1997 between the supporters of co–prime ministers Hun Sen and Prince Rannariddh, in which Rannariddh had to flee the country. Thousands of expatriates were trying to get out of the country, and hundreds had taken refuge in the huge Cambodiana Hotel. As I had been accompanying a speaker to Auckland, I was unaware of what was going on in Phnom Penh until I got back to Wellington and heard that the CPP had closed down the Phnom Penh airport. I panicked when I realized that I didn't know if my family had gotten out before the airport closed. When I called the Sukhothai Hotel in Bangkok where they had been scheduled to stay, I was told that they were not there, which was inconclusive. I finally woke up our friends in Paris where they were supposed to stay next and was told rather grumpily that it was 1:00 a.m. and that my wife and daughter were there and asleep. I broke down and cried with relief in front of all my staff.

My family and I had mixed feelings about New Zealand. While it is an extremely beautiful country and a pleasant place to be, we tended to prefer postings to countries that are less similar to our own in terms of their cultural heritage. Both the United States and New Zealand have a colonial history, both are immigrant societies with English as a unifying language, and both are democracies based on the rule of law and respect for human rights. While New Zealand has historically taken an anti-nuclear stand, they have fought alongside the United States in every major war. At least half of the twenty-four cabinet members and one-third of the members of Parliament have participated in our International Visitor Program.

In spite of this rosy picture, there is an undercurrent of anti-Americanism, concern about the influence of American pop culture, and opposition to what they see as American military hegemony and support for globalization. It can be argued that the job of USIS is more challenging in New Zealand than in less similar countries, since public diplomacy must be quite nuanced and sophisticated to be effective.

My family, interestingly, had preferred Cambodia. My daughter Samantha, then in her early teens, found Cambodia fascinating, with people from all countries and cultures. In addition, she spoke French and a bit of Cambodian. Another thing that appealed to her was that there were no rules except those imposed by her parents; she and her friends were able to go out to clubs and dancing at night. And it must be admitted that the slight undercurrent of danger that existed in Phnom Penh appealed to a teenager's adventurous spirit. In contrast, in New Zealand Samantha attended the all-girls Chilton St. James private school, where she had to wear a uniform and where her classmates had never heard of Phnom Penh. I think she found all these blonde rosy-cheeked shepherdesses a bit boring. So my family, and I must admit I as well, found New Zealand much less exciting than places like Cambodia, Morocco, and Burma.

The Charms of New Zealand

Wellington is justifiably one of the most highly sought-after posts in the Foreign Service, especially by families with children. The capital itself has the reputation of being unpleasantly windy and with little of particular interest for tourists. I don't deny that Wellington's location in the Cook Strait between the two islands makes it a bit of a wind tunnel, but on a clear day the bay around Wellington sparkles in the sun, the pastel colored houses stand out against the green mountains, and the sky is like an inverted blue bowl. And the new National Museum of New Zealand, completed in 1998, is well worth a trip to Wellington. Tourists typically arrive in Auckland, New Zealand's major metropolis, and after checking out the traditional Maori cultural center at Rotorua, head for the South Island to visit the charming English look-alike city of Christchurch (at least as it was before the devastating earthquake the city suffered in February 2010) and picturesque Queenstown, with its marvelous glaciers and mountains and valleys and outdoor sports.

I was surprised to learn that the country is bigger in area than Great Britain but has only 3.5 million people—about 5 percent of the population of Great Britain. There are more people in Auckland—about a million—than on the entire South Island. So when we drove down to Queenstown, the roads were quite good but with one-lane bridges. That a one-lane bridge on a main highway causes no backup at all indicates how few people there are. You can drive for hours without passing any car. With an estimated sixty million sheep, the joke is that New Zealand has about twenty sheep for every human. I was impressed to learn that New Zealand actually has more cattle than sheep and that the country supplies fully one-quarter of worldwide trade in dairy products.

New Zealand has been called "a nation of poet-farmers." This epitomizes the contradictions, and challenges, of public diplomacy programming in New Zealand. On the one hand, New Zealanders are sophisticated and well informed, yet they pride themselves on their rural sheepherder image. They are patriotic, even chauvinistic, about the virtues of New Zealand but at the same time defensive about their diminutive size and geographic isolation. The first question they ask a visitor is "How do you like New Zealand?" and become visibly upset if you don't answer that you are highly impressed. They like to project the tough rugby player/Maori warrior image, yet they must have the highest proportion of sensitive artists, writers, and musicians of any population anywhere. They have a proud military tradition and reputation as tenacious soldiers, having fought in every major war of the past century; yet pacifism is pervasive, and New Zealand prides itself on having stood up to the United States with its antinuclear stance in the mid 1980s.

Finally (or at least I'll let this suffice), having moved from a cradle-to-grave welfare system to a competitive market-driven system in record time, New Zealand has become a pacesetter in free trade. Yet the expectations of the population with regard to social services—health, education, and social security— remain extremely high. And with some justification. At dinner one evening Dr. Alex Sundakov, director of the NZ Institute of Economic Research, told me that New Zealand governments had been extremely efficient over the past several decades—so much so that even though the government was privatized and downsized by some 25 percent, social services have not really been much reduced. He opined further that New Zealanders get a high return on their taxes in terms of free medical care, subsidized tertiary education, and guaranteed pensions for an average tax rate of 35 percent vs. the U.S. average of 30 percent, for which we don't get nearly as much.

I have always believed that Americans would be willing to pay higher taxes if they got something for it besides increased military expenditures (for weapons systems that the military doesn't even want; guess who profits from that!), agricultural subsidies to millionaire farmers that distort the market and impoverish third-world farmers, and unnecessary wars, such as in Iraq. It is a conservative myth that citizens of other industrialized countries, all of whom have government-funded health care (to avoid the highly charged term "socialized medicine"), hate their systems of health care. My firsthand experience in France, Great Britain, New Zealand, and Canada has confirmed that, on the contrary, they are happy with their health care, as well as with their free higher education and pensions. And why in the world should the insurance industry be involved in health care? This simply ensures profits for the insurance industry and drives up the price of health care in the United States. It would no doubt be too revolutionary to achieve such a system in the States in one fell swoop; for one thing the insurance and pharmaceutical industry lobbies are too powerful. Now that we have an adult in the White House with the election of Barack Obama, we may begin to make progress on some of these pressing issues—and start to repair the damage that Abu Ghraib, Guantánamo Bay, support for creationism, and denial of global warming have wreaked on the prestige of this country around the world. But I digress.

The Maori Issue

Known by the Maori as "The Land of the Long White Cloud," New Zealand was explored and mapped by Captain James Cook in the 1790s, and settlers from Great Britain founded the modern country only in 1840. About 14 percent of the population consists of Maori— South Sea Islanders who arrived about 700 years before the British. The Maori feel that they have been discriminated against, had their culture repressed, and been dispossessed of their native lands by the British (all of which, unfortunately, is essentially true, and uncomfortably parallel with the situation of Native Americans). The striking thing about current New Zealand society, or at least official policy, is how politically correct they are with regard to the Maori. New Zealanders insist that they are a "bicultural society," and affirmative action, the rights of the Maori, and Maori claims to ancestral land are hot topics. When the impressive new national museum of New Zealand was completed in Wellington, it was decided to give it the official name "Te Papa," which means "Our Place" in Maori. That was a nice gesture, but it seems like bending over backward to name a national museum after a 14-percent minority.

Since the Maori claim to be the "natives" of New Zealand, the Maori situation in New Zealand is rather like a combination of the issues surrounding both the African Americans (roughly the same percentage of the U.S. population) and the American Indians. But the truth is that the Maori are not, strictly speaking, natives of the land, since they dispossessed and stamped out the natives who had been there when they arrived 700 years earlier. New Zealand is more properly a "multicultural society" rather than a "bicultural" one, since other European, Asian, and Pacific Islander immigrants make up perhaps 20 percent of the population. In fact Auckland, with its large population of Polynesians from such places as Samoa and Fiji, has the largest Polynesian population of any city in the world.

Dealing with the Ambassador

Our ambassador to New Zealand was Josiah Beeman, a political appointee who had been active in both Presbyterian and Democratic politics on a national level, having served as secretary for international affairs for the United Presbyterian Church, staff director of the Democratic caucus in the House of Representatives, and director of the Washington office of the State of California, after which he established his own consulting agency, Beeman and Associates, lobbying for California state agencies, before President Clinton appointed him ambassador to New Zealand in 1994.

Beeman had a good sense of humor and a realistic understanding of the (relative) unimportance of his job in the overall scheme of U.S. foreign policy. But I think he was extremely effective. He was indefatigable in attending social events and entertaining. He was busy almost every night either entertaining at the Residence or attending some other function, such as a government reception or a wedding of the cousin of some minister, and he knew them by name—their spouses and cousins and children. As my predecessor had been a speechwriter for the ambassador, I inherited that job and must have written dozens of speeches for him while I was there. I remember once writing four versions of a Fourth of July speech for four different venues. (Sir Edmund Hillary, first conqueror, along with Tenzing Norgay, of Mount Everest, attended one of the venues in Auckland. It was a particular thrill to meet him, as I had visited their mountaineering school in Darjeeling, India, during my motorcycle jaunt in 1958.)

But Beeman was not universally popular among the staff. The DCM in particular felt that Beeman was a control freak who did not delegate enough authority to the second in command and who hogged every speaking engagement and press contact for himself. I learned that he had had a falling-out with a previous DCM, who he felt didn't keep him informed of crucial information (I don't know the details), as a result of which he shut the current DCM out of embassy actions and decisions. This became clear early in my tour when Beeman instructed me to send memos concerning requests for interviews or educational exchanges directly to him, without sending them through the DCM, the standard operating procedure in other embassies.

I had only one major confrontation with the ambassador. Washington had sent a cable asking me to go to Cambodia in July–August 1998 to cover their parliamentary elections, as they were expected to be rather contentious, if not violent, and the post was temporarily without a PAO. At the same time the New Zealand embassy was preparing for a possible visit in August by Secretary of State Madeline Albright. Washington had said that if the SecState visit materialized, they would send someone to replace me in Wellington. The ambassador, however, understood that if the SecState visit were to take place, I would stay in Wellington, and Washington would send someone else to Phnom Penh. I was personally and professionally interested in covering the elections in Cambodia, but in the interest of avoiding a last-minute cock-up, I presented the issue squarely to the ambassador. He dug in his heels, instructing me to say to Washington that unless State announced definitively that Albright would not be coming, he would not approve my going to Phnom Penh nor my replacement in Wellington by another officer, experienced or otherwise, arguing that New Zealand had not had a SecState visit in fourteen years and that a successful SecState visit following the ASEAN (Association of South East Asian Nations) and Australia-U.S. Ministerial Meetings in Sydney was all the more important in view of New Zealand's upcoming presidency of APEC (Asia-Pacific Economic Commission) in September 1999.

Finally, the ambassador modified his stance somewhat by saying that the only officer he would accept as my replacement for the SecState visit would be my predecessor as PAO, Tim Randall, whom the ambassador had greatly liked. I relayed this to Washington, asking if sending Randall would be a possibility. They contacted Randall, who was delighted with the chance to revisit Wellington, where he had spent four pleasant years. So I went to Phnom Penh, Tim went to Wellington, and a tug-of-war was averted.

The PAO residence was a rambling one-story house surrounded by spacious gardens in the same compound as the ambassador's residence in the suburb of Lower Hutt. The ambassador's residence was an imposing mansion that had inherited its picturesque name "Camperdown" from its days as a large sheep ranch station. Living in the same compound with the ambassador had its advantages and disadvantages. It was protected and well maintained, and it was easy to contact the ambassador in the event of an emergency — a not-too-likely occurrence in New Zealand. The disadvantage was that it was easy for the ambassador to contact me on any matter, trivial or otherwise. As a case in point, my daughter organized a lawn party on the occasion of her sixteenth birthday and invited a number of her school friends. The problem was that, as the compound was not guarded, some uninvited guests crashed the party (a fairly common event in the neighborhood), there was loud music, drinking, and an attempted rape (the attacker was driven off by Samantha's large Maori girlfriend, who reportedly broke his nose). Fighting broke out, and there was general mayhem. In the end we had to call the police to break up the fracas.

The inevitable call came from the ambassador: "Frank, what the hell's going on over there?" I described the situation as briefly as possible, downplayed the seriousness of it, and assured him that so far as I knew no press had been alerted to the event. Although I was later interviewed by the police in response to a complaint from the parents of the alleged rape victim, there were no local press reports such as "Police Break up Wild Party at U.S. Ambassador's Compound."

U.S.–New Zealand Relations

Our biggest public diplomacy issue was the antinuclear stance that New Zealand took in the mid 1980s prohibiting nuclear-powered ships from coming to New Zealand. This pretty much torpedoed the ANZUS (Australia-New Zealand-U.S.) defense treaty. The issue was a constant undercurrent, more so among the general population than on the part of the New Zealand military, who would have liked closer security cooperation with the Americans.

The ambassador, who liked to tease Prime Minister Jim Bolger, on one occasion asked him, "Would you like to have a visit by the president?" When Bolger answered, "Oh yes, indeed," the ambassador said, "Well what if he comes on a nuclear-powered ship?" We thought their position was rather head-in-the-sand, since New Zealand after all enjoyed the protection of the U.S. nuclear umbrella in the Pacific.

On the matter of free trade—usually a workhorse issue for U.S. public diplomacy—New Zealand was a bit ahead of us. A perfect example was the flap over New Zealand's decision to lift the ban on parallel importing. This meant that franchise and copyright holders in New Zealand would no longer be protected: if an importer could buy a particular branded product (such as Toyotas, Barnes and Noble books, Gucci clothing, Nike shoes) more cheaply in, say, Australia, he could bring it into New Zealand and undersell the franchised dealer for that product—in other words, they legalized the "grey market" in all sectors. The USG position was that this is an IPR (intellectual property rights) issue, that parallel importing stifles innovation, debases franchises, and increases the risk of copyright piracy, while the New Zealand government argued that it was a free trade issue, that it would lead to lower prices for the NZ consumer, and that the USG was being inconsistent in opposing it while claiming to support trade liberalization. The NZ parliament passed the measure "under urgency" as part of their budget bill, as they knew the United States would oppose it.

When we learned of it just twenty-four hours before its passage, the ambassador wrote a rather strong letter to various ministers concerned advising them that the USTR would take a very dim view of such action. One of the ministers leaked the letter to the press, and all hell broke loose—I took about fifteen calls a day from the press. The ambassador gave two television interviews on the issue and several to the print media. He finally asked me and the economics section to prepare a statement giving the rationale for our opposition to the measure to hand out to the press, but the press was not interested so much in the issues as in the conflict between the New Zealand and U.S. governments, especially after U.S. Trade Representative Charlene Barshefsky announced an "out-of-cycle Special 301 Review" of the issue. As the issue was not all that clear-cut, it was difficult not to sympathize with the New Zealand position; they were definitely getting ripped off by franchise holders, especially with regard to cars, books, and brand-name clothing. I rather thought we had chosen a poor issue to go to the mat on— that we should pick our fights more carefully— but, acting on orders from Washington, Ambassador Beeman took the issue by the horns and seemed quite prepared to squander four years of hard-won goodwill with the New Zealand government over this murky issue. When I suggested as much, he said, "At least I'm popular with USTR," which was not a surprising position for him to take, as his term was nearing a close and he was heading back to Washington to resume his profession as a trade lobbyist.

We had good relations with the New Zealand press. They were friendly and relatively pro-American, and we sent a lot of them to the States on journalistic exchange programs and international visitor programs. I can't say that press relations were a strenuous part of my job in New Zealand, other than dealing with the mild anti-Americanism over the nuclear thing and some trade issues. But New Zealand had changed enormously from the early days, when they opposed the nuclear ships and were a quasi-socialist government with a cradle-to-grave welfare system. When they realized they couldn't afford the system, they had to go through a major revision of their policies in the 1990s. They slimmed down and cut benefits and became much more committed to free trade. In other words, they had to make many of the same reforms that other countries, especially in Europe, had to make to become more competitive in the world market.

Handmaiden for a Shotgun Marriage

About the only unpleasant aspect of my tour in New Zealand was the imminent merging of State and USIA. This actually took place after my departure, at the beginning of fiscal year 2000, that is October 1, 1999. But we had to make all kinds of changes in preparation for this merger which all of us in USIS felt was a shotgun marriage. The idea was to get efficiencies from combining admin staffs, information technology staffs, drivers, and all the rest. But we felt that USIA had been an efficient operation because it was small and because it didn't have all the levels of hierarchy that the State Department had. Although there was a good deal of resistance to the change, we knew it was coming and had to accommodate it. The bitterest conflict arose in personnel matters. We had highly qualified local personnel who had been with USIS for twenty years who, at worst, were going to be let go and, at best, were going to be required to change jobs. They would have to go work in Admin and B&F (budget & fiscal) and the other sections of the embassy, and they didn't want to.

On the other hand I had my marching orders to cut down my staff, who tended to feel that I was not being supportive enough of them if I failed to protect their positions. If we could claim that this person or that was essential to USIS programs, then we could keep him or her in the USIS section. I made the case for a number of employees in certain areas where I knew we could operate more efficiently with people familiar with our operation. I ultimately failed to prevent some people from being "cross-walked," as they called it, but my attempts to salvage what I considered the more sensible parts of our programs put me at loggerheads with the DCM, Terry Miller, who had recently arrived and didn't know where the bodies were buried.

When he learned that I was receiving back-channel advice from Washington on how to best deal with the upcoming merger, he charged that I was not negotiating "in good faith." He got so furious with me that he said, "Huffman, if you keep opposing me on this thing I'm going to ruin you!"

I laughed and said, "Well, you know, I'm almost sixty-five, and if I'm not ruined by now you're a bit late." Nonetheless, the whole thing was very unpleasant.

They All Come to New Zealand

Many diplomats from the United States and other countries have chosen to retire in New Zealand, and the country is indeed an idyllic place to live, except that it is so incredibly isolated. When I had first gone to New Zealand to attend a CAO conference a few years earlier, I had thought it was an island off the coast of Australia. But no. When you get to Australia you're already way "down under" and you still have some 1,500 miles to go to get to New Zealand. So you don't get many people stopping through. Surprisingly, two of my brothers and their wives decided that if they were ever going to visit Frank abroad before he retired they'd better get on with it, so they came all the way out to New Zealand for a visit. It would have made much more sense to have visited us in Paris or Morocco or even Cambodia, but they just never got around to it. In spite of its isolation, New Zealand has a mystique that attracts people to take a "once in a lifetime" trip to the "Land of the Long White Cloud." A Harris poll taken in 1997 showed that if cost were not a consideration, New Zealand would be the thirteenth most popular destination for American tourists (Australia was number one, followed by the standard European countries; interestingly, Japan tied with New Zealand for thirteenth).

One of the high-profile speakers I was able to recruit was Walter Russell Mead, the Henry A. Kissinger Senior Fellow on U.S. foreign policy at the Council on Foreign Relations. He addressed the "Foreign Policy School" organized annually at one of New Zealand's excellent universities—in this case the University of Otago in the southern city of Dunedin. Another effective speaker was George Washington University President Stephen Joel Trachtenberg (now retired), who addressed audiences on tertiary education financing in Wellington, Christchurch, and Auckland. Trachtenberg is a genial and entertaining fellow, and I thoroughly enjoyed accompanying him on his travels in New Zealand. He is also a *bon vivant* who enjoys scotch and cigars. As we dined together one evening in a restaurant in Auckland, he confided in me—facetiously, no doubt—that as soon as he turned seventy, he planned to drink scotch and smoke cigars to his heart's content because "it takes about fifteen years for those things to kill you, and eighty-five is good enough if you're enjoying yourself."

Other high-level visitors to the embassy during my tour were the ubiquitous Under Secretary of State Strobe Talbott (I had had him also in Cambodia), a congressional delegation (CODEL) of eleven senators led by Senator Thad Stevens (all of whom had urgent business to attend to in Antarctica), CODELs led by Representatives Tom Lantos and Philip Crane, CINCPAC (Commander-in-Chief, Pacific Command) Admiral Joseph Prueher, Lt. Gen. William Steele, Commanding General, U.S. Army Pacific, and Minnesota governor Arne Carlson on a business development mission. Beyond the embassy, New Zealand attracted such high-profile Americans as former secretary of labor Robert Reich (invited by the then–out of power Labour Party), World Masters of Business General Norman Schwarzkopf, Lee Iacocca, and Stephen Covey (author of *The Seven Habits of Highly Effective People*), and even Noam Chomsky, billed as "the renowned professor of linguistics and radical critic of the American political system."

Following the visit of Strobe Talbott, I sent the following self-congratulatory note back to Washington (for inclusion in the "Director's Weekly"):

> USIS Wellington provided up-to-the-minute reports on a change of government leadership which occurred in the middle of the visit to New Zealand by Deputy Secretary of State Strobe Talbott November 2-4. The 25-member delegation included representatives from the Departments of State, Defense, and Interior, the National Security Council, and USAID, and involved four separate schedules. In addition to providing the Wireless File and transcripts of Deputy

Secretary Talbott's major policy address and interview with Radio New Zealand on Nov. 3, USIS kept the delegation up-to-date on the ouster of Prime Minister Jim Bolger which culminated at midnight the same evening."

Bolger was ousted in a Nationalist Party "palace coup" by Jenny Shipley, his minister of transport. The next election was won by Helen Clark of the opposition Labour Party. Earlier I had briefed Clark before sending her on an International Visitor program to the United States and had found her a friendly, down-to-earth person, as are most New Zealanders.

The informality of New Zealand politics is extraordinary. I once had the experience of telephoning the office of a minister and having him answer the phone personally. At a reception one evening at the ambassador's residence I shook hands with the highly popular Foreign Minister Don McKinnon (who later was elected Secretary-General of the British Commonwealth of Nations).

Although I had met him before, I thought it a bit much to assume that he remembered me, so I said, "Hello, Mr. McKinnon. I'm Frank Huffman, counselor for public affairs at the embassy."

He aimed a kindly smile at me and said, "Of course you are."

I've never decided whether he actually remembered me, or whether it was the ultimate put-down, but knowing New Zealanders, who actually mean it when they say, "Have a nice day," I suspect the former.

The Visit of Joe Duffy

Perhaps the most entertaining visit for me personally was that of USIA Director Joseph Duffy and his wife Ann Wexler, in the company of Mr. and Mrs. R. W. (Johnny) Apple, Jr., chief correspondent and later associate editor of the *New York Times*. My wife and I were invited to a dinner for the visitors at the Residence, to which NZ Prime Minister Jim Bolger and his wife were also invited. Apple, a brilliant conversationalist, engaged in a virtual *tête-à-tête* with Prime Minister Bolger, totally dominating the more passive Duffy. Although Duffy had been president of the University of Massachusetts system and had served as head of the National Endowment for the Humanities under Reagan, he was not an inspiring agency head. For example, when he was appointed director of USIA while I was serving my brief Washington tour in 1993–94, he called a meeting of all the Washington-based agency employees. His goal as director of USIA, he told us, was to "engage the American people in a dialog about the role of public diplomacy in the post–cold war world"! Not exactly an exciting slogan to rally the troops.

When the Clinton administration ordered the incorporation of USIA (and USAID) into State in response to the ill-informed demands of Senator Jesse Helms, Duffy folded immediately, putting his position as an "FOB" (Friend of Bill) above loyalty and duty to his employees. USAID's administrator, Brian Atwood, more of a fighter, was able to hold off (at least for the time being) USAID's consolidation with State. Who would have thought that we would feel nostalgia for the days of Charlie Wick, who, despite his faults (see Act One: Striped Pants Duty), was able to expand the budget and influence of USIA as a bosom buddy of President Reagan.

Medical Misadventures

In October 1998, I scored a long-sought-after personal victory—I quit smoking after thirty years of smoking an average of a pack and a half a day. I had tried for years to quit, once quitting for as long as three months, but had always failed in the end. As Mark Twain is reported to have said (or was it Will Rogers?), "It's easy to quit smoking; I've done it many times!" My success this time was due to several factors, one of which was no doubt the healthy outdoor lifestyle of New Zealand, but more important was inbred German stinginess. During a visit to the Navy Exchange in Christchurch (the U.S. Navy had a base there in support of the U.S. Antarctic Research Program), I found Nicoderm patches on sale for about half-price, so I bought a six-week course. But even at half-price, they cost several hundred dollars, and I was determined not to have spent that money in vain. I learned quite early on that, like a recovered alcoholic, I could become an ex-smoker, but never a nonsmoker; it was impossible to have "just one"; I had to go cold turkey. So I persevered and have never smoked since.

Ironically, a chain of health problems immediately followed my cessation of smoking. First I developed a hernia requiring surgery. Then the week after that I had to have emergency laser surgery on my left eye for a partially detached retina. Some weeks later, we took a long-planned vacation to Fiji, where I tried to show my daughter how to water-ski, and aggravated a groin injury, requiring six weeks of physiotherapy. I was tempted to go back to smoking.

I never achieved a satisfactory tennis regime during my two years in New Zealand, in spite of the country's reputation for outdoor sports. There were only about two tennis players in the embassy, neither of whom was as enthusiastic about the game as I was. I joined the Lower Hutt Tennis Club but was never fully accepted by the members, most of whom had played together for decades, usually on weekends. When I told them I was interested in singles, they advised, "You're too old for singles; you need to play doubles." This annoyed me for two reasons, first because I was not a particularly good doubles player and second because, while they could make me look silly on the doubles court, I knew I could beat any one of them at singles (and sometimes had the occasion to do so). After becoming a bit more familiar with the club, I realized they thought I wanted to *compete* on the club's singles team, made up mostly of younger guys, who competed with other clubs, when all I wanted was to play singles with other guys who enjoyed playing singles at my level.

Once while playing at the net during a doubles match, I was struck just above the groin by a hard-hit tennis ball. The spot became increasingly painful, until it developed into a hernia. When I outlined this theory to the surgeon, he dismissed it, saying, "Hernias always develop from the inside, pushing out through a weak spot in the stomach lining. They are not caused by an external injury." He was merely repeating the mantra he had learned in medical school, but it made eminently good sense to me that the spot, damaged and weakened by the tennis injury, had then allowed the hernia to develop from the inside. After all, I knew the sequence of events in my own body better than he did. Fortunately, New Zealand medical practice is excellent—probably superior to ours. For the hernia repair, the surgeon recommended a procedure called bilateral laparoscopic inguinal hernia repair, to use the medical jargon, in which they insert a television eye into the stomach cavity and a mesh to cover the breach, a procedure that was less invasive, resulted in fewer recurrences, and had a shorter recovery time than the old-fashioned method of simply making an incision and sewing the hernia shut. (My only reservation was the surgeon's proposal to put a screen on both sides; when I asked him if he saw evidence that I had a hernia on the opposite side, he said, "No, but you will." I was not too happy about this kind of preventive maintenance, but I bowed to his superior knowledge.) However, the State Department's RMO (regional medical officer), on a visit from Jakarta, refused to authorize the new procedure, claiming it was too experimental, and said the State Department would pay only for the traditional cut-and-sew approach. At this point, the ambassador, who himself had a long history of surgery for heart and back problems, intervened and got the department to authorize the new procedure, dismissing the RMO with the comment, "If he was any good, he wouldn't be working for the State Department."

As for the eye problem, I was walking down the street in Wellington one morning when suddenly I had spider webs and phantasmagorical patterns in my left eye. On the advice of Dr. Crutchley, the embassy doctor (the embassy dentist was named Dr. Paine; I'm not making this up), I saw a Dr. Wellings, who it turned out was the only ophthalmologist in town; the other half-dozen were attending a medical conference in Sydney. I was fortunate he had not considered it necessary to attend the conference; maybe they drew straws.

When Wellings looked into my eye, he said, "You've got a torn retina. I want you at Wellington Hospital this afternoon for laser surgery."

When I asked, "Does it have to be done today?" he replied bluntly, "Yes, unless you want to go blind."

Wellings, who was president of the New Zealand Society of Ophthalmologists, was a rather crusty old fellow. When he was performing the laser surgery ("spot-welding," as he called it), I would groan when he zapped different spots on the back of the eyeball with the laser beam. "Does it hurt?" he asked rather impatiently.

"No, not really," I replied bravely, although it was a decidedly weird and uncomfortable feeling.

"Then quit groaning," he said crossly, "it's off-putting."

The next week the right eye began to show some of the same symptoms, but has never required surgery.

I have gone into rather more detail than necessary about my physical ailments, and certainly more than you wanted to know. But these experiences left me with rather unpleasant memories from the end of my tour and tempered the nostalgia I should normally have felt for New Zealand.

Sanda, with her usual resourcefulness, found ways to pursue her profession as an interpreter. In addition to working at the Alliance Française, she joined the New Zealand Society of Interpreters and Translators, interpreted for a UNESCO conference in Christchurch in February 1998, and that same year spent a week in Samoa as interpreter for an international conference of the South Pacific Regional Environment Program.

Back to the World

Since you have to retire from the Foreign Service on the last day of the month in which you turn sixty-five, I was going to turn into a pumpkin at midnight on January 31, 1999. We began to make plans to leave post a week or so in advance of that date, but we still hadn't decided what to do or where to live. We wanted Samantha to finish high school in the United States and had planned to rent an apartment in Falls Church, Virginia, so she could attend the highly rated George Mason High School, where they offer the International Baccalaureate accepted in European universities. (The school was rated number two in the nation that year by *U.S. News and World Report,* based on the percentage of students taking advanced placement courses.) The problem was that the New Zealand school year runs from February through December, so she would be set back one year, since schools that grant the IB require that students attend for the last two years. We played with the idea of bumming around South America for three or four months, since that half of the year is wasted anyway, and it's cold in D.C. in February, but the devil was in the details.

I thought about buying a four-wheel-drive vehicle in Washington and driving down the Pan-American Highway all the way to Buenos Aires, but was advised that it was not really safe to drive a single vehicle (meaning, not in a convoy) through such countries as Colombia, Bolivia, and Peru. Also, we'd have to modify the car to use leaded gasoline, install heavy-duty shocks, put grills over the headlights, and so on. We learned that there is a stretch of about 120 miles of impassable highway in Panama, so we would have to ferry the car around to Cartagena in Colombia. (I had ignored such trivial considerations in 1958, when the only question I asked in striking out on a motorcycle from Laos to London was, "Which way is west?" But when you get older and have a family to think about, you get a lot more cautious.)

Then we hit on the idea of flying directly from Auckland to Santiago, Chile (which is actually the closest South American city to New Zealand), renting a car and driving around the five countries in the southern cone that are considered safe (Chile, Argentina, Paraguay, Uruguay, and Brazil), but we ran into the "Catch 22" that the U.S. government Fly America Act would prohibit such a plan, even on a cost-constructive basis, since there is no American carrier between New Zealand and Chile. In the meantime, Sanda was applying for a job again at FSI that would begin in February, conflicting with plans for the South America trip.

In the end, we settled for the route more traveled, flying to Los Angeles via Hawaii, visiting my son David in San Francisco, thence to Washington We rented an excellent three-bedroom apartment in Falls Church City (so Samantha would be eligible to attend George Mason High School without paying tuition), leaving our house in D.C. occupied by renters.

Mandatory Retirement

I've never quite understood just why retirement from the Foreign Service is required at age sixty-five, since experienced officers should be at the peak of their effectiveness at that age and thus of greatest value to the country's diplomatic efforts. When the law against age discrimination in employment was passed in 1967, certain types of employment were exempted in cases where public safety could be affected, as for example air traffic controllers, who have to retire at sixty. Educational institutions were also granted a temporary exception, claiming that they needed the right to require mandatory retirement at age sixty-five in order to get rid of deadwood otherwise protected by tenure rules, but the limit was raised by stages to seventy and then to seventy-five and eventually phased out altogether.

Why the exemption for the Foreign Service? Perhaps they consider that when we reach the advanced age of sixty-five our brains become soft, making us a security risk. It is surprising that this exemption has never been successfully challenged by AFSA (the American Foreign Service Association, which represents the rights of Foreign Service officers). Like universities, the State Department claims the exemption is necessary in order to move out placeholders at the top and allow promotion of younger officers up through the ranks. But another consideration, not explicitly mentioned, is that younger officers' salaries are much lower, and the practice thus saves money. And it is true that life in the Foreign Service takes such a toll on one's energies and family life that few Foreign Service officers who join at an early age make it to the mandatory cutoff at sixty-five. Furthermore the "time-in-class" limitations weed out many officers before they ever reach sixty-five. To illustrate, you are allowed a total of twenty-two years to make it into the Senior Foreign Service; once you have made OC (counselor, the first grade of the SFS) you have seven years to make it to MC (minister counselor) and a total of twelve years to make it to CM (career minister, the top grade of the SFS). Fortunately, I never came up against these time-in-class limits, as I didn't join until I was fifty-one, made it to SFS in eleven years at age 62, and had to retire three years later.

The Foreign Service retains the ability to rehire retirees when needed for specific jobs or to fill gaps in hard-to-fill positions, under a program with the strange acronym WAE (when actually employed). The rationale for this designation is the rule that, in order to prevent "double-dipping," your total income from both your government pension and your WAE salary may not exceed the salary at which you retired. This limits the time you may be employed in any one calendar year to six months, or 1,040 hours. And they can get around even this restriction by hiring a retiree on a PSC (personal services contract), which allows them to claim that the retiree "is not a government employee." Go figure.

When I returned from New Zealand, I took the two-month

retirement planning seminar offered to retiring officers at the Career Transition Center at FSI. It is called the Career Transition Center because the great majority of retirees are younger officers who have been "TICed out," that is, who have retired because of time-in-class limitations, rather than people who have reached mandatory retirement age. As I recall, out of about forty-five people in the seminar, only two of us were sixty-five. They spend a lot of time talking about how to write the perfect résumé, how to network, and how to behave in an interview—things I didn't particularly need instruction in—and they also had a number of speakers (usually former FSOs) who gave testimonials about how they had succeeded in their post-retirement enterprises. We took the Myers-Briggs personality test and talked about self-analysis (what do you really want to do?). Talking about oneself is always fascinating. All in all, it was a pleasant way to spend two months at government expense.

Act Seven: Chad

"Once More Unto the Breach"

After about six months of retirement, I began to get wanderlust again, so I went in to USIA and said, "Look, have you got any PAO jobs that you can't fill?" I went to the Africa Bureau because I had heard that they always need people, and I knew the deputy director, Pat Corcoran. Pat said, "Well, yes, it happens that we have openings in both Niger and Chad."

At that same time my wife was interpreting for a group of International Visitors from Francophone Africa—from Senegal, Côte d'Ivoire, Cameroon, Niger, and others, and they all said, "You know, Niamey (the capital of Niger) is a nice place; that's a real sleeper, but don't go to Chad." (One reason they could say that was that there was no participant from Chad.) So I went back to USIA and told Corcoran that I might be willing to go to Niamey.

He said, "Well, we've assigned that job, but we'd still like you to go to Chad."

So I agreed to go to Chad. I'd been posted to Morocco but I had never been to sub-Saharan Africa, and even though I was too senior for the job (rated, as I recall, as an FSO-2), I just thought it would be an interesting experience. Besides, to work another year would shore up the old retirement reserves. But again, the devil was in the details.

Corcoran said, "OK, I'd like you to bid on a two-year assignment as PAO N'Djamena."

I said, "Pat, I can't 'bid' on a two-year assignment! I'm no longer a Foreign Service officer."

He said, "OK, whatever. Just work it out with Personnel."

When USIA approached State Personnel, they objected to the assignment; when we asked why, they first said, "He's too old."

We said, "Come on, you send older guys than that abroad all the time as WAEs and PSCs."

Then they said, "Well, we don't think USIA should encumber that position for two years when it will become a State position just a month after he gets there."

We said, "Why, do you have State bidders on the job?"

"Well, no, but..."

The compromise was that I would go for only one year, while they opened the position to bidding by State officers after that. Thus my assignment was a strange bird—it was neither a regular two-year assignment nor a WAE. In my letter of appointment as "Public Affairs Officer in N'Djamena, Chad," they called it a "Foreign Service Limited (Non-Career) Appointment." I don't know if there was any precedent for such a thing. I do know that the appointment was to cause all manner of administrative mischief for some time to come. Since I left Washington as a USIA employee and returned as a State Department employee, they had no slot they could put me in, and the State Department administration is notoriously averse to ad hoc solutions.

First Impressions of Chad

The following excerpt from my first letter home will describe my first impressions of Chad in more authentic terms than I could reconstruct now, ten years later:

> Sunday, September 26 (1999)—I'll start this letter now, but probably won't finish it in one sitting (nor will you!) It's Sunday morning, and I have come in to the Embassy to have access to the computer. The whole Embassy compound is overshadowed by towering trees which are white with cattle egrets, cawing and fluttering in their nests as they turn the ground—and all the cars below—white with their droppings. They're rather ominous, and make one think of Hitchcock's *The Birds*—all the more so when the sky is dark with an approaching storm. Apparently the previous

ambassador thought they were picturesque until he was ordered by the regional medical officer to get rid of them as a health hazard, so they sprayed them and fired off guns to scare them away, and they moved to the treetops adjoining the compound, but now have come back. The entire compound—even inside my office—smells rather like a chicken house.

On Friday I moved from the hotel into my temporary house. I was not feeling well—had nausea and dizziness for some reason—and the challenge of setting up housekeeping on my own, rather than simply relying on the hotel, was all rather depressing. This is a house that nobody seems to like and whose lease they plan to drop as soon as I get out of it. I must say it doesn't look much different from the others I've seen; it is quite spacious, with three bedrooms, four and a half baths, kitchen, laundry room, storage room, huge living room and dining room. Of course everything is dingy, but it would take the entire two months I plan to be here to get it into anything like acceptable shape, so I'll just ignore it. You tend to overlook grime after a while. For example, when I first walked into my office with my predecessor (with whom I overlapped a week), it struck me as dark, dingy, and oppressive—the whitewashed walls are peeling, leaving dust and broken plaster at the edges of the faded burgundy-colored wall-to-wall carpet. My first thought was "I'll get my staff in here and really clean this place up, and show them what it ought to look like." But now, I've forgotten about it; you realize after a while that there is no point because if you clean that up, then you notice that the plaster around the baseboards is missing, the electrical wiring is exposed and falling off the wall, the wood-paneled ceiling is warped, water-stained and about to fall down, and the windows have large cracks around them which let the insects in—so you just learn to lower your expectations. (I've almost gotten used to the smell of bird manure.)

The worst shock I got when I arrived here was the condition of the roads. When I got to the airport, a low yellow structure with a big black and white sign saying

"Bienvenue à N'Djamena," it reminded me somewhat of Vientiane, Laos—I wish! As my sponsor the GSO (an old Africa hand named Don Huth, rehired on TDY as GSO in various African posts—wearing shorts and a floppy straw hat) was taking me around showing me some of the significant points of interest, we were frequently required to change into four-wheel-drive in order to get through a bog or swamp in the road (we're talking here streets in the middle of the city, with houses and buildings inside concrete walls on both sides). Sometimes they would stop in front of a particularly wicked-looking bog and debate whether one could get through with 4WD or whether it would be advisable to take another street, all the while making such comments as "Abdul said he got through here yesterday." And "Yes, but it rained again last night, and it looks deeper than before."

So now I realize that when I was advised to bring a 4WD to Chad, it was not idle gossip. The car of choice here is the Toyota Land Cruiser, although one does see such things as Jeep Cherokees (mostly among the Americans), Isuzu Troopers, Nissan Pathfinders, etc., so I tremble to think what will happen to my poor new front-wheel-drive Honda Accord when it gets here. But I am encouraged by the fact that there are dozens of 2WD yellow Peugeot taxis (of about 1970 vintage) plying the main streets. There are some hard-topped streets, especially those that go past the Presidential Palace (so he doesn't get his Mercedes muddy), the Avenue Charles de Gaulle, and the main drag along the river. I have been told that taxi drivers refuse to get off the hardtop in the rainy season. In any case, the rainy season is coming to a close now, and by the time my Honda gets here it will have to contend only with dust and potholes until the rains start again next May or June, by which time I will be almost ready to come home—I'll just leave the car in the garage (if I have one) when it rains.

Anyway, to get back to the house, it is crowded with so much standard-issue State Department furniture that it looks like a furniture store, with pieces along all available walls. I had them move the four couches around a square coffee table in one end of the living room to form a conversation nook, and move   the dining table and ten chairs out of the other end of the living room into what obviously is supposed to be the dining area. There are eleven bookcases and desks—six in the living-dining area, and a desk-like thing and bookcase in each of the bedrooms. There are about ten transformers—and I still managed to plug the USIS stereo into 220 current and burn it out.

When I got to the house on Friday, I was immediately besieged by a gardener who said he had always worked on that compound (without impressive results, apparently), and a "houseboy" named Benjamin, whose odor was so strong I had to stand several meters away to talk to him. He gave me a copy of a recommendation from a previous occupant of the house (in fact it was a former PAO—an Egyptian-American named Fawzi Friej), dated August 1997, saying that Benjamin always kept the house spotless. It was difficult to understand what had happened to the house in the two years since. Anyway, I told him to come back Monday and we would discuss it, but that I didn't need a full-time houseboy—just someone three times a week to clean, do the laundry, and go to the market to buy meat and vegetables and that sort of thing so they wouldn't rip me off. There is no point in cleaning the surface of the house three times a week—what it really needs is steel wool and scrapers to get down to the original surface. I finally did hire Benjamin, and he is useful in buying vegetables and disinfecting them by soaking them in chlorinated water (they use *eau de javel* here—two tablespoons per gallon of water), but although I encouraged him to use the shower at the house, his personal hygiene has never noticeably improved.

Just to give you an idea of prices here, I went shopping yesterday to buy some of the basics to set up housekeeping—a ten-pound box of Omo (the French laundry detergent) cost almost $30! And I didn't get ripped off, as some French customers in the store confirmed that that was the standard price. I bought some very nice locally woven baskets for wastebaskets and dirty clothes—four small baskets cost about $15—and there I probably did get robbed, in spite of giving bargaining my best shot. There are fruit stands along the street, but Chadian fruits are not spectacular—another unfortunate comparison with Southeast Asia! All of this takes place along Avenue Charles de Gaulle —the main drag of the "European" part of town—it has whitewashed arcades of the kind fairly universal in Africa, I take it, occupied by grocery stores, tailors, jewelers, restaurants, the butcher (whom I have yet to visit), the "Carrefour" (where French cheeses and pâtés can be had at exorbitant prices—yesterday I bought about 250 grams of Port Salut cheese for about $8.00, but I couldn't resist). I have been eating entirely too much sweet stuff—coffee with sugar, orange Fanta, cookies (how I crave some salted crackers or potato chips!). I had a craving for a lunch with high protein, so I went home and fried two eggs in olive oil and ate them with bread, butter and Port Salut cheese—delicious. I also got the French coffee press and the Café du Monde out of the air freight and made the best coffee I've had since I got here.

The Restaurant Scene

There were actually some pretty good (if expensive) French restaurants in N'Djamena, for the most part operated by French expats for French expats. There was one pretty bad, but less expensive, Chinese restaurant popular with Americans in the embassy. But the best food in town was to be had at a hole-in-the-wall restaurant run by a Senegalese lady whom everyone knew by the name of Mom Djara. Her *chepujen* (sometimes spelled *ceebujen* or, in French *thiéboudienne*—a dish of roasted fish, eggplant, squash, and chili peppers) was so good that ambassadors and ministers came to sit around crude tables with rickety benches and get their shoes muddy just for the gastronomic experience. Everybody eats from a large platter in the middle of the table, accompanied by sweet orange, red, or green Fanta to blunt the power of the chilis (alcoholic beverages are not served). Indeed, Mom Djara's *chepujen* was better than any we found in Senegal itself during a later visit to that country, perhaps because of the sweet and delicate Chadian fish, known as *capitaine*, found in the Chari River.

One night several people from the embassy, along with about twenty-five local missionaries, arranged to have a special performance of the Chadian Etoile Ballet at the Caravelle Restaurant (so called because they have a wrecked Air Afrique Caravelle airplane in the courtyard for kids to play in). The ballet was probably pretty good, but with only one fluorescent light tube we couldn't see much of their costumes or their movements, and certainly not their faces. The music, however, was quite enjoyable, basically because of the origins it shares with American jazz.

The darkness reminded me of a dinner I had hosted shortly after my arrival for media types—directors of Chad National TV and National Radio and editors of half a dozen newspapers—at the Auberge la Metropole, back a deep-rutted road in a low mud-walled building. It was dark inside, lit only by dim blue and red lamps. I asked where the lights were and they said bright lights would attract insects—a very persuasive argument here, where insects thrive—so I couldn't see the faces of the guests, or hear them either for that matter, as a TV mounted in a corner of the bar was showing a soccer game. I asked them to turn it down at least for my welcoming speech in French, but most of my guests were watching the soccer game anyway. I thought the evening was a total disaster, but my staff thought it was perfectly all right, and that everyone had enjoyed the food (and pretty good Chadian beer). I later learned that one member of my staff was related to the owner of the restaurant; needless to say, I never used that particular venue again.

Chadian Politics

Chad is perhaps the poorest and most desolate country I have ever seen. I have lived and worked in such poor countries as Laos, Burma, and Cambodia, but those countries, with their lush tropical vegetation and bamboo houses, somehow don't seem as desolate as the arid drought-stricken countries of sub-Saharan Africa, where villages consist of mud huts, straggly herds of goats and cattle trying to find forage, while desertification marches inexorably southward and encroaches on former agricultural lands. Chad has been in a state of almost constant war since achieving its independence from France in 1960. In addition to poverty and corruption, Chad, like the other sub-Saharan countries of Sudan, Niger, Mali, and Mauritania, suffers from the schism between the predominantly Muslim, Arabic, pastoral nomads of the northern deserts and the predominantly Christian, black African farmers of the agricultural south. During the colonial period, the French generally favored the Christian south and groomed southern Christians as national leaders. But since independence in the early sixties, in most of these countries the northern Arab Muslims have increasingly dominated politically and economically at the expense of the black Christian south.

The political situation when I arrived in Chad was fairly quiet (except for a rebel guerrilla group in the Tibesti Mountains in the north) but was considered rather "fluid" (translation: anything can happen). While President Idriss Déby was saying all the right things about democracy, human rights, open markets, and social programs, the cynical view was that his government was no more interested in the welfare of the people than any previous government and was dedicated to enriching his cronies and the members of his own ethnic group. Someone said it is rather a testimony to his skill that he has stayed in power so long (since 1990), as he has had to balance the interests of the various tribal and ethnic groups that put him in power.

Meanwhile the great hope for Chad was the anticipated exploitation of major oil reserves in the south of the country by an international consortium of companies led by Esso and Shell and the French conglomerate Elf/Total/Fina. The World Bank was debating whether to endorse the deal, which would involve building a pipeline across Cameroon to a seaport at Douala (since Chad is landlocked), and various environmental groups were opposing the venture. Basically we supported it since it was the only obvious way to bring some development and benefit to the six million inhabitants of one of the poorest countries in the world—but there was considerable skepticism as to whether the revenues would ever trickle down to the people. As one Chadian put it, sugar was cheap until the government started producing it through a sugar monopoly, so by that reasoning the exploitation of the estimated $20 billion in oil reserves would simply cause the price of gasoline to go up for the ordinary citizen. And it cannot be denied that wherever oil has been found in Africa, it is an unmitigated disaster for the people— Nigeria would be Exhibit A.

The most pessimistic predictions turned out to be true. At one point, just as the deal seemed about to go through, and Déby could already taste the proceeds, the French consortium decided to back out of the deal. Déby was so angry with the French that he declared the French ambassador *persona non grata* and organized demonstrations against the French community. As the demonstrators marched through my section of town, beating on tin pans and throwing rocks into foreign compounds, I opened the gate to my compound a crack to see what was going on. Just at that moment a brick came hurtling through the opening in the gate, just missing my head but hitting my gardener in the leg; he had to be taken to the hospital to treat the wound. The Chadian demonstrators couldn't distinguish French from Americans or any other Westerners; we all looked alike to them!

Another oil company replaced the French, and the World Bank eventually endorsed the deal when Déby pledged that he would spend the first $25 million in revenues from the oil pipeline on health, education, and welfare. When the ambassador, persuaded by the World Bank representative, announced in a country team meeting his satisfaction with Déby's pledge, the young political officer, who had been in Chad for several years and was simultaneously political, economic, trade, and consular officer, said, "Boy, Mr. Ambassador, you're really naïve."

This was an incredibly brazen thing to say to an ambassador, and a more vindictive ambassador would surely have reprimanded her, but she was right; as she predicted, Déby spent the money on military weapons to maintain himself in power. The World Bank later withdrew its support for the pipeline out of frustration with Déby's obvious misuse of the proceeds, but the project has continued and is now in operation, without perceptible benefit to the people.

Chad has been mired in civil wars for thirty years, as one tribal chieftain after another unseated the one in power, along with a history of hostility between Chad and Sudan. In 1990 Déby himself, after mustering the forces of his Zaghawa tribe inside Sudan, roared across the desert and overthrew the French-supported President Hissène Habré; Déby later fought off periodic invasions by rebel forces based in Sudan, most recently in January of 2008, when a rebel force briefly occupied the capital before Déby, with French help, was able to push them back. The situation was so bad that the American embassy had to close down and evacuate its personnel to neighboring countries.

A Culture of Dependency

Over a hundred languages are spoken in Chad, but the official languages are French and classical Arabic. This is rather strange given that the majority language of the country is Chadian Arabic. There have been attempts to make Chadian Arabic the official language, but it has been resisted by—surprise—the Muslim scholars, on the grounds that it is a degenerate form of classical Arabic. This is equivalent to saying that French shouldn't be the official language of France because it is a degenerate form of Latin. Nevertheless, educated Chadians speak excellent French, and they love to use the language for intellectual, if sometimes vacuous, discussion and debate. This makes Chad a receptive place for USIS-sponsored speakers and seminars on U.S. policy toward Africa, economic development, and democratic institutions.

These seminars frequently revealed the culture of dependency on Western donors and an attitude of "it's not our fault ... we were screwed up by colonialism ... you have to help us ... forgive us our debts ... give us money ... give us ... give." One particularly outspoken Chadian participant at a seminar put it bluntly, "We don't need your ideas; we have plenty of ideas; we need things; we need money." He claimed that the West is imposing its ideas on them—ideas that are not native or original to Africa—such things as democracy, free trade, freedom of the press, transparency, human rights, and so on. He further claimed that civil rights don't make any sense in the African context; the African tradition is to solve problems by consensus.

At this point, although I was supposed to be a neutral facilitator of the discussion, I couldn't resist saying, "But if that is the case, why are there currently some fourteen different interethnic wars and tribal rebellions going on in Africa, killing millions of people since independence?"

Most African countries gained their independence from France, England, Portugal, and other European empires at least forty years ago, and nobody has come up with a uniquely African solution. It seems to me that at some point over the past forty years some bright African would have said, "Wait a minute, this isn't working. Let's set up an African alternative." Libya's President Muammar Qaddafi did try to do that, but his attempts to use his ill-gotten gains to purchase the leadership of a Pan-African campaign for a United States of Africa was rejected by his neighbors. (Qaddafi's current brutal massacre of his own people in an attempt to save his regime after forty years in power is unresolved as of this writing.)

Musical Diversions

One of our more amusing programs, on the cultural side, was the USIA-sponsored visit of a classical pianist named Roman Rudnytsky. A former child prodigy from a prominent Ukrainian musical family in New York, Rudnytsky apparently used his considerable talent as a means to satisfy his love of traveling to remote and exotic places—following his program in Chad, he was scheduled to tour Guinea (Conakry), Mali, Burkina Faso, and Togo. Finding good pianos in Africa is a challenge, and there appeared to be no satisfactory piano in all of Chad. The ambassador had inherited a baby grand that was so out of tune that it just would not do, and Chad had no piano tuners. The French told me of a circuit-riding piano tuner who used to come out from France every year and tune people's pianos in former French colonies—Chad, Mali, Central African Republic, Niger, Senegal, Guinea, Cameroon, Côte d'Ivoire, Burkina Faso—but the man had died. However, the Filipina wife of the World Vision rep in N'Djamena had an electric Yamaha Clavinova that she generously offered to lend us in the interest of some cultural uplift in the capital. When Rudnytsky, as a professional pianist, readily agreed to perform on such an instrument, it did not

inspire confidence in his professionalism. But his two concerts—
one at the French Cultural Center and the other at the ambassador's residence —were a *tour de force*. Although his style might be
described as somewhat bombastic, his renditions of Mendelssohn,
Beethoven, Debussy, Chopin, Mozart, and Liszt were impressive,
and his encore performance of Gershwin's *Rhapsody in Blue* was
especially rousing. One could not help but be amazed that such
triumphalism could be coaxed from an electric keyboard.

We had the occasional Embassy Talent Night in the American
Club (basically the embassy cafeteria), where I was inspired, given
the modest level of available talent, to sing and perform on my bari-
tone ukulele. My toe-tapping renditions of the old classics "Five
Foot Two, Eyes of Blue" and "Cool Water" were received politely,
but with some mystification, as most of the younger crowd had
never heard of them. I was even inspired to write and perform the
following parody of the Rogers and Hart show tune "Manhattan"
(also not familiar to my audience):

Original Version	My Version
Summer journeys to Niagara,	R and R to London and to Paris
And to other places	On Air Afrique
Aggravate all our cares;	Aggravate all our cares;
We'll save our fares;	We'll save our fares;
I've a cozy flat in what is	I've a cozy flat in what is
known as old Manhattan,	known as CNPS Compound,
We'll settle down,	We'll settle down,
right here in town.	right here in town.

Refrain	
We'll have Manhattan,	We'll have 'Djamena,
The Bronx and Staten Island too,	And with the rain a storm or two.
It's lovely going through the zoo;	It's lovely sliding through the goo;
It's very fancy	It's very fancy
On old Delancey Street, you know;	On Charles de Gaulle Street, you know;
The subway charms us so,	The "Carrefour" charms us so,
When balmy breezes blow	When there's croissants to go

To and fro;
And tell me what street
Compares with Mott Street in July,
Sweet push carts gently gliding by;

The great big city's a wondrous toy
Just made for a girl and boy,
We'll turn Manhattan
Into an Isle of Joy.

And there's no snow;
And tell me what stream
Compares with th' Chari in July,
With hippopotami swimming by;

So if you're feeling a little down
Don't let it make you frown,
We'll turn 'Djamena
Into a happenin' town.

Travels with the Ambassador

The ambassador, Christopher Goldthwait, was the first member of the Foreign Agricultural Service ever to have been named an ambassador. He was way overqualified to be ambassador to Chad, as he held the rank of Career Minister (CM). He had served as General Sales Manager for the Department of Agriculture, administering some $8 billion annually in food aid and exports. But I suppose the idea of being the first FAS ambassador appealed to him. Goldthwait was a nice gentleman; his hobby was archaeology, which was perfect because Chad is rich in archaeological lore. At the same time he was writing a novel about archeological exploration, set in Chad.

During the dry season in February 2000, the ambassador invited me to accompany him on a trip up-country, which proved to be one of my most fascinating experiences in Chad. In the interest of preserving the freshness and immediacy of the event, I will reproduce here the letter I sent to my family describing the trip:

On my 66th birthday I was in quite exotic surroundings. I took a four-day road trip with the ambassador and Les McBride, our democracy and development officer, to inspect some of our humanitarian and self-help assistance projects in two prefectures some 300 kilometers north of N'Djamena.

The first was Mao, capital of the ancient Sultanate of Kanem-Bornou (ninth to nineteenth centuries). This place is really exotic—rather like Timbuktu, only better. Built on top of a sandy mound, the mud brick they use turns white in the sun, so it looks like a fortress on a hill, complete with a sultan's palace with parapets and all, although it is crumbling and of rather faded elegance. We stayed in the compound of the World Food Program (to which the U.S. is a major contributor), and were entertained to dinner the first night. Their official dinners consist of huge platters of mutton, beef, chicken, tripe and various other unidentifiable meats, with very few vegetables or salads. The ambassador complained that after four days of eating pure meat, he had enough protein for the rest of the year.

The staple dish for ordinary Chadians is a lumpy pasty mixture made from millet and called *boule* (so-called because it is shaped like a hemisphere from the bowl it is made in), on which you put a sauce made of pureed okra ("gumbo," as the French call it), and if you're lucky, also some stringy meat sauce—not a gastronomic treat. About six times a day you find yourself sitting around on a carpet trying to find something to say to the *préfet* (prefect), *maire* (mayor), *sous-préfet*, or sultan and drinking strong sweet tea, or worse, soft drinks (how I longed for a diet Coke). On our arrival at the palace, the sultan greeted us with horsemen on prancing horses, swordsmen on brightly caparisoned camels, bugle blowers and drummers—quite an impressive reception. When we drove into the palace compound, I thought it a real waste not to be able to film it, so when we were sitting down on the Arabian carpets in front of the sultan (in flowing robes) to drink yet more tea, I whispered to the ambassador that I had forgotten the book we were to present to the sultan, so I went out, bypassed the car with the book for the moment, and went back out of the gates with my video camera. Dressed in my suit, the horsemen and the others thought I was the ambassador and put on a wild performance, clashing swords, blowing bugles, and prancing their horses, while children danced and shouted all around me—really rare video footage.

The culture of dependency was evident wherever we went. We delivered several hundred books to the *lycée*, where the *proviseur* pulled out a prepared speech asking for U.S. assistance to fix the roof on his school. We visited the museum, where they asked for aid to build an addition. We were taken out to a site where the town is being cut in two by huge ravines caused by erosion; the mayor read a prepared statement asking for U.S. help to stop the erosion and prevent the houses from falling into the ravine. The sultan even asked for help to renovate his crumbling palace (despite the expensive carpets throughout the building). We visited three U.S. embassy-supported self-help projects—a reforestation project (to address the creeping desertification endemic in all of sub-Saharan Africa), a project to build a masonry abattoir to improve the city's sanitation, and a clinic for undernourished children run by *Action Contre la Faim* in collaboration with the World Food Program.

The second day (on my birthday) we had one of those sandstorms called *harmattan*, with wind howling and sand swirling into our eyes, mouths, and noses, gritting between our teeth. You have to clean your glasses every five minutes. At night I had to wipe the dust off my watch to see what time it was. Visibility was severely limited. I could appreciate why the nomads of the desert wear those white turbans around their heads covering everything except their eyes (and the more fashionable ones have dark glasses to complete the attire).

After two nights in Mao, we went on to Bol, capital of the Prefecture of Lac-Tchad (Lake Chad, a really big lake that borders Chad, Niger, Nigeria, and Cameroon, but which is shrinking due to desertification). On the way we stopped at a smaller lake that the sultan wanted us to see in order to ask for assistance to stock it with fish. He said there were carp in it, but they don't get big because there is not enough nourishment in the lake. We pointed out that stocking a lake with fish is pointless if there is not enough nourishment. The roads were atrocious; you have to wear your seatbelt to keep from bashing your head against the roof of the car—in our case, one of the embassy's Toyota Land Cruisers (the vehicle of choice in Chad for those who can afford one, such as government officials, embassies, and NGOs). Bol is relatively prosperous because they raise crops—corn, wheat, sorghum, millet, onions, etc.—in the "polders" or reclaimed arms of Lake Chad. They have quite an impressive agricultural station there of about 2,500 acres, but the roads are so bad they can't get their crops to market. It took us five hours to go 150 kilometers on leaving Bol. The road was built by the Italians only fifteen years ago but has entirely fallen apart; the ambassador commented that he'd seen roads in Italy just as bad! In Bol they took us to see four projects in rapid succession for which they wanted aid—a water tower built 10 years ago by the Italians which had rusted and was leaking and the water was not potable; the museum whose roof had collapsed; the weekly market, which needed a tin roof; and finally a slaughterhouse that needed running water. Later in the evening they took us on a boat excursion on the lake, then took us to see a rare species of cow called "Kouri" which are unique to the region around Lake Chad—they have horns each of which is about 8–10 inches in diameter at the base, and they use these horns as flotation devices while swimming in the lake—really impressive horns!

Finally, we stopped at the weekly stock market in the subprefecture of Massakoury, where they had massive pens of camels, cattle, horses, donkeys, sheep, and goats for sale—makes for great photography. All in all, it was an exhausting but fascinating trip. Fortunately both the ambassador and Les McBride are intelligent and sensitive companions for a four-day road trip. McBride is the only embassy employee who remains from the former USAID operation in Chad that left in 1995, ostensibly for security reasons but really because the Cold War is over and we basically don't care anymore. Les has been in Chad since he was a Peace Corps volunteer twenty-five years ago, married a Chadian woman and has about five kids, speaks fluent French (if with an atrocious accent), some Chadian Arabic, and several other of the 100-some languages spoken in Chad.

Well, that's probably more than you wanted to know about Chad, so I'll close and go home. Cheers, Dad.

One interesting thing I learned on the trip was how to drive in the desert. I have always been pretty smug about my skill in driving in mud or snow; where you put the car in the highest gear that will pull it so as to retain traction. This strategy does not work at all in the desert. There, the worst thing that can happen is to stall the motor, especially if you're climbing a sand dune. You therefore have to put it in jack low to avoid stalling, then jerk the steering wheel violently from left to right to maintain traction against the sides of the ruts; otherwise the wheels will simply dig holes in the sand while the vehicle sinks to the point of hanging up on the sand in the middle of the frame. In these conditions, four-wheel drive is highly recommended, if not mandatory.

At War with My Own Embassy

The consolidation of USIA with State was to take place on October 1, 1999, one month after my arrival at post. I had already had an unpleasant experience with that in New Zealand, but I wanted to see sub-Saharan Africa, and I told myself cynically, "What the hell; I'll do whatever they tell me."

Well, I found out that didn't work. You still have to feel that you are doing something useful. Chad is the poorest country I've ever seen in my life, but it was still interesting and exotic. The problem was not Chad; my problems were with my own embassy. On October 1 my status changed from director of USIS to head of the public affairs section of the embassy. I was no longer the head of an agency at post. I was under the thumb of various layers of bureaucracy that I wasn't accustomed to, and my staff were all unhappy. They claimed that the previous PAO promised this and that and fought for them, but she had left the problems for me to resolve. It was quite traumatic, actually—as the head of an agency in previous assignments I had had my own budget, I had had my own cars and drivers and my own computer specialists and so on, and suddenly my status had been revised downward and my autonomy shackled.

There was a brash young admin officer who took great pleasure, I think, in telling me at one point that I no longer had "procurement authority," which is bureaucratese for "you can't buy anything." I couldn't go out and buy a pencil. He had to do it for me; I had to put in a requisition for it, which he might or might not approve. The best example of this situation was when the Fourth of July came along. USIS would traditionally take the pictures for official events, and we would have established relationships with shops where we could get pictures developed in two hours and have them back. But I wasn't allowed to do that under the new regime, so I said to the admin officer, "Okay, how am I going to get these pictures?"

He said, "Well here's what you do. You fill out a requisition and send that to me and then I'll send that to GSO (general services office) and then GSO (which was not co-located with the embassy) will assign somebody to come back to the embassy and pick up that film and then they will take it to a shop with which we have negotiated a vendor agreement and then in three days, when they notify us they are done, GSO will send someone to pick them up and deliver them to me. At that point I will call you and you can come get them."

I went to the ambassador and said, "Mr. Ambassador, you know those pictures you wanted from the Fourth of July celebration? I'm not going to be able to get those to you for about three days."

He said, "Oh? Why is that?"

I was prepared. I said, "Here, Mr. Ambassador, is a list of the fourteen steps I'm required to go through to get this film developed."

"Well, this is just unacceptable," he said. "Get me the admin officer in here." Well, we got the admin officer in and he cited multiple regulations from the Foreign Affairs Manual, such as FAM 632, section 3, subparagraph 6, which specifies thus and so, and as a result of State cables 21376 and 42723 dealing with the consolidation, we have to jump through this hoop and that, and he snowed the ambassador, who didn't understand that he had the authority to cut through such nonsense.

Another example, at the risk of belaboring the point: When they made the changeover, we were no longer to use the acronym USIS on our letterheads; we were supposed to use something like "Public Affairs Section." Well, the USIS office had reams and reams of stationery with the USIS letterhead on it; I told my staff to just go ahead and use it up, and we would put the new designation on the next order. I based this decision on the obvious fact that even if our Chadian audience knew anything about the consolidation, the change in terminology would be meaningless to them. My mistake was to mention to the DCM what I had done; he was horrified, and said I should have solicited guidance from the department before making such a crucial decision. This ludicrous advice was typical of my dealings with the embassy, and I found the whole thing just extremely frustrating.

Another problem that I had was that I was taking Mefloquine for malaria. State Med was continuing to recommend the drug, even though a lot of people had had unfortunate reactions to it ("We have no reliable clinical evidence to support…" etc.). It affects some people very badly, you become paranoid, you have nightmares, and you can't sleep. I began to have emotions that I'd never had before in my life. I was extremely irascible, I'd get angry, I would throw furniture, had anxiety attacks and depression—all the classic symptoms of culture shock. But I had never had culture shock in any other third-world countries, such as Laos and Burma and Cambodia, so why now? I wondered if it was just the frustrations of dealing with the State Department. And finally I realized no, this is not me, there's something wrong.

And so when the medical officer came to post he said, "Look, we're going to take you off Mefloquine and put you on Doxycycline, which doesn't cause these reactions, but you'll have to take one every day instead of once a week."

When I got off Mefloquine my outlook improved considerably.

A Comedy of Errors

I had such a series of disasters in Chad it was almost comical. First of all, they didn't have a house ready for me, so I spent my first several weeks in the rather shoddy Chari Hotel, so named because it had a view over the Chari River that divided Chad from Cameroon. True, I could have gone into my predecessor's house, which was a huge thing, because a PAO has representational duties. But I didn't particularly like the house, whose large dark living room and low ceiling reminded me of a church social hall. Besides, a family with two children was coming and could make much better use of the house, which was in the housing compound with the school. They said, "Well, we'll put you in GSO house no. 36 until we get another house ready." So I moved into no. 36, which they were going to relinquish because it was too old and ratty and too hard to maintain. I didn't care much because I was to be there for only a year, and the house didn't seem to be much worse than the other choices in the housing pool.

After several months, my official house was ready—a nice airy house with high ceilings and an abandoned swimming pool. I had been in it about six weeks when a fire burned out the interior, including my books and pictures and personal effects. It was determined that a short in an air-conditioner had caused the fire.

So I moved back into the Chari Hotel. Finally they said, "Well, we think we'll try to renovate #36 after all, but it will take several months. In the meantime we'll put you in a TDY apartment." So I moved into a TDY apartment in the housing compound that included about ten embassy houses. Shortly thereafter I went over to Bamako in Mali to help out with the visit of Secretary of State Madeleine Albright to several African countries. When I got back to post they said, "We have bad news: there was a fire in your office." So both my house and my office had caught fire.

Another disaster: not knowing I was going to go to Chad, I had just bought a new Honda Accord. The post report said you should take a four-wheel-drive vehicle to Chad. And I thought well, it'd be nice but I don't have a four-wheel-drive vehicle, I have this car; it's the only car I have so I'll take it. Big mistake. When I got there I realized that they didn't mean that you "should" have a four-wheel drive, they meant you "must" have one. You couldn't get to the office without a four-wheel drive, because when it rained the streets became a slough of mud that you could disappear into. So it was the wrong vehicle to have in Chad.

One day, as I was leaving the housing compound, the guard opened the left side of the double gates, then went around to open the right one. Just as I started to go through, the left gate swung shut on my car and before I could stop it had torn off the sideview mirror. Seeing that, the guard left the right gate to run around to the left, and the right gate blew shut against the right side of the car. New car. When I shipped the car home I waited and waited for it to come and finally I got a call from our dispatcher in Baltimore, saying, "Mr. Huffman, I'm afraid there's been considerable damage to your car."

Well, it turned out that the train car in which it was shipped had derailed in Cameroon, and the car had bounced around inside the container. It cost $8,000 to restore it, which my private insurance paid, minus a $250 deductible. But even though it was restored to new condition, the fact that it had been wrecked caused it to lose $4,000 more in market value. Now, the State Department will pay you the deductible on your private car insurance, which was $250. I said you really need to pay me $4,250. I made no progress there at all. I don't think they ever even paid the $250. So the whole thing was a comedy of errors.

Across Cameroon by Caravan

But there was one adventure I had in Chad that made the whole posting worthwhile. We had ordered seven new Toyota Land Cruisers from the Toyota dealer in Douala, Cameroon, for donation to the Chadian de-mining operation, which our military was supporting. They were to come into Douala and come up by train to the railhead at Ngaoundere in northern Cameroon and then be driven across the border to N'Djamena, Chad. But the train tracks had been blown up and some trains had derailed, so the embassy decided we'd just send seven or eight drivers down to Douala and drive the trucks all the way across Cameroon to Chad. I volunteered immediately. They wanted volunteers from FSNs in admin and GSO and didn't expect senior American officers to volunteer; but I have always loved driving adventures. I had ridden a motorcycle and other conveyances overland from Laos to Europe in 1958; driven from New Haven to Guatemala City in 1970; and five years ago my brother and I had driven from D.C. to San Jose, Costa Rica. So I jumped at the chance to drive all the way across Cameroon. And it was a fascinating experience to see the condition of the country and of the roads. Since we had neglected to get diplomatic plates, we were stopped at innumerable roadblocks and shaken down for money, maybe twenty times in the course of five days getting across the country.

It was fortunate that I was along, because the GSO in charge of the expedition didn't speak French, and I had to negotiate with the police. Sometimes we'd get hauled back to the nearest police station, but usually we would get out our diplomatic passports and point out that we were diplomats and the cars were for donation to the Chadian government. We only paid bribes at two or three places where our passports didn't impress them. In the course of the trip one of the trucks slid off the muddy road and rolled over; the driver was okay, but we had to tow the truck back to the nearest town to get it back in drivable condition, although with the windshield broken out.

The GSO, a former Marine sergeant rather impatient with diplomatic niceties, later said, "Frank, if you hadn't been along to smooth the way, we'd still be in a Cameroonian jail somewhere." It was revealing to experience, for the first time really, what it is like in these corrupt countries for ordinary citizens who have no diplomatic privileges.

Keeper of the Royal Stool

My trip to Mali to assist with the visit of Secretary of State Madeline Albright was fascinating. I volunteered to go because I was interested in seeing as much of Africa as I could, but Air Afrique, while nominally under the tutelage of Air France, is so unreliable that it is almost impossible to fly from one African capital to another without going through Paris. I had to get to Bamako (the capital of Mali) via Paris and Nouakchott in Mauritania. The secretary was scheduled to visit Timbuktu, which I had always wanted to see, but the trip to Timbuktu was canceled at the last minute because of the death of Julius Nyerere, former president of Tanzania, and it was decided that she should attend his funeral.

By one of those coincidences common in the Foreign Service, the DCM in Bamako was Bob Porter, who had been my DCM in Phnom Penh, and he invited me to stay in his rather palatial residence. The patio leading to his swimming pool was adorned with a Cambodian cyclo (a three-wheeled pedicab) that he had brought with him from Phnom Penh.

Secretary Albright is an extremely short lady, so she needs to stand on a riser so she can see over the podium. One of my duties during the visit was to make sure the stool was in place at each venue where she was to make remarks to the press; I dubbed myself "Keeper of the Royal Stool."

I had a bit of a run-in with the Bamako PAO, who was in charge of the press center at the Grand Hotel. When I finished my duties at the end of the final day of the secretary's visit, I dismissed my car and driver, as I wanted to walk back to the press center in order to see a bit of the city. The PAO was highly incensed that I had assumed the authority to dismiss my car (one of twenty or so at his disposal) rather than sending the driver back to him at the press center. I could understand the appeal, especially to a younger officer, of being in charge of the "command and control" center for a high-level visit, but I was never able to muster the required gravitas for such occasions. While in charge of the press center for President Clinton's brief visit to Bangkok several years earlier, I had never found it necessary to shout at any of the twenty-one officers and FSNs under my command. Just not a born leader.

Problems with Security

A highlight of my tour in Chad was the ability to go over to the Waza Game Preserve in northern Cameroon, just an hour away from N'Djamena, where you could see lions, giraffes, elephants, wild boar, and other wildlife. The first time I saw a family of giraffes stalking across the road in front of our land cruiser—not in a zoo—was a great thrill for me. And I played a lot of tennis, which was good for my mental health. We had a clay court—or rather a mud court, as it got a bit slippery in the rainy season—behind the Embassy, and I even got the ambassador and the DCM to take up tennis again to supplement my matches with various Chadian contacts. I partnered with the French ambassador in a tournament at the French club, where we lost in the second round. The first time I invited the French ambassador to play on our rather pitiful embassy court, he came to the embassy gate at the appointed time and was held up by the security guards. I got an urgent call from the security office enquiring about the situation, and by the time I got to the gate, the French ambassador was furious. "You need to change your silly procedures! Don't they know who I am?" he thundered.

I apologized profusely and let him win the match to mollify him. But he was right. We had a rule that whenever we were to be visited by a Chadian or other contact, we had to send a memo to the regional security officer twenty-four hours in advance requesting access. Not realizing that my very efficient secretary had been sending the required memos for all official visitors, I had neglected to mention to her that I was planning to play tennis with the French ambassador.

I had a number of run-ins with the RSO, or regional security officer (I don't know why they are called "regional," since so far as I could determine, their duties were typically limited to one embassy). Once when I had finished a tennis match on the embassy court, I found that the gate between the court and the compound was locked. I was locked in the tennis court. Swallowing my embarrassment at being locked out of my own embassy in front of my Chadian visitor, I yelled at the top of my lungs until a guard finally came and unlocked the gate. On another occasion, I found myself locked out of my own conference room. The USIS library and conference room, which to be effective had to be open to the public, was closed off from the higher-security embassy compound by a door controlled by a cipher lock. It was my custom to work in my office until the audience had arrived for an event, then leave my office just in time to proceed to the conference room to introduce the speaker or film or whatever the program was to be. On one occasion, when I got to the door to the conference room, it was locked with a padlock. Furious, I yelled for a guard to come and open the door.

"Why the hell is that door locked?" I demanded.

"The RSO, he say must lock with padlock when have program," replied the guard.

"I don't give a damn what the RSO said. Unlock it now, and don't ever do that again!"

When I cooled down, I realized that the guard was only following orders, no matter how stupid. So I confronted the RSO and pointed out that since the door was already controlled by a cipher lock, members of the public could not access the embassy compound. I'm afraid I also made some rather strong statements about the arrogance of locking me out of my own conference room without letting me know he had done so. But it is impossible to win an argument with security types. Their inevitable comeback is "What if..." To them success is measured in how many rules they have been able to impose, rather than on whether those rules are reasonable or necessary. This has long been an area of contention between USIS, whose success depends on public access, and the embassy security officers, whose objective is to limit—or ideally, prohibit—public access. When the ambassador inquired about my ruckus with the RSO, I advised him, "Look, Mr. Ambassador, you can't let the security types have their head. Otherwise they'll shut us down completely."

Foreign Service Kids

When I took the job in Chad, it was decided that my wife Sanda would stay behind in the apartment in Falls Church so our daughter Samantha could attend George Mason High School. But Sanda was a bit miffed at this decision, as she would have much preferred going along to Africa to accepting full responsibility for Samantha as she transitioned from the Foreign Service to an American high school.

Foreign Service kids often have great difficulty adapting to life in the United States after many years abroad, as they tend to have lost touch with the social fads and technological preoccupations of their U.S. peers, who exclude them from their long-standing cliques and have little interest in their foreign adventures. Foreign Services kids in the D.C. area had formed a support group called AWAL (Around the World in a Lifetime) to help them deal with the transition. Samantha joined the group and attended some of their meetings, but if truth be told I don't think she has ever made the transition to U.S. society. Most of her friends in high school tended to be foreigners—Indians, Cambodians, Chinese or Russians—with whom she felt a closer kinship than with the U.S. students. She opted to attend McGill University in Montreal because of its location in a bilingual city and majored in international development. She later served an internship with Project Hope in Almaty, Kazakhstan, during the summer break from her Master of Public Health program at Emory University in Atlanta.

Children react to the Foreign Service experience in unpredictable ways. Our son Christopher found it mildly interesting, but I think he felt a bit resentful at having been denied a normal American childhood. In any case, after seven years abroad (in London, Rangoon, Marrakech, and Paris), he returned to the United States, took a five-year professional degree in architecture from Pratt Institute in Brooklyn, and has apparently never felt any inclination to live or work abroad. Samantha, by contrast, after spending essentially her entire school career abroad, is totally fascinated by foreign languages and cultures, and is currently working for The Global Fund for AIDS, Malaria, and Tuberculosis in Geneva, Switzerland.

West African Safaris

Sanda and Samantha came to Chad for the Christmas–New Year holidays, four months after my arrival in the country. It was a festive season, with dinners in the homes of various embassy colleagues. My wife and I even undertook to cook a traditional Christmas dinner on Christmas Eve, with the ambassador, the DCM and family, the UNESCO representative, and the director of the USIS English Language Center as guests. I borrowed a cook named Pierre who had the reputation of knowing how to cook Western food, but his "candied yams," flavored with garlic and onions, were rather strange. Otherwise the turkey dinner was a great success.

During their visit, I took them to the Waza game preserve across the border in Cameroon, a trip organized by the CLO (community liaison office, usually headed by the spouse of an embassy officer). One day I undertook to take them to the traditional pottery-making village and museum of Gaoui, some ten or fifteen miles across the desert from N'Djamena. I had been there before with an embassy driver and thought I could easily find it again, but I quickly got lost among the random tracks in the featureless desert but finally made it with the help of a camel driver, who indicated the correct direction with a vague wave of his hand, thus sparing myself terminal embarrassment.

On the following day, the CLO had organized a trip for embassy personnel to Elephant Rock, a massive limestone formation that vaguely resembled an elephant's head. Finally, on New Year's Eve, we organized a hippopotamus-spotting trip in a small boat on the Chari River. The CIA station chief had brought along a couple of bottles of French champagne for the occasion. After much effort we spotted two pods of hippos, their heads and eyes barely breaking the surface of the water, and considered the outing quite successful. (Little did we know that later on in the dry season, when the river was low, you could see entire families of hippos strolling along the banks of the Chari in full view; sometimes they would come into town, and there were stories that they would occasionally attack and kill town residents. I read somewhere that more people are killed by hippos than by any other wild animal.)

That evening we all went to the New Year's Eve party at the Marine House, where Samantha was very much in demand as a dancing partner by the seven or eight homesick Marines (to avoid a more pointed adjective). As a result of all these activities in a compressed period of time, Sanda and Samantha were enchanted with N'Djamena, and declared Chad a fascinating place. What they didn't understand, however, was that during their ten-day visit we had covered all four of the major amusements of N'Djamena.

Fortunately for me, they were sufficiently impressed by their first visit that they decided to return to N'Djamena in July and stay until my scheduled departure in August. Samantha was interested in doing some volunteer work during her visit, so I had arranged for her to work in a French-run orphanage named Béthanie, about nine miles outside of N'Djamena. She got on their bus every morning at 7:45 and returned in the afternoon. The orphanage had some sixty-five children ages newborn to seven, and Samantha helped to feed them, devised games for them, and taught them drawing and the alphabet. Once when we visited her at the orphanage, it was obvious the children loved her and she them: she had one kid in her arms and one on her shoulders, while two others tugged at her free hand. The French directors, a M. et Mme. Burkhardt, invited us to lunch with the staff, where we were served the traditional Chadian *boule*, but in our honor, they served a kind of chicken sauce with the millet instead of okra, rendering it somewhat more edible. As a seventeen-year-old, Samantha found her experience with the orphans fulfilling, but she was heartbroken when several of them inevitably died from malnourishment and disease.

On our trip home from Chad we visited several countries of West Africa along with Christopher, who flew from New York and met us in Abidjan, Côte d'Ivoire. After exploring Abidjan (which was in the early stages of the unrest that eventually resulted in a coup), we went up to the new capital in former president Houphouet-Boigny's home village of Yamoussoukro, which boasts a stunning Catholic cathedral that is second only to St. Peter's in Rome in size. From Abidjan we hired a car and drove along the coast to Accra, Ghana, visiting the castles along the coast that had played a large role in the African slave trade. From Accra we flew to Dakar, Senegal, and visited the Ile de Gorée and its slave house museum. The trip was a mixed blessing for Christopher, who was suffering from both mild culture shock and separation from his fiancée, but Samantha, typically, reveled in the exoticism of the whole scene.

Chad in Retrospect

Throughout my adventures and misadventures in Chad, my wife kept asking me if I thought the whole thing had been worth the effort, given the family separation and the almost comical series of problems I had suffered. On balance, I feel that the experience was positive. It enabled me to understand the problems of Africa in a way that I could never have done had I not spent a year there. Chad has all of the problems common to most countries of sub-Saharan Africa—poverty, corruption, disease, and the tension between the nomadic Arab Muslim herdsmen of the north and the black Christian farmers of the south.

The more serious problem is that most of the national leaders are more concerned with lining their own pockets and those of their immediate tribe than with the welfare of their country as a whole, which in any case is usually an unnatural construct carved out by the Europeans. President Idriss Déby is no exception—he overthrew the French-supported President Habré in a coup in 1990 and is using the revenues from the country's recently exploited oil resources to maintain himself and his Zaghawa tribe in power rather than to relieve the desperate poverty of his people.

Cambodian Postscript

Return to Phnom Penh

When I returned to the United States from Chad in August of 2000, we decided to finally move into our house in the Palisades section of northwest Washington, even though Samantha would have to commute to George Mason High School some six miles away and we would have to pay tuition as nonresidents of the city of Falls Church. The house had been rented out since our departure for Paris in January 1995 to a series of tenants that included the sister and brother-in-law of Queen Noor of Jordan and the U.S. bureau chief for France Inter, the French international radio network. We had fairly good luck with our tenants, except for the agent's unfortunate decision at one point to rent to a group of American University students, who trashed the house and whose parents had to put up $10,000 to repair the damage.

Our decision to reoccupy the house was motivated partly by the return of the France Inter rep to France and partly so Sanda would be nearer her work with the Department of State. The Frenchman had been a heavy smoker and the house reeked of stale smoke, but his wife had been a meticulous housekeeper and left the house in relatively good shape. We had all the wall-to-wall carpets removed and refinished the beautiful red oak floors that had been hidden beneath them, thus getting rid of some of the tobacco smell.

Once we got settled, I decided that, as I appeared to be fully retired, I would set to work on writing a book that had been germinating in my head for forty years—about my two years as a volunteer in Laos in 1956–58 and my trip across Asia, the Middle East, and Europe by motorcycle and other land conveyances in 1958

(*Monks and Motorcycles: From Laos to London by the Seat of my Pants*, 1956–1958, published in 2004). But the hardest part of writing a book, or anything for that matter, is getting started. Once I got into it, after a year I had written about half the book and was on a roll, when I got a call from the State Department asking if I would be willing to go to Phnom Penh for six months—February to August 2002—as public affairs officer. The previous PAO had curtailed for medical reasons several months earlier, and they needed somebody to fill the gap while the PAO-designee finished Khmer language training. My separation from State on my return from Chad in 2000 had been so painful (requiring a full eight months of badgering the Offices of Personnel Management, Payroll, and Retirement to deal with my case), that I swore I would never again become enmeshed in the bureaucratic morass of the State Department. But that was eighteen months earlier, and the memory dulls. Besides, my wife and daughter both had fond memories of Cambodia and were intrigued by the prospect of visiting the country again. So I decided to go for it. As I had already served in Phnom Penh and knew the language, I was the logical person to send. That I was well known in Khmer academic circles also worked to my advantage.

The Good, the Bad and the Ugly

The second time around, I found the situation in the country to be both better and worse. Prime Minister Hun Sen had consolidated his power over the country, and security was much better than it had been in the nineties. The Khmer Rouge movement had totally collapsed, partially as a result of Hun Sen's offer of amnesty, through which several thousand Khmer Rouge troops had defected to the government side and several high-ranking officials had been given monetary inducements to defect. Pol Pot himself had died in isolation in the mountains in 1997; some people think maybe his own people turned against him, but it's not terribly clear. You could travel freely throughout the country, with the result that tourism had increased, especially to Angkor, and the more remote provinces had been opened to tourism.

On the other hand, democracy and human rights were in retreat, as Hun Sen had cowed the opposition through intimidation and threats of violence, local human rights organizations were weakened, and the press had become more restrained. Foreign investment from Western sources had essentially dried up, replaced by those countries and businesses willing to pay kickbacks to corrupt officials. Companies from China, Malaysia, South Korea, and Thailand accounted for the majority of investment in the country. Corruption was rampant, with government officials, especially military officers, claiming land traditionally owned by the peasants for their own purposes, and engaging in illegal logging and smuggling. Extravagant mansions and expensive cars had multiplied in Phnom Penh, while the countryside, as had been true for centuries, benefited very little from development.

So it was a mixed bag. All in all I felt pretty good about the tour. Knowing the country and the terrain as I did, I felt that I was at the top of my game. I managed to get the educational and cultural exchange programs in shape, recruited all the candidates for the following year's Fulbright and International Visitor programs, allocated all of our budget for grants to various human rights, educational, and civic society organizations, organized a performing arts visit by an American jazz group, dealt with the press, and gave four or five outreach speeches myself.

Mission Impossible

I was less successful, however, in completing the three main assignments I had been given in Washington. The first was to persuade Ambassador Kent Wiedemann, whom they considered a bit of a loose cannon, to clear his speeches and statements to the press with Public Affairs at State—in other words, go out there and whip the ambassador into shape. I smiled.

When I got to post, the ambassador said, "I know what they told you in Washington, but I know the situation here better than they do in Washington, and I'll say whatever I please. If they don't like it, they can fire me."

In fact, he was eventually fired, or at least called home early. He stood up for what he believed, and I admired him for it. A conservative cabal in Congress had instructed USAID to throw their support to the Sam Rainsy Party, which they were convinced was the only democratic party in the country. Sam Rainsy knew how to push the right buttons in Washington and Paris, but he was not inherently any more democratic than his opponents. Even if he had been, the ambassador argued, to support only one party constituted unwarranted interference in the country's internal affairs, and the United States should be even-handed among all the parties in supporting democracy. I believe he was right, but you can't fight city hall.

My second "mission impossible" was to reclaim space for the PAS (public affairs section, as USIS was now called) that had been usurped by the embassy. The problem was that the ambassador had requisitioned the USIS building containing the USIS library and offices for his own use while OBO was hard-walling another building for his office. The PAS offices had been shoehorned into a tight space in the admin building, and the library relegated essentially to a stairwell. I was unable to correct the situation at that time, but I did manage to secure the promise of generous space for the PAS offices, library, and auditorium in the plans for the new embassy being built, which was completed and dedicated only in early 2006. (Although I was unable to accept the invitation to attend the dedication, I later learned that they had named a conference room in my honor.)

My third mission was to improve the morale of the public affairs staff, demoralized by the confiscation of their physical space, the downgrading of the library, and the vacancy in the PAO slot. I feel that I achieved a certain measure of success in this third assignment, by involving the staff in the planning for space in the new embassy, getting stalled programs in shape, and raising the profile of our programs both within the embassy and in the Phnom Penh community. So I did complete about one and a half out of the three assignments—not bad for government work.

The Saga of the Two Heads

Shortly after my arrival in Phnom Penh in February of 2002, I became embroiled in a saga that was a perfect microcosm of the inefficiency and bureaucracy of the U.S. government. Two sculptured heads on display in the Honolulu Academy of Arts had been identified as ninth- and twelfth-century sculptures from Angkor. The proof came from pictures in a valuable little book published by the International Council of Museums called *One Hundred Missing Objects: Looting in Angkor*. The Honolulu Academy of Arts agreed to repatriate the heads to Cambodia but wanted somebody else to pay for shipping them, as they involved two rather large wooden crates. The primary issue was whether the heads could be shipped from Hawaii to Cambodia on a military aircraft (which was in any case making periodic flights to Cambodia to support the POW-MIA program of the Joint Task Force–Full Accounting, based in Hawaii) and, if so, who would pay the required $1500 and to whom.

This was a trivial sum of money, but there followed a bureaucratic dance involving three months of emails among dozens of officials from the Department of State, the Department of Defense, the U.S. Embassy, and the Honolulu Academy of Arts as to how the money could be legally transferred from the Department of State to the Department of Defense. The imbroglio even threatened to involve the secretaries of State and Defense.

An email from a brigadier general states, "We do have an aircraft taking a team to Cambodia in about a week. If we can't make that, we do have milair [military air] support for other teams later and can possibly use intertheater milair for movement."

But a later email from the office of the CINCPAC [Commander-in-Chief Pacific] explains, "It appears to me that this would fall under the 'other' category for movement on non-DOD cargo on a space 'A' basis under DODD [Department of Defense Directive] 4500.9 and would require SecDef [Secretary of Defense] approval."

As if anticipating State Department bureaucratic foot-dragging, one email from the military states, "I have kept this out of State for the time being, so as not to cloud the issue of 'who wants to do this mission?' If State becomes the driver we run the risk of not meeting the set aircraft departure time while staffing this to a higher approval level."

Once State's legal office got involved, an email to all concerned stated, "I understand that, once I have the L (Office of the Legal Advisor) green light I need to draft a memo for S/ES [Office of the Secretary of State/Executive Secretariat] to send to DOD/OSD/ISA [Department of Defense/Office of the Secretary of Defense/International Security Affairs] approving the shipment. OSD/ISA will then authorize the use of milair on a space-available basis."

A later email from a State lawyer wonders if he needs the approval of Secretary of State Powell: "It's unclear to me whether Secretary Powell himself has to make the certifications mentioned, or whether someone further down the food chain has the authority to do so for State...."

On March 1, two months into the controversy, I sent the following email to Ken Foster, my counterpart at the Department of State: "Help! This head repatriation thing is a many-headed hydra....Who wants the $1500 and why? And if JTF-FA can't pay for getting the heads here, why would they be involved in the turnover? Finally, if in fact the availability of $1500 is a deal breaker in this whole thing, I would try to come up with it one way or another."

I proposed to pay for the shipment out of my Public Diplomacy budget in the interest of international cooperation and understanding, which is after all our mandate, but this excellent idea was shot down in the following email from a State lawyer: "A review of both the Smith-Mundt Act and the Fulbright-Hays Act (which provide the justifications for PD's operations) didn't disclose any basis for spending appropriated funds for the proposed repatriation."

Later on, my proposal to pay out of PAS funds at post attracted some support at State, but an email from the Cambodia desk officer cautioned, "Before we get ahead of ourselves, there is still a bit of red tape to cut through in State. Chief issue is: Does State have authority to expend monies on such a DOD milair shipment. Because the 7th floor [reference to the office of the Secretary of State] has to cut the order for milair, it gets more attention than you'd think. EAP/BCLTV [Bureau of East Asia and the Pacific/Burma Cambodia Laos Thailand and Vietnam Desk] is working it, but it appears to be an uphill battle, with the lawyers split on the issue. Bear with us."

Three months into the imbroglio, Ambassador Wiedemann in exasperation wrote to John Holzman, the U.S. ambassador to PACOM [Pacific Command], explaining that "The matter has worked its way through the Pentagon and State bureaucracies and legal shops (at the cost of several multiples of the $1500, no doubt) to a point where it must be presented to SecState Powell in a decision memo." He continued, "I wonder if you might be able to cut through the red tape and interagency trauma in Washington by either (a) calling JTF-FA and asking them to swallow the paltry $1500;

(b) getting Adm. Blair to fund it out of any pot of money that may exist for such odds and ends; or (c) convince the museum big shots that milair at $1500 is a bargain for which they should be happy to pay."

A response from the Office of Regional and Security Policy Affairs of State's Bureau of East Asia and Pacific Affairs perpetuated the impasse: "We are working with our lawyers on this, but their views differ. I am trying to...broker the differences...."

At one point Greg Lawless, the Cambodia desk officer at State, wrote, "After an incredibly long discussion among five lawyers here lasting the entire week, we are still not sure that we have 'legal authority' to expend PD monies for the Milair shipment of the Khmer stone busts from Honolulu to Phnom Penh on March 23."

It must be said that Lawless fought a valiant fight, but in one message to State's legal department he says plaintively, "The bureaucracy is stuck on payment and efficiency, when all I wanted was a legal opinion on getting involved in repatriating art pieces."

Obviously, where he went wrong was to turn the question over to State's legal shop. I'd bet my pension that if USIA had not been incorporated into State in 1999, the whole matter would have been resolved expeditiously between USIA, their public affairs advisor to CINCPAC in Hawaii, and their public affairs officer in Phnom Penh (in this case, me). Thus the goals of public diplomacy would have been promoted, and all those lawyers at State would not have had to get their knickers in a twist over it. The entire folderol would be amusing if it weren't so painful. At one point, one of the lawyers complained, "This is heartbreaking. Really. I fear that we have gone collectively mad."

I ultimately received the two crates at Pochentong Airport and turned them over to the National Museum of Cambodia. They were formally presented to the Royal Cambodian Government in a ceremony that involved representatives from the Honolulu Academy, the Cambodian ministries of culture and tourism, the International Council of Museums, and the U.S. embassy. The whole affair was followed by a reception at the ambassador's residence. The total time and effort devoted to this trivial matter by ambassadors, generals, government lawyers, and other high officials dwarfed the $1500 in dispute, which in the end was never paid to anyone.

In a final email to me after the ceremony, Ambassador Wiedemann said, "Thanks, Frank. You've worked hard on this and will receive your reward in heaven."

Extracurricular Activities

My wife joined me in Phnom Penh in April, after completing an interpreting assignment with the State Department. Samantha also joined us in the summer following her first year at McGill. True to form, she explored possibilities for volunteer work and got a job with an NGO called RACHA—Reproduction and Child Health Alliance—which had the clever idea of training monks, nuns, and traditional healthcare providers such as mediums to spread the word to villagers about AIDS prevention. She used the data collected that summer as the basis for her honors thesis on international health at McGill.

Sanda and I went back to Cambodia in December 2004. I had offered to donate my collection of Cambodian books to the Buddhist Institute Library, and I was invited to give a lecture at the Buddhist Institute on that occasion. The event was attended by our ambassador, Charles Ray, and by the Cambodian minister for religions and cults. It was quite a nice affair. On the same trip we visited our friend the consul general in Chiangmai and her husband, stopped off to see friends in the embassy in Rangoon, and made another trip up to Mandalay and the ancient capital of Pagan, which for some reason they now spell "Bagan."

Southeast Asia continues to hold great appeal for my family and me. In fact we are thinking rather vaguely that when my wife and I both retire, we might like to spend our winters in Thailand or Cambodia.

The Triumph of Hun Sen

In the July 2008 elections, Hun Sen and his Cambodian People's Party predictably won by a large margin, through intimidation, suppression of votes, and voter fraud. The CPP won 90 out of 123 seats, with the Sam Rainsy Party coming in a distant second with 27, and various other small parties taking the rest. It was reported that Hun Sen had paid up to $200,000 to Sam Rainsy Party officials to defect to his CPP. An SRP-affiliated union leader was gunned down in 2004. The FUNCINPEC (Royalist) party, formerly led by Prince Rannariddh, had split into two splinter groups. Rannariddh himself was charged with corruption in the sale of FUNCINPEC's former headquarters and sentenced to eighteen months in prison. Rannariddh had been such an ineffectual leader that Hun Sen probably didn't even have to trump up the charges. He fled the country, and resorted to giving speeches over the telephone from exile in Malaysia, while begging Hun Sen to return his private jet.

Hun Sen and his cronies continue to profit from illegal logging, expropriation of peasant land, and kickbacks from foreign investors. Wronged citizens who attempt to find justice in the courts, frequently supported by Western NGOs, are typically frustrated by corrupt judges who are easily bought off. Hun Sen's party has a monopoly of the media, the National Election Commission, the judiciary, the military, the civil service, and educational institutions. Hundreds of schools, hospitals, and bridges all over the country are named after Hun Sen.

I recall that once when the FUNCINPEC party accused Hun Sen of spending public money to buy votes, he denied the charge angrily, saying, "I donated two million dollars of my own money to the building of those schools." Where would a former officer in the Khmer Rouge army, with an official salary of only several hundred dollars as prime minister, get two million dollars if not by devious means? Apparently he didn't realize—or more likely didn't care— that the statement was self-incriminating.

The Khmer Rouge Tribunal so long sought by the UN Human Rights Commission was delayed by CPP procedural challenges and regime foot-dragging. Hearings finally got underway in early 2009, and in July 2010 the infamous Comrade Duch, convicted of exterminating some 17,000 prisoners at the notorious Tuol Sleng prison in Phnom Penh, was sentenced to eighteen years in prison. But only about three major figures are still alive and may well die before being brought to justice at the current rate of the proceedings. One reason for Hun Sen's lack of enthusiasm for the tribunal is that it could lead to the prosecution of some former Khmer Rouge officials in his own regime, and possibly Hun Sen himself.

Some observers point out that the party's victory may be due in part to the stability imposed by the regime, which has led to considerable economic growth in recent years and made Cambodia more attractive to foreign investors. As a result of the discovery of major oil and gas deposits off Cambodia's coast by Chevron, the United States has lifted its ban on direct aid to Cambodia and resumed direct military aid, adding further proof, if any were needed, of the influence of oil on U.S. foreign policy. If the deposits turn out to be true, it will further enrich Hun Sen and Chevron, but will likely have little beneficial effect on the lot of the peasants.

In July of 2010, I was invited to give a talk on U.S.-Cambodian educational and cultural relations at a symposium in Phnom Penh commemorating the 60th Anniversary of United States-Cambodia Diplomatic Relations (1960–2010). Having spent my diplomatic career programming VIPs, it was quite a change to be treated as a VIP myself, met at the airport and ferried to the hotel, invited to dinner at the Residence, and provided a car and driver for the weeklong events. At the three-day symposium I shared the podium with academic specialists such as the historian David Chandler and political scientist Dr. Kenton Clymer, along with current Ambassador Carol Rodley and former ambassadors to Cambodia Charles Ray, Joseph Mussomeli, and Kent Wiedemann, as well as various Cambodian officials, including Deputy Prime Minister Sok An, whom I sent to the United States as an International Visitor in 1995 and who is probably the second must powerful man in Cambodia after Hun Sen himself. At the conclusion of the symposium, a gala dinner was held at the elegant Raffles Le Royal Hotel, with music provided by the Pacific Fleet Band. But given the history of our contentious relations with Sihanouk, our bombing of Cambodia during the Vietnam War, and our disgraceful support for seating the Khmer Rouge at the UN in the 1980s, I wasn't totally convinced that U.S.-Cambodia relations deserved to be celebrated. No doubt Ambassador Rodley was technically correct in saying that U.S.-Cambodian relations have never been better, but it is obvious that the embassy has opted for the "engagement" side of the engagement vs. confrontation conundrum.

Following the festivities, Sanda and I, along with our friends Kem Sos, director of the Khmer Service of Radio Free Asia, and his wife Thura, made a weeklong trip upcountry, visiting the tenth-century temple of Banteay Chhmar near the Thai border and the even older Sambor Prei Kuk ruins in Kampong Thom Province. Having driven through ten provinces, at one point on a new Chinese-built highway from Kampong Cham to Mondulkiri, it was clear that some development is taking place, especially along the main roads. Motorcycles and cars have replaced bicycles and oxcarts. Motorized plows appear to predominate over traditional ox-drawn plows in the rice paddies. Satellite dishes sprouted from one-room shacks, even in a Phnong hill tribe village in Mondulkiri Province. Don Jameson, a former FSO who served in Phnom Penh and an ardent Cambodia observer who visits the country regularly, feels that, in spite of the corruption and dismal human rights situation in the country, conditions are nevertheless slowly improving. But Hun Sen has bragged that he plans to stay in office until the age of ninety. Given his record of outsmarting not only his domestic opponents but also the UN and foreign donors, I wouldn't bet against him.

Life in the Foreign Service

I am often asked (and I have often asked myself) whether it was a good decision to leave academia and join the Foreign Service. In attempting to answer that question, I made a list of the PROs and CONs of life in the Foreign Service.

The Good News

The Foreign Service provides an exciting and challenging career for those who are intrigued by foreign travel and residence abroad and fascinated by foreign languages and cultures. Those who do not have these interests are well advised to avoid the Foreign Service.

The Service provides a fulfilling way to serve one's country in exotic and challenging environments. The State Department ranks high in job satisfaction among the various U.S. government departments and agencies. Duties can range from carrying the secretary of state's luggage to negotiating a life-or-death hostage situation. The unofficial, if facetious, motto of the Foreign Service is "No job too small."

Housing is one of the remaining perks of the Foreign Service and ranges from good to excellent. My experience has been that housing, especially in large urban areas, tends to be much more elegant, centrally located, and expensive than the officer could normally afford on his own.

Compensation is quite generous, especially if one includes the benefits of free housing, medical care, travel to and from post as well as during home leave and R&R, tuition for children through secondary school, educational travel through college, incentive pay for language skills, and pension programs.

The Bad News

The Shotgun Wedding of USIA and State. The abolition of USIA—a longtime objective of the late North Carolina senator Jessie Helms—and the absorption of some of its functions by the Department of State was a huge mistake. Helms saw himself as a foreign policy watchdog and believed that educational and cultural exchanges were fluff that didn't really contribute to our immediate foreign policy goals. What he didn't understand was that the long-term impact of educational and cultural exchanges is much greater than the day-to-day preoccupations of the other sections of an embassy. Some two hundred current and former heads of state and government leaders were former participants in the International Visitor and Fulbright exchange programs. That pays incalculable dividends for U.S. foreign relations over the long term. What is amusing, if it weren't so sad, is that during the soul-searching that followed the tragedy of 9/11, when people were asking "Why do they hate us?," some of the same members of Congress who had voted to abolish USIA were asking, "Why don't we have more and better public diplomacy?" So now they have to reinvent the wheel.

Paul Blackburn, the former director of the public diplomacy office of the Bureau of East Asia and the Pacific and former PAO in both Tokyo and Beijing, says in his interview for ADST's oral history project, "As long as [public diplomacy] stays in the State Department it will inevitably be hamstrung. Without some autonomy and with no possibility of a direct link to the White House, public diplomacy may hold its own but can never thrive." Further on he says, "The USIA and CU culture of long-term relationships and long-term programs really conflicts with the fundamental State Department culture of short-term objectives set by whatever administration is currently in power."

It can not be denied that the intrinsic cultures of the State Department and the former USIA are in basic conflict. USIA's traditional objective has been to provide information, to communicate with foreign publics, and to "tell America's story to the world," while State's objective is the exact opposite: to collect information, to keep it from foreign publics, to classify it whenever possible. Put another way, USIA's job was to send information from Washington to the world, while State's job is to send information from the world to Washington. A perfect example is the differing approaches to the Internet: USIA was far ahead of State in adopting and making use of the Internet to enhance communication with foreign publics, and USIS officers tended to have Internet access on every desk, while State was wary of the Internet and didn't want it in their offices because of the possibility that leaks would compromise their classified system. Some argued at the time that USIA's comparatively advanced communications technology would have a beneficial influence on State, but the reverse has been true—public diplomacy has been constrained by State's culture of secrecy.

A frustrated PAO, writing in the September 2008 issue of the *Foreign Service Journal*, complained, "Here we are in 2008, and we're still not allowed to use a Google search bar in the Internet Explorer browser on OpenNET."

State's Stifling Bureaucracy. The hierarchy and bureaucracy of the State Department are stifling and detract from both morale and efficiency. As an academic, as well as a professor of linguistics, I was accustomed to writing letters, memos, and articles that were clear, articulate, and self-sufficient. However, in the State Department, a memo or cable must be "signed-off on" by a whole hierarchy of superiors, from the composer to his supervisors, through all the office directors who could possibly have an interest (or not), to the deputy assistant secretary, to the assistant secretary, to the under secretary, and so on before it can finally be presented to the secretary, usually so watered down and bland as to be useless or overtaken by events in the meantime. A memo typically requires six or seven signatures before it reaches its destination, and each signatory feels compelled to make niggling little changes to justify participation in the process.

This charade reveals two undesirable attitudes on the part of supervisors: first, distrust of their subordinates' ability to produce a satisfactory memo, and second, a typical CYA mentality. If the supervisor knows what he wants the memo to say in its final form, he should write it himself and obviate the need for so many plebes down the line.

Foreign Service officers are highly intelligent and capable people whose abilities have already been proven by the rigorous entrance exam, and it is wasteful and inefficient not to make use of their independent skills. For an authentic illustration of this bureaucratic constipation, see "The Saga of the Two Heads" in the previous chapter about a decision concerning a trivial matter that required hundreds of emails over a period of three months. On many occasions during my tours to seven different countries, it was abundantly clear that things could be accomplished much more efficiently when several members of the supervisory hierarchy were absent from post. Even when the United States suspended contacts with the Burmese regime in response to the massacres of 8/8/88, the sixty-man embassy was as busy as ever just perpetuating itself.

Problems for Two-Career Families. In a day and age when two-career families are the norm if not a necessity, a career in the Foreign Service presents a challenge. State does attempt to provide jobs for family members at post, but in general they are low-paid jobs for which most "trailing spouses," as they are called, are overqualified, such as director of the Community Liaison Office, or director of the Embassy Recreation Club. My capable and resourceful wife, a person with unsuspected administrative skills, was able to find career-enhancing employment wherever we went. At one point she served as Acting AID representative in Burma and supervised a Georgetown University training program in Cambodia, in addition to occasional assignments in her specialty as a conference interpreter for French, English, and Romanian, but that is not the norm.

In the rare cases where both spouses are Foreign Service officers, State makes an honest attempt to provide them a "tandem assignment" to the same post, but since one spouse may not supervise the other and write the all-important performance evaluation, assignment possibilities are limited to large posts where spouses can occupy coordinate positions with separate supervisors. Since in many cases the nonofficer spouse is a professional in his or her own right, such as a doctor or a lawyer, who cannot be expected to find career-enhancing employment in a foreign country, one solution would be to provide generous travel and visitation rights for spouses who remain in the United States for career reasons. At the risk of being accused of male chauvinism, it has been my observation that life in the Foreign Service is a particularly bad choice for single women, as their scope of social contacts outside of embassy personnel is severely limited in many foreign societies.

Finally, again treading on treacherous ground, when the "trailing spouse" is a man, the venture is more likely to end in failure. This is no doubt due to ingrained attitudes in our society, where it is considered inappropriate, either consciously or subconsciously, for the husband to be subservient to the wife or to live at her expense. However that may be, the divorce rate in such situations is high.

Russian Roulette with Your Children's Education. Schooling for one's children is an important consideration. When children are small, it can be convenient to be posted to countries where labor is cheap and nannies can be hired quite reasonably. But as they grow older, the Foreign Service begins to pose problems for their education. Most posts have either American or international schools, at least for students K–8; but the problem becomes more acute when the children reach high school age. At that point officers are limited to bidding on posts that have adequate American or international secondary schools. When such schools don't exist at post, alternatives are sending one's children to local schools, which may be substandard or present language problems, or sending one's children to boarding schools at a young age—a practice more common in certain European countries than in our own.

Frequent changes of schools required by a Foreign Service career present another problem. Our own children attended nine different schools and, in the case of my daughter, had to cope with four different educational systems—British, French, New Zealand, and American.

When I was a graduate student doing research in Bangkok, my colleagues and I used to make fun of "embassy types," shielded behind the walls of their housing compounds from meaningful interaction with local society. At the same time there was an undercurrent of envy for the perks and logistical support they enjoyed. After I became a Foreign Service officer, I saw things from a different perspective. When academics go out to a third-world country on a research sabbatical, they pride themselves on roughing it for six months or so, while their families remain safe and secure back home. Foreign Service families, on the other hand, commit to living abroad as a career, and they have to be concerned about the children's education and the family's exposure to unhealthful conditions and possible violence. I particularly admire some USAID families that I have met who, because of the nature of USAID work, have spent thirty years or more raising their families exclusively in developing third-world countries.

Silly Travel Restrictions. Among my pet peeves about the Foreign Service are the ridiculous travel restrictions. You certainly don't join the Foreign Service to see the world, contrary to popular perception. One of the silliest and most expensive practices is vouchered travel. It costs millions to administer and monitor the maze of regulations concerning the Fly America Act, city-pairs, and contract fares (many of which are higher than can be obtained on the market). When as an academic at Yale I had a Guggenheim grant for research in Southeast Asia, I visited with colleagues in London, Paris, Heidelberg, and Prague, and stopped in Delhi, Kabul, Madras, Kathmandu, and Rangoon on the way to research in Thailand, Laos, and Cambodia. But in the Foreign Service, an officer cannot spend three days in a city en route if the contract fare calls for only a six-hour stopover. As my academic research was in Southeast Asia, I would typically travel to Bangkok via Europe and return via the Pacific, thus circumnavigating the globe. But with government travel, if you were posted to the Far East, you were required to travel to and from Bangkok via the Pacific, as it was several hundred miles shorter than via Europe. You could not afford to travel by Europe and pay the difference, because no American carrier flew between Bangkok and Bombay.

The Fly America Act no longer makes any sense, since government travel is insignificant given the size of most airline operations, and in any case, all major U.S. airlines now have code-sharing arrangements with non-U.S. carriers. We should adopt the sensible practice followed by many other governments—simply give the officer an allowance based on the cost of economy air fare between points A and B, and say, "Be there on such and such a date." Not only would this save millions in administrative costs, it would give individual officers the flexibility to travel to post by whatever means and whatever route they wish. Once when I proposed this solution to one of the green-eyeshade types resident in every government agency, his reaction was, "Think how many people would lose their jobs!"

I said, "Exactly."

Ethan Allen Furniture. Another silly—and expensive—practice is stocking everybody's house with typical Ethan Allen (or other American brand) furniture. You see the same overstuffed couches and flowered patterns in Foreign Service housing whether you're posted to Brussels, Bangkok, or Bamako. Think how much it costs to purchase, ship, and warehouse thousands of tons of American furniture at every embassy as well as at regional warehouses. If you want to have a truly foreign experience, why does your furniture have to look like it came from Peoria? It would be much more economical to require—or at least encourage—FSOs to furnish their homes on the local market, especially in developing countries. When I visited the homes of our French or British counterparts at various posts, I was impressed with their use of local furniture and indigenous art objects—both appropriate to the local climate and reflective of the local culture. To adopt this practice would not only be more economical but would also provide a valuable opportunity for FSOs to interact with the local society and economy and to practice the language. When I expressed this opinion to a veteran FSO, she pointed out that many of the support staff in our embassies are specialists who are not interested in the local culture. This is certainly true, with exceptions, but one wonders, if that is the case, why they chose employment abroad as a career.

Make-or-Break Evaluations. The system of evaluating an officer's performance for promotion (or not) is seriously flawed. The dreaded OER (officer evaluation report, more recently dubbed EER—employee evaluation report) is written by the officer's supervisor and optionally reviewed by that supervisor's superior, who may or may not know very much about the officer involved. Thus one person can make or break an officer's career. I think an officer should be rated by at least three colleagues of equal or higher rank. Thus if one of the three writes a vindictive report, the bias will be revealed (or at least balanced) by the other two. (If all three are negative, then that is also useful to know).

I would further recommend that OERs be confidential. I suppose that in this age of egalitarianism and transparency, such a suggestion would be seen as a step backward, and no doubt at some point in the past confidential OERs were jettisoned in favor of the present more "enlightened" system. It seems to me, however, that confidentiality would solve a whole host of current problems. When a rating officer knows that his negative comments will be read, and perhaps contested, by the rated officer, it leads to a lack of candor and an inflation of OERs that distorts the objectivity of the OER. Raters have to use increasingly bloated terminology to praise a good officer, such as, "Mr. X is one the most brilliant officers I have encountered in my thirty years in the Foreign Service." Raters have to resort to certain well-known code words if they want to impugn one's performance: to be called "competent," for example, is the kiss of death. And the frequent epithet "He's a real people person" means "He's a nice guy, but..."

Another gripe is that OERs are simply too long. They are too much of a chore, with too much repetition and overlapping of information. A better format would be a list of relevant qualities, skills, and abilities that could be checked in one of three or four categories, such as "Excellent," "Satisfactory," or "Unsatisfactory." Thus the evaluation would not depend so heavily on the verbal virtuosity of the evaluator.

Finally, the "Rated Officer's Comments" section is a minefield. Some veterans warn, "Leave it blank," while others recommend using it to justify one's failings, to butter up one's raters, or to show off one's writing skills. When commenting on a reviewer's criticisms, there are two strategies the rated officer can take: "He's right, but I'm doing my best to improve," or "He's wrong." Self-interest dictates that he take the second approach. But the whole problem of OER inflation, the use of code words, and commenting on oneself could be avoided by OER confidentiality.

Mandatory Retirement
Mandatory retirement from the Foreign Service at age 65, when an experienced officer is at the top of his game, should be scrapped,

and an officer's tenure and promotion should be based on a fair and objective evaluation of his performance, rather than on the arbitrary criterion of age.

Conclusions

My list of "cons" is admittedly much longer and more detailed than the "pros," but they do not necessarily outweigh them. After all, it is harder to make a case for change than for the status quo. On balance I think my decision to join the Foreign Service was a good one. I must admit that it's hard to beat the academic life. One of the great luxuries of academia is the freedom to wake up in the morning (preferably late) and ask oneself, "What do I really want to do/ think about/pursue today?" In government service, you are told what to do and what policies to support.

My colleagues at Cornell were mystified when I resigned to join the Foreign Service; to them, when you're a full professor at an Ivy League university, the only place you can go is down. The director of Cornell's Southeast Asia Program at the time told me, rather plaintively, "Frank, you're the first person ever to leave the program voluntarily," implying that many were called but few were chosen to such a high honor. To join the government was to prostitute oneself and to compromise one's academic freedom. And I must admit that I had some qualms about swearing to support and defend U.S. policies, but it was seldom a serious problem (with the possible exception of Cambodia, where I knew enough about the country and its history to see where some of our policies were wrongheaded). Usually I agreed with our policies abroad, especially during the Clinton administration, although I would have had some trouble supporting the policies of the Bush II administration. I always rationalized that if I couldn't support and defend our policies, I could at least explain them in the context of American history and society, which after all was consistent with "telling America's story to the world."

I also had to deal with some ego problems. After having been a specialist in my field (a reviewer of one of my books called me "the leading authority in the United States on the Khmer language," perhaps because he was the only other one), I was now a generalist who programmed other academics as speakers and specialists.

And, as mentioned before, some of my former students were now my superiors.

But it is true that my reputation as a Cambodia specialist and the author of several widely used textbooks on the Cambodian language was a definite asset to my effectiveness as a cultural attaché during my tour there and played an important role in my continued involvement with Cambodia. In 2004, when I donated my collection of Khmer vernacular publications to the Buddhist Institute in Phnom Penh, I gave a lecture at the Institute titled "The Importance of Khmer to Southeast Asian Studies," attended by the minister of cults and religions and then-U.S. Ambassador Charles Ray. When the new U.S. Embassy was officially inaugurated in 2006, I was amazed (and honored) to learn that they had named one of the conference rooms the "Franklin E. Huffman Room" (a rumor that I confirmed during a visit to the Embassy in 2009). Finally, in July 2010 I was invited by U.S. ambassador Carol Rodley to speak on "the history of U.S.-Cambodian educational and cultural exchanges" on the occasion of the embassy's commemoration of the sixtieth anniversary of U.S.-Cambodian diplomatic relations.

If I had stayed at Cornell, I would have returned over and over to the same research sites in Southeast Asia and continued to write articles read by maybe forty specialists in the world, whereas the Foreign Service provided the opportunity to live and work in countries and cultures that I would not otherwise have experienced. In a span of only fourteen years, I managed to serve on all the continents of the world except Latin America. I conclude that my decision to join the Foreign Service has resulted in a much more varied, exciting, and challenging experience than I would have had had I stayed in academia, and has given me the opportunity to have two interesting careers rather than one.

Index